P9-DOE-380

AN

262.9   93433
Cor   Coriden, James A
        An Introduction to
        Canon Law

DATE DUE			

RIORDAN HIGH SCHOOL LIBRARY
175 PHELAN AVENUE
SAN FRANCISCO, CALIFORNIA 94118

93433

Published with the approval of ecclesiastical authority; *nihil obstat* issued by Norbert F. Gaughan, Bishop of Gary, October 24, 1990.

Copyright © 1991 by James A. Coriden

All rights reserved. No part of this book may be reproduced or transmitted in any form or by any means, electronic or mechanical, including photocopying, recording or by any information storage and retrieval system without permission in writing from the Publisher.

Library of Congress Cataloging in Publication Data

Coriden, James A.
    An introduction to canon law/James A. Coriden.
      p. cm.
    Includes index.
    ISBN 0-8091-3231-1 (paper)
    1. Canon law. I. Title.
  LAW
  262.9—dc20   91-7188
                                       CIP

Published by Paulist Press
997 Macarthur Boulevard
Mahwah, N.J. 07430

Printed and bound in the United States of America

DEDICATED TO MY COLLEAGUES
AT THE WASHINGTON THEOLOGICAL UNION
AND IN THE CANON LAW SOCIETY OF AMERICA.
MAY THIS BOOK CONTRIBUTE IN SOME SMALL WAY
TO THE UPBUILDING OF A CHURCH
WHICH IS BOTH FREE AND WELL-ORDERED.

Outline

Contents

A CANONICAL CONSTITUTION
OF THE CHURCH

THE PEOPLE OF GOD:
BOOK TWO OF THE CODE

Consecrated and Apostolic Life ....

THE TEACHING FUNCTION:
BOOK THREE OF THE CODE

THE SANCTIFYING FUNCTION:
BOOK FOUR OF THE CODE

THE GOVERNING FUNCTION:
BOOK ONE OF THE CODE

TEMPORAL GOODS OF THE CHURCH:
BOOK FIVE OF THE CODE

SANCTIONS IN THE CHURCH:
BOOK SIX OF THE CODE

PROCESSES:
BOOK SEVEN OF THE CODE

APPLYING THE RULES

APPENDIX I:
DOING RESEARCH IN CANON LAW

APPENDIX II:
CASES AND QUESTIONS

Preface

The Roman Catholic Church is a highly organized community of religious belief, worship, witness and action. "Canon Law" is the name for its church order and discipline, its structures, rules and procedures. This book attempts to introduce the reader to Roman Catholic canon law.

The book is intended for use in introductory courses in canon law in seminaries and schools of theology where men and women prepare for ministry in the church. It should also be helpful for anyone, lay or religious, who seeks to understand the way the Roman Catholic Church is structured and actually works. A sense of the church's organization and operation is essential for anyone to function well in ministry, just as it is for anyone who takes an active interest in the life of the church.

The Code of Canon Law is the central and coordinating compilation of rules for the Western (or Latin) church. It must be the primary source and reference in any introductory course in canon law. Students must get to know the Code itself. They should become familiar with it, so that they can consult it with ease and understanding. This book is a guide to the Code. It points to and leads into the Code; it refers constantly to the canons of the Code. It offers a way of organizing the material for a course based on the Code.

Commentaries on The Code of Canon Law offer detailed explanations and applications of the individual canons. Several good commentaries on the 1983 Code already exist. This book does not attempt to rival or replace them. Instead, it introduces the reader to the basic structures and areas of the church's rules, so that the student can then refer readily to the Code and make intelligent use of the commentaries. In this sense the book is like an introduction to the New Testament. It leads a person to the text itself so that the words can be understood and their meaning appreciated. It does not repeat the text, nor does it comment on chapters and verses.

Handbooks or manuals of canon law, pastoral companions or handy references, select and summarize the canons most relevant to ministry. This work, in contrast, offers an introductory orientation to all of canon law, like a map which gives an overview of the entire terrain. It is well-suited for those initially exploring the canonical landscape.

This is a teaching and learning tool. It provides outlines and overviews of relatively complex areas of canon law, but it is not "Canon Law Made Easy." It attempts to describe canonical structures accurately, and to explain technical terms so that their meanings are clear.

An introduction is about basics. This work sketches the basic structure and design of the various offices and functions within the church, and describes how they relate to one another. This is rudimentary material, but necessary for a correct perception of the church's organization.

The book is certainly not "The Compleat Canonist" or "Everything You'll Ever Need To Know About Canon Law." It gives an orientation to the more important areas of canon law, and it provides a background and context within which more detailed rules can be understood. Indeed, professional canonists will immediately recognize that many nuances, distinctions and qualifications have been omitted. Some matters of lesser importance to the beginner, e.g., cathedral chapters, personal prelatures, computation of time, prescription of property, canons penitentiary, etc., have been deliberately left out. Other areas, like the lengthy book on Processes, are summarized very briefly. Every teacher of introductory courses must make such judgment calls.

The book begins with five introductory chapters on the nature, origins and development of canon law. Then "A Canonical Constitution of the Church" (a draft text which was never promulgated) is presented for the sake of its comprehensive vision. There are fourteen expository chapters on the books of The 1983 Code of Canon Law. They generally follow the order of the Code (except that Book One, General Norms, which is quite abstract and dry, is inserted after Book Four, for pedagogical reasons). A final chapter deals with the interpretation and application of canonical norms. The first appendix offers guidance for doing canonical research, and the second provides a set of case studies for use as learning exercises. Two bibliographies are provided, one after the chapter, "The History of Canon Law," the other in the appendix on canonical research.

This modest effort results from more than twenty years of teaching. The author fondly hopes that students will find it a helpful guide through the canonical thickets.

In 1983, when Pope John Paul II promulgated the revised Code, he wrote that the church must have canonical norms

> ". . . so that the exercise of its divinely-given functions may be appropriately organized, and so that the mutual relations of the faithful may be regulated according to justice based on charity, with the rights of individuals guaranteed and well-defined . . ."

This book was written for that same purpose.

INTRODUCTORY ISSUES

Rules in a Church Community

Names

Every church, although based on what its members believe to be divine revelation, is also a human institution. As human communities, churches require rules.

The Roman Catholic Church is a particularly large and far-flung community of faith. It claims about 850 million members worldwide. And it is ancient. It traces its orgins back to Jesus Christ in the first century of this era, and considers itself to be in continuity with his teachings and those of his disciples. The church, through the centuries, has accrued a lot of rules.

The generic name in English for the rules of the Roman Catholic Church is "canon law." "Law" is a familiar term; its meaning is well-known. It is a measure or norm of conduct. We are induced to act or refrain from acting in accord with the law. Laws are products of reason, and they are directed toward the common good of the society for which they are given.

"Canon" is not as common a word, but it has been used to describe the church's rules from very early times. "Canon" comes from the Greek word *kanon*, which means reed, rod or ruler. It described the measure or ruler used by a carpenter or designer. It was a standard by which things were measured. It came to mean a rule of conduct. (It is used in this sense in the New Testament; cf. Gal 6,16 and Phil 3,16.) In English, we speak of the accepted standards of art or professional practice as canons. The Latin word *regula* also means rule, pattern or model, and from it our term "regulation" is derived.

Both Greek and Latin have other words for "law": *nomos* and *lex.* But the church chose to name its rules "canons" because it recognized that its rules were different from the laws of the Roman Empire. Indeed, canons are compared to the advisory opinions of the Roman Senate, *senatus consulta.* They gave a "sense of the Senate," and were not lightly disregarded, but they were not the same as the laws of the realm.

"Canon law" is a rather unfortunate English translation of the Latin *ius canonicum. Ius* does not have an exact English equivalent. It can mean a legal system (e.g., *Ius Romanum*, Roman law), or a subjective right (e.g., *ius ad rem*, right to a thing), or the objective of justice, that which is right, due or just. Most other modern languages translate *ius* as right: *droit, diritto, derecho, recht.* In English, in reference to the church's system of rules, we translate it as law. (To translate *ius canonicum* literally as "canonical right" just wouldn't work.) The other languages clearly distinguish canon law from civil or secular law, but in English there is a tendency to equate the two very different systems of rules, because of the use of the same word, law.

So "canon law" is a slightly redundant and infelicitous descriptive title for the rules which govern the public order of the Roman Catholic Church. It names our ecclesiastical regulations.

Those norms which describe the basic structures of the church, e.g., the papal and episcopal offices, the sacramental system, constitute Roman Catholic "church order." Those which set forth individual regulations, e.g., the age for confirmation, the requirements for ordination, are considered to be "church discipline." Canon law includes both order and discipline.

Canons are rules or norms for the governance of the external life of the church.

Scope

The canons have to do with church order and discipline rather than doctrine and dogma. It is important to recognize that canon law contains guidelines for actions, not beliefs. It presents norms of conduct, not the content of faith. For official church teaching one consults the teaching documents, e.g., the documents of the Second Vatican Council, not the Code of Canon Law.

Theology is concerned with God's revelation and the church's teachings. Canon law is concerned with the patterns of practice within the community of faith. They are distinct but closely related disciplines. Systematic and moral theologians teach about the divinity of Christ and the morality of war. One might consult a canonist about the limits of the teaching office or the defense of someone accused of teaching falsehood.

Canon law governs the external order of the church, the public life of the faith community. It does not attempt to measure or compel personal conscience or moral judgments. Canon law pertains almost exclusively to the "external forum," the arena of the church's public governance, as over against the "internal forum," the arena of conscience.

Purpose and Functions

The church is a radically different kind of community than the state or other secular societies. As a result, its system of rules has a different purpose than other legal systems.

The church is a mystery, a reality imbued with the presence of God. It is the temple of the Holy Spirit, resplendent with the Spirit's gifts. It is the sacrament of Christ, the visible and effective sign of his saving work in the world. The church is a communion, that is, a unique set of interrelationships among its members and with God, based on faith and love. But the church is also a human community made up of ornery, erring and sinful people.

The church is *sui generis*, in a class by itself. It differs from all other human societies in its origins, its history, its inner dynamism and its destiny. Consequently, the church's system of rules must function differently from that of any other society.

Pope John Paul II, when he promulgated the Code of Canon Law in 1983, described its purpose as follows:

> The purpose of the Code is not to substitute for faith, grace, charisms, and especially charity in the life of the Church or of the Christian faithful. On the contrary, its very purpose is to create an order in the ecclesial society so that, while giving priority to love, grace and charism, their ordered development is facilitated in the life of the ecclesial society as well as in the lives of the individuals who belong to it (Apostolic constitution, *Sacrae disciplinae leges*).

This is true not only of the Code, but of all of canon law as well.

Law has at least four functions in any society, and, by analogy, canonical rules fulfill these functions within the church:

1. Law is to aid a society in the achievement of its goals. It is to facilitate the attainment of the purpose or common good of the society. Canon law helps the gathered community of the Christian faithful to be what it is meant to be, and to carry out its mission in the world. The church is to proclaim the life and message of Christ, to be a communal witness to the loving presence of God, and to be of service to the world of today. The church's discipline is to aid it in carrying out those central tasks. The church has a transcendent spiritual purpose as well: the ultimate salvation of its members, their reconciliation and communion with God. Hence, the classic canonical maxim: "The salvation of

souls is the supreme law" (*salus animarum suprema lex*; cf. canon 1752). All else must defer to this end.

2. Law is to afford stability to the society, that is, provide good order, reliable procedures, and predictable outcomes. The church needs the tranquillity of order in its life, just as other societies do. Leaders need to be elected, sacraments celebrated, the word of God preached, decisions made, property administered. The community of faith has a right to expect reasonable, appropriate and predictable ways of doing these everyday things. The canons govern these functions, which are vital as well as stabilizing.

3. Law is to protect personal rights, provide avenues of recourse and redress of grievances, and means for the resolution of conflicts. What the church has in common with all other visible, human societies is relationships involving rights and obligations, that is, a juridic order. Its juridic life must be conducted with justice and fairness for all its members. This is another task of its canons of discipline: to articulate the rights and duties of the faithful, and to provide means for their protection.

4. Finally, law is to assist in the education of the community by reminding everyone of its values and standards. The church requires such continual education and, although much of its teaching is done in other ways, the canons help. Canon law spells out the expectations of members, the qualifications for office-holders, and the ideals of religious life. The church's discipline is concerned to lead people to a virtuous life, not simply an external compliance with rules. Not satisfied with justice, canon law, at its best, challenges the church to strive toward love as its goal.

The canons also help to create and maintain the metaphors and symbols which influence the faithful subtly but strongly. For example, the canons call marriage a covenant rather than a contract, and a parish is described as a community of the faithful rather than a territorial part of a diocese. The effects of these characterizations, over time, are profound.

Canon law shapes and guides the life of the church in many ways. For those who care about the church, it is important to understand its rules.

New Testament Roots
of the Rules

The most sacred and revered of the classic sources for the Christian tradition is the New Testament. The books of the New Testament emerged from the living churches of the first century. We believe, their authors were moved by the Holy Spirit, but they also wrote from their own experiences and memories as members of or visitors to what we now call "local churches." The gospels and letters, in addition to all they tell us about the life, words and works of Jesus, tell us a lot about those early congregations of believers in Jesus. Part of the message is about their rules.

Every human society develops patterns of action, which eventually become rules of behavior. The first Christian churches developed regulations to help them live in orderly and Christlike ways. The New Testament is replete with indications of these earliest rules. Indeed, many of our present "canon laws" are rooted in these originating writings.

What follows is simply a range of examples of rules or policies of those early churches drawn from the pages of the New Testament. They are not arranged in any special order, nor are they analyzed. The examples are simply presented to bear witness to the fact that the very first Christian communities received or evolved rules for their lives. They were not amorphous or spontaneously charismatic groupings. The churches had orderly structures and procedures.

The local congregations were linked to one another in a fellowship of faith and caring (e.g., Paul's collection for the church of Jerusalem, Rom 15,26). There was a structured authority within each local church (e.g., lists of ministries, 1 Cor 12,28; Eph 4,11; references to elders and over-seers, i.e., presbyters and bishops, Acts 20; Phil 1,1). The church had a conciliar, consultative process for making decisions, especially on major policy matters (e.g., the "Gentile question" and the "Council of Jerusa-lem" in Acts 15 and Gal 2). The participants were obviously conscious of being guided by the Holy Spirit (Acts 15,28).

To hold a position of authority among the disciples of Jesus meant to serve the others, after the example of the Master (Mt 20,25; Mk 10,42; Lk

7

22,25). The qualifications for office-holders were enumerated (1 Tim 3 & 5; Tit 1,7), and the responsibilities attached to those offices were spelled out. The charges to preach and teach were presented clearly and forcefully in the pastoral epistles (1 Tim 4; 2 Tim 4).

The sacramental life (as we now call it) of the communities was delineated. Baptism with water was necessary for incorporation in Christ (Mt 28,19; Jn 3,5; Acts 2,38; 1 Pet 3,20). The discipline for celebrating the Lord's Supper was given in detail, along with instances of abuses which occurred (1 Cor 11). The powers of binding and loosing from sins were announced (Mt 18,18; Jn 20,23). The procedure for praying over and anointing the sick was described (Jas 5,13). Mention was made of the laying on of hands, evidently an early form of installation in office or commissioning for ministry (1 Tim 4,14). Regulations for marrying "in the Lord," the conduct of married life, and the prohibition of divorce were enunciated with unusual specificity (Ephs 5,21–33; Mt 5,31; Mt 19,3,9; Lk 16,18).

An explicit process for the resolution of disputes or offenses within the community was given in Matthew's gospel (18,15). Indeed, chapter 18 of Matthew's gospel has been called "Jesus' sermon on church order and life." Much of it is directed to those who act with authority in the church and have pastoral responsibility. Examples of excommunication, or at least "corrective quarantine," for offenders are also mentioned, showing that a rudimentary system of sanctions was in place (Mt 18,17; 1 Cor 5,1–5).

One must not conclude too much from these examples. There was great variety among the New Testament churches. Diversity was the standard, not the exception. Titles, offices, functions, all varied greatly. There was no sense of uniform regulations or coordinated government for the churches. But there was, clearly present, at least the beginnings of church order and discipline. The earliest churches had begun to come to grips with routine, authority, succession and conflict.

The History of Canon Law

The history of the church's juridical structures from the post-apostolic times to the present day is very complex. The church was not born with its administrative organization in place. It evolved rules and procedures as it grew and spread. In that process, the church's rules were shaped by its internal needs, the surrounding cultures, and the pressures of changed circumstances.

This evolutionary process was anything but a smooth, unilinear trajectory. It more resembled the vicissitudes of a pilgrim people making their way across a strange continent, buffeted and benefited by the things they encounter. They react to and learn from their surroundings. They defend themselves from occasional adversaries, but they also discover and adopt new ways. They borrow the customs of others out of need and out of wisdom.

This brief synopsis of the long history of canon law is divided into periods:

(a) from the end of the first century to late fourth: The Post-Apostolic and Early Church;

(b) from the fourth to the eighth centuries: The Church of the Empire;

(c) from the eighth to the twelfth centuries: The Church and Feudalism;

(d) from the mid-twelfth to the mid-fourteenth centuries: The Classical Period;

(e) from the mid-fourteenth to the eighteenth centuries: Decline and Reform;

(f) the eighteenth and nineteenth centuries: The Church in the Modern World;

(g) the twentieth century until the Second Vatican Council: The Codification of Canon Law.

Of each of these periods, we ask three questions:

1) Who made the rules? From what authority did they emerge?
2) What forms did they take? What was their scope and style?
3) What were the major influences which shaped the rules?

The rule-making process is stimulated in periods of church reform. Enactment and enforcement of rules is an integral part of the process of church renewal. We are now in the midst of a reform period. It may be valuable, after surveying the historical development, to revisit some of the major moments of renewal of our church's life and recall the role that canon law played in them.

A. *The Post-Apostolic and Early Church*

After the New Testament period, local churches were scattered all around the Mediterranean basin. There was mutual recognition and some communication between them, but there was no central authority or single rule-making power. Yet some of the earliest records we have about the life of these churches are canonical.

The *Didache* or *Teaching of the Twelve Apostles*, an anonymous collection of moral, liturgical and disciplinary instructions, is one of the first and most precious post-apostolic writings. It was written about the year 100. It contains clear directions on how to baptize, on keeping the Lord's day, on prayer, and on the election of bishops and deacons.

The *Didache* formed the pattern for several other small collections of rules about the life of the church in the first two hundred years after New Testament times; for example, the *Traditio Apostolica* of Hippolytus of Rome (ca. 218), the *Didascalia Apostolorum* (ca. 250), and the *Canones Ecclesiastici Apostolorum* (ca. 300). They were not issued by any formal authority. They were simply compiled customs. People wrote down the accepted practices of their own community. Then they were circulated and accepted by other communities.

The earliest form of church discipline was the recorded customs of the believing communities. They told of the ways that sacraments were celebrated, leaders elected and sinners reconciled. They also reflected the conflicts and disputes which troubled the local churches, e.g., whether to rebaptize those who had fallen into heresy and then returned.

The writings of the apostolic Fathers and apologists of this same period confirm and bear witness to these early church practices; for example, the letters of Clement of Rome, Ignatius of Antioch and Polycarp of Smyrna.

The most significant development of this early period for canon law, however, is the synodal or conciliar process. It was patterned after the example of the Council of Jerusalem depicted in Acts 15. The leaders of the local churches of an area would come together, either regularly or as need arose, to deliberate and seek consensus on matters of doctrine and discipline. This practice was common and well accepted from at least the early third century.

Local councils were held in North Africa, Spain, Italy, France and Asia Minor. The disciplinary decisions of these local councils were frequently communicated to other churches when they gathered in council. It was a lateral process of mutual acceptance and common usage.

In the fourth century this conciliar process expanded to what we now call "ecumenical councils," that is, gatherings representative of the entire communion. (The term ecumenical comes from the Greek *oikoumene*, the inhabited world, the universe.) The first of these "universal" councils, called by the Roman Emperor Constantine, met in Nicea (in present-day Turkey, not far from Istanbul) in the year 325. It was attended by about 318 bishops. It is known chiefly for its debate about the nature of Christ. The council gave us the Nicene Creed, which we still use in eucharistic celebrations today. But the bishops of the council also debated, agreed upon and issued twenty "canons," that is, various rules of discipline. And such was the authority and prestige of the council that those canons were widely circulated and accepted thoughout the churches which made up the communion.

The canons of Nicea dealt with a range of topics which apparently represented abuses or disputes at the time; for example: self-mutilation, clerical chastity, ordination of bishops, mutual recognition of excommunications, reconciliation of those who denied their faith, clerical stability or non-transferability, clerical usury, distribution of holy communion, and the appropriate posture for prayer.

In this early period the church was relatively free to develop its own regulative structures. It was a minority religious group, widely established in the urban centers of the Roman Empire. Before Constantine the church was either ignored or persecuted by the government. It retained the offices and practices first used in the New Testament period, those derived from Jewish tradition (e.g., the conciliar process) or the Greek context (e.g., offices like *episkopos*, overseer, bishop, and *presbyteros*, elder, presbyter). However, the church's world was organized by the law of the Roman Empire and, naturally enough, when the church needed new structures, it often borrowed from that source (e.g., "diocese" and "province" were terms directly taken over from the subdivisions of the empire).

Perhaps the most important thing to remember about these first centuries of the church's rule-making life is that its earliest modes were customary and conciliar.

B. *The Church of the Empire*

Early in the fourth century the church was recognized by the Roman emperor, Constantine, and was granted not only freedom but a position of preference and privilege. Gradually it became the established religion. But its relationship with the imperial authority was not worked out satisfactorily until later. Throughout the middle of that century successive emperors sought to dominate the church, to favor heretical factions within it, and even to persecute members of the church.

In the late years of the fourth century, Bishop Ambrose of Milan and Emperor Theodosius I worked out a relatively balanced alliance: a positive, close and collaborative relationship in which both authorities, church and state, recognized each other as supreme in their own realms. The church respected and supported imperial authority and policies, and the state honored the church's authority in matters of faith, the discipline of the clergy, liturgy and the administration of church property. The empire supported the social and charitable works of the church, exempted the clergy from taxes and military service, and even made the bishops administrators of the state's justice. The church had become the church of the empire.

In this new status the church could not help being strongly influenced by Roman law. It borrowed freely from the well-developed legal structures and procedures of the empire. In fact, the church was compelled to adopt elements of Roman law because the Christian emperors, especially the great legal compilers of the fifth and sixth centuries, Theodosius II and Justinian I, legislated for the church. They included large sections of ecclesiastical rules, many of their own making, in the collections of laws promulgated for the empire (e.g., the *Codex Theodosianus* of 438, and the *Corpus Iuris*, 535). It would be difficult to exaggerate the influence of Roman law on the church's regulatory system, at this period and permanently thereafter.

Two demographic factors affected the development of the church's organization and ministry at this time; namely, its huge numerical growth and its spread into the countryside. It became socially and politically advantageous to be a Christian, and many desired to join the church. The result was a vast increase in membership, but a decrease in the levels of preparation and commitment. This newer population extended the church outside its traditional urban areas into rural towns and villages. This caused the bishops of the cities to depute presbyters to lead the outlying communities. Congregations of the faithful were dispersed and multiplied, but the bishop gradually lost all personal relationship with the members of the local churches.

The gradual evolution of the Bishop of Rome into a figure of central authority is another key factor in the development of canon law. Because of its connections with the apostles Peter and Paul, and because of its importance as the imperial capital, Rome had significance as an ecclesiastical reference point as early as the third century. During the tumultuous changes of the fourth century the Bishop of Rome grew in stature and influence.

In the West, bishops referred questions to Rome, and they received answers which were treated as authoritative. By the time of Leo I (440–461), the Bishop of Rome was recognized as the Patriarch of the West with an undisputed primacy. This unique leadership role was not yet acknowledged in the East. Leo articulated the theory that the Bishop of Rome is the heir of Peter. Christ is the true and eternal bishop of all his people, but he granted Peter an enduring share in his episcopal power, and each successive Bishop of Rome inherits it.

The bishops of Rome, referred to as popes (from *papa*, father), began to issue preceptive letters or decretals (*decretales*, decrees) with some frequency during the fifth century. These letters were seen to have broad authority, even though they were addressed to one bishop or one region. The decretal letters, therefore, are the first manifestation of papal legislative power. They began to be collected and placed alongside the earlier customary and conciliar regulations for the life of the church.

The two most important canonical collections from the early centuries are:

1) The *Syntagma Canonum Antiochenum* (the collection of conciliar canons made at Antioch), probably begun in the late fourth century and completed in the late fifth. This collection, with its later additions, is the central basis for Oriental church law.

2) The *Dionysiana*, a collection of conciliar canons and papal decretals made at Rome by a monk named Dionysius Exiguus (Dennis the Little) at the outset of the sixth century. This compilation, in its

various subsequent editions, had an immense influence on all medieval canon law.

A final example will illustrate the relationship of church to empire and the effective use of a canonical collection. In the year 751, long after the decimation of the Roman Empire by the invading tribes from the north, Pepin, the *de facto* ruler of the Frankish kingdom, was given the title of King of the Franks by the pope. Pepin and his son, Charlemagne (768–814), set about the work of consolidating the kingdom, and they knew that the restoration of church discipline was an integral part of that task. They also assumed that church renewal was their responsibility as Christian monarchs. In 774 Pope Adrian I gave to Charlemagne a revised version of the *Dionysiana* collection of canons (called the *Dionysiana-Hadriana*), which the vigorous Christian king did his best to enforce throughout the kingdom. He convened reform councils in various parts of Europe to restore good order to the church. He appointed reform-minded metropolitans and bishops, and they brought the message home to their diocesan synods. On Christmas Day in the year 800, Pope Leo III crowned Charlemagne the Holy Roman Emperor.

To conclude this section on the Church of the Empire, it should be noted that the growth and territorial organization of the church, together with the influence of Roman law, contributed greatly to centralization and monarchical (from *monos archein*, to rule alone) rule within the church, with a simultaneous diminution of local congregational autonomy and participatory governance. The groundwork was laid for the sole authority of the bishop in each diocese, the metropolitan in the province, and the Roman pontiff in the entire church.

C. *The Church and Feudalism*

The peoples of northern Europe who overran the crumbling Roman Empire had a profound effect on the church's regulatory system. These changes took place over a long period of time, however, not as a result of the invasions. They emerged in what we now describe as the feudal period (roughly mid-ninth century until early thirteenth), and they are related to some basic legal concepts developed among these peoples. The tribes had become quite settled, and also quite Christian.

Their system of laws was customary, more dependent on the oral traditions of how things were done than on laws written down in collections. It was closely entwined with the life and livelihood of the people, rather than inherited from the distant past. And it was tied to the land on which and from which they lived.

The feudal system was based on the concepts of vassalage (a personal promise of loyal service in return for protection and recompense), fealty (an oath of fidelity), and benefice (*beneficium*, income for the performance of a specific task). These and other features of feudal law impinged on the life of the church. For instance, the local lord gave priests the revenue from certain lands in exchange for the performance of their parochial duties. The pastorate became a benefice, an office tied to a source of income. And the lord, owner and protector of the land, dispensed the pastoral offices to whomever he wished, often without regard for the priest's qualifications or the spiritual welfare of the people.

The same was true of bishoprics and monasteries. Greater nobles and kings used these offices and the lands of the church to consolidate their power and income. The clergy promised faithful service to the secular rulers.

Many other elements of this tradition found their way into the church's discipline; e.g., the extensive use of oaths in judicial proceedings, stipends and stole fees on the occasion of sacramental ministries, personal penances replaced by offerings of money or performed by a substitute, etc. There were also certain participative procedures which were encouraged; e.g., the collegial forms of self-governance in religious orders, chapters of canons, confraternities, and lay associations.

Eventually the "privatization" of the church's public offices led to the great church-state conflict known as the "lay investiture controversy" of the late eleventh century. A restored papacy faced determined German kings in a struggle to regain control of ecclesiastical offices. The practice had been for the lords (laypersons) to install their chosen bishops and abbots in their offices by investing them with the symbols of office (pastoral staff and ring). Pope Gregory VII in 1075 decreed:

> . . . that no one of the clergy shall receive the investiture with a bishopric or abbey or church from the hand of an emperor or king or of any lay person, male or female. But if he shall do so he shall clearly know that such investiture is bereft of apostolic authority, and that he himself shall lie under excommunication until fitting satisfaction shall have been rendered.

The matter was not ended with a decree, for the practice of investiture was deeply embedded in the structure of feudal society. But after nearly fifty years of conflict, theological and political as well as military, the issue was fairly concluded with a compromise (at the Synod of Worms in 1122): bishops would be canonically elected and lay lords would no longer invest them with ring and staff, but they could be present for the elections and receive the homage of newly elected prelates for the feudal lands of their churches. Hence, the secular ruler still could exercise an effective veto over a candidate unacceptable to him. It was probably the best solution possible in the context of the times.

These were not transitory episodes in the medieval life of the church. Strong influences of Germanic law remain in the canonical tradition. Parishes were considered to be benefices and the *ius patronatus* (right of the patron to name the pastor) continued until the middle of the twentieth century. Mass stipends and oaths of fidelity and veracity are with us still. The gesture in the ordination ceremony of placing one's folded hands within those of the ordaining bishop while promising reverence and obedience is a replica of the feudal act of vassal homage. (It is a symbolic expression of the obligations of reverence and obedience of c. 273.) And the participative practices, e.g., election of leaders, deliberations in chapters, within religious communities and lay associations also endure.

The review of the period should not conclude without mention of five significant canonical collections:

1) in the East, the *Nomocanon* (from the Greek *nomos*, law, and *kanon*, rule), compilations which combined the civil laws of the empire and the canons of the church councils, edited in the ninth century and revised in the eleventh;
2) the *Collectio Dacheriana*, a lasting product of the Carolingian Reform, compiled in the middle of the ninth century (and named after its seventeenth-century French publisher!);
3) the *Decretum* of Bishop Burchard of Worms, a collection completed in 1012 which was widely used in schools and church offices;
4) three collections, *Tripartita, Decretum,* and *Panormia,* completed in 1094, by Bishop Ivo of Chartres, works influential in the debates of the Gregorian Reform;
5) the *Pseudo-Isidorian Decretals,* of unknown mid-ninth century authorship, attributed to the seventh-century Bishop Isidore of Seville, and containing fictitious decrees of several early popes; an influential collection of false documents, whose falsity was not discovered until the fifteenth century.

Here it is a sad necessity to note that, owing to the tragic events of 1054 which broke the bonds of unity between Eastern and Western Christianity, the two canonical traditions further diverge and cease to interact.

D. *The Classical Period of Canon Law*

The canons of the church were assembled into an organized and rationalized body of knowledge in the twelfth and thirteenth centuries.

This body of canonical knowledge was studied as a science and practiced as an art from that time on.

Three factors coalesced to make this period, from the mid-twelfth to the mid-fourteenth centuries, the "classical epoch" of canon law, a time of critical development and great influence: 1) a new and unparalleled collection of canons, 2) the systematic study of this new science in major educational centers, and 3) its mutually reinforcing relationship with a very strong papacy.

1) At the University of Bologna in the early twelfth century there occurred a major revival of interest in and study of Roman law. In that context, a Camaldolese monk, John Gratian, who taught in one of the faculties, compiled a collection of canons which he called *Concordantia Discordantium Canonum* (A Harmony of Discordant Canons). He completed the work about 1140. It became more commonly known as the *Decretum Gratiani* (Gratian's Decree), but it was a scholarly compilation, not a decree. Gratian's work surpassed and superseded all preceding canonical collections because it was more comprehensive, better organized, and because he applied to this mass of canonical literature a systematic process of scholastic analysis. Gratian analyzed the meaning of the terms used in the canons, examined the sources for the canons, and determined which canons had greater authority. When rules on the same issue diverged or were contradictory, he worked out a reconciliation (or harmony) of the canons by means of these principles of comparison and preference.

2) Gratian's *Decree* quickly became the one book used in all of the universities where canon law was studied, and their number multiplied in the decades following its publication; e.g., at Paris, Oxford, Salamanca, Montpellier, Padua. Teachers lectured on it, students studied it, and authors commented on it. (Those earliest commentators are called "decretists.") It was the unifying point of departure for a whole new field of study. More gradually it also became the standard reference work for those in papal and episcopal offices.

3) In this same period the papacy was establishing itself in Europe as a centralized and dominant power, both spiritually and temporally. The newly organized system of canon law assisted this growth and, in turn, the popes, now claiming wider legislative, judicial and administrative powers, issued more rules and decisions which further expanded the canons. The leading popes of this period were all canonists: Alexander III (1159–81 who had been a student of Gratian), Innocent III (1198–1216), Innocent IV (1243–54), and Boniface VIII (1294–1303). In their frequent negotia-

tions with the kings of Europe as well as in their daily governance of the church, these strong men relied heavily on the canonical system.

At the apogee of papally asserted "fullness of power" (*plenitudo potestatis*) Boniface VIII stated that the spiritual authority of the church was superior to the temporal power of civil rulers, and that church leaders could both instruct and sit in judgment upon those rulers. The highest spiritual powers could be judged by God alone. He concluded:

> Therefore we declare, state, define and pronounce that it is altogether necessary to salvation for every human creature to be subject to the Roman Pontiff. (The Bull *Unam Sanctam*, 1302.)

Papal decrees were not the only source of canons during this period. Four ecumenical councils were held during this time (two in Rome, Lateran III in 1179, IV in 1215, and two in Lyons, in 1245 and 1274), and each of these issued its own canonical regulations.

Popes and bishops used the newly developed canonical craft to undergird their authority and actions, but they also advanced the canonical science. Gregory IX (1227–41) ordered a Dominican scholar, Raymond of Peñafort, to compile all of the decrees and conciliar canons issued since Gratian's collection (as well as some materials Gratian had omitted). Gregory issued this collection of decretals (which became known as the *Decretales Gregorii IX*) in 1234. And for the first time it was promulgated as an authentic, official and exclusive source of rules for the whole church. All previous canonical collections had been essentially private and unofficial. (The commentators on Gregory's decretals are known as "decretalists".)

Decretal and conciliar legislation continued, and subsequent popes issued similar, well-ordered collections of canons. The quality of the scholarship surrounding this growing body of canons was exemplary. The canonical commentators and teachers were among the finest minds of the time. Three stand out:

1) Huguccio (Hugh of Pisa) taught at Bologna and was later Bishop of Ferrara; his *Summa* (about 1190) was among the finest works of the decretalists.
2) Hostiensis (Henry of Susa), taught at Paris and later became Cardinal-Bishop of Ostia; his *Summa* (1253) and *Lectura* (about 1270) place him at the head of the decretalists.
3) Joannes Andreae (John of Andrea), a layman and distinguished professor at Bologna, wrote two *glossa ordinaria* (commentaries, 1301 and 1322), and surveyed the whole of decretalist literature in his *Novella Commentaria* (1338).

Two other important canonical developments of this period should be mentioned. First, the mendicant religious orders (e.g., Franciscans, Dominicans, Carmelites, Servites), which were founded and flourished at this time, developed enduring constitutions and statutes which enabled them, under papal protection, to launch splendid apostolic initiatives and remain in control of their own destinies. Parallel to them and often related were the foundations and activities of Third Orders, confraternities and other lay organizations, which sponsored vast charitable and educational undertakings, supported by participative canonical structures.

Second, Roman law once again had a profound effect on canon law. The two systems were studied side-by-side. Many canonists also earned degrees in Roman law. The principles of interpretation were parallel. And the canonical system recognized Roman law as supplementary, i.e., when there was no canon to cover a certain matter, it was appropriate to harken to Roman law. (Throughout this and the following period the word "laws" referred to Roman laws, while "canons" referred to rules enacted by church authorities.)

Joannes Andreae died in 1348, a victim of the terrible Black Death which decimated Europe in the ensuing years. His death marks the end of the classical period of canon law and, to some extent, a decline in its vitality.

E. *Decline and Reform*

The Black Death (1348–49) broke the spirit of Western Europe, the Avignon Papacy (1309–77) weakened the papal office, and the Great Western Schism (1378–1417) shook the church to its foundations. The church had not really recovered from the schism and its aftermath, a woeful decline in discipline and morality, when its unity was splintered by the Protestant Reformation (1517–1560).

These tragic events did not trace a single, steady spiral of decline, but they severely buffeted the church, eroded its authority, and muffled its attempts to proclaim the gospel. Cries for "reform in head and members" arose on all sides.

Canonists were active in both directions, decline and reform. The powers of the papacy, so carefully crafted and enhanced in the classical period, now served to centralize church authority as never before. The popes of Avignon reserved to themselves the right to fill ecclesiastical offices all over Europe. They employed a litany of pretexts for intervening in the normal course of elections and appointments, not only to major archdioceses and dioceses, but to all manner of offices: canons, chaplains, houses of monks and friars. Sometimes these "reservations" of offices to the Holy See were due to abuses or disputes in the legitimate electoral processes, but more often the reasons were political or financial. The papal coffers at Avignon were filled by the taxes, required gifts, and revenues from these endowed offices. They were the principal means of support for a lavish papal court.

The reservation of appointments to church benefices was perhaps the most offensive exercise of the fullness of jurisdictional authority. However, an even greater abuse was the practice of "pluralism," that is, the simultaneous possession of several benefices by the same person. Some cardinals of the papal curia held more than fifteen offices at the same time. They were ecclesiastical positions, with incomes, all over Europe. Their holders never even visited the places, to say nothing of fulfilling the sacred duties attached to the offices. They coveted the income. They might hire a substitute to perform the local ministries, if they were keen of conscience. (One extreme example: As late as 1556, Cardinal Alessandro Farnese, grandson of Pope Paul III, possessed ten episcopal sees, twenty-six monasteries, and 133 other benefices—canonries, parishes and chaplaincies.)

Canonists designed and ran the machinery which drove the whole system, and it was both elaborate and effective. But the canonists also labored as agents of change. During the shameful disgrace that was the Western Schism, when two or three rivals simultaneously claimed the Chair of Peter for nearly forty years, canonical writers strove to resolve the conflict. They studied the relationships between pope, councils, emperor and people. The issue was finally resolved at the Council of Constance (1414–18), called the greatest representative assembly of the whole Middle Ages. There were more canonists than bishops in attendance!

The Council of Constance, in addition to its chief achievement of ridding the church of anti-popes and restoring the papal office, made a constitutional change. It decreed that general councils should be convened regularly and frequently (every ten years) as an effective means of ongoing church reform. Two following popes complied with that conciliar provision, but then it was allowed to fall into desuetude. High papalists interpreted the rule to imply that a council was superior to a pope and could sit in judgment on him (as Constance had done in order to clear the papal throne). High conciliarists had given reasons for concern but, in retrospect, such regular conciliar consultation might have mitigated the monarchical style of the papacy, and perhaps spared the church the greater grief which lay ahead.

The worldly Renaissance popes of the last half of the fifteenth and early sixteenth centuries (from Nicolas V, 1447–55, to Leo X, 1513–21) had some serious concerns, but church reform was not among them. Their need for huge amounts of money precluded any real consideration of the gross abuses related to church offices. Toward the end of this period a general council was called, the Fifth Lateran Council (1512–17), but it was so poorly attended that it scarcely merits the name ecumenical. It enacted lengthy reform decrees, but no one seemed committed to making them work.

The Protestant Reformation began with Martin Luther's actions of 1517. It precipitated the fracturing of Western Christianity.

> No one desired a reformation that would lead to a division in Western Christendom. The reformers wanted the reform of the one Church common to all. Because this reform in head and members was thwarted, the split occurred. Consequently, the Reformation would be the revolutionary rejoinder to the failure of reform in the fourteenth and fifteenth centuries. (E. Iserloh, *Handbook of Church History*, V, 3–4.)

Luther's burning of books of canon law at Wittenberg on December 10, 1520, symbolized not only his defiance of papal authority but also his view that the church leaders "constantly exalt their own ordinances above the commands of God." He complained that the volumes of canonistic literature "say nothing about Christ," but within a decade he had come to terms with the need for "good order and tranquility in the church." He then claimed that "we are more faithful to the canons than our opponents are" (Apology of the Augsburg Confession, 1530).

As Luther and the other leaders of the Reformation began to modify and refashion the canonical tradition to fit their own theology and practical needs, the Roman church slowly began to come to terms with its need for reform. The two successors of Pope Martin V could not or would not call for the necessary reform council. But Paul III (1534–49) did convoke a general council, after frustrating delays, in the city of Trent at the end of 1545. He accomplished three other things which set reform in motion: named a number of reform-minded men to the college of cardinals, urged on the reform of the major religious communities, and appointed a special commission on the reform of the church (*Consilium de Emendanda Ecclesia*). The report of the commission (in 1537) candidly pointed to the papal office, the College of Cardinals, and the Roman curia as most in need of reform.

In spite of enormous political obstacles and two long interruptions (it finally concluded in 1563, eighteen years after it began), the Council of Trent succeeded in enacting a series of decrees on the internal reform of the church, in addition to major doctrinal clarifications. It did not radically alter existing structures or create many new ones; instead it made rules about the qualifications for ordination and performance in office. It assigned clear responsibilities for bishops and parish priests. The restoration of the episcopate, morally and administratively, was a central focus. It outlawed simony, the possession of multiple benefices, absenteeism (the obligation of residency was a major point), and it stressed attention to the needs of the people. The chief aim of the council's reform decrees was the restoration of pastoral care.

Canonists played a key role in the deliberations at Trent, and the regulations which the council issued breathed new life into the canonical enterprise. Canon law, since the end of the classical period, lacked originality and drifted from its pastoral purpose. It had become repetitive, defensive, and increasingly distant from its essentially religious function. From the end of the council to at least the mid-eighteenth century, the reforming spirit and decrees of Trent dominated the canonical agenda.

Church renewal is never accomplished by rules alone. It takes determined leadership as well. To the extent that the Catholic "counter-reformation" actually succeeded in reforming the church, credit must be given to a series of convinced popes (Pius V, 1566–72, Gregory XIII, 1572–85, and Sixtus V, 1585–90, stand out) and a legion of committed bishops (some examples: Giberti of Verona, Fisher of Rochester, Borromeo of Milan, Thomas of Villanova, Francis de Sales in Savoy). They acted out in the life of the church the script written at Trent and, in doing so, set the standard for others.

Remarkably enough, the papal office emerged from the council even stronger and with greater authority than before, and the local power of bishops was enhanced by having them act in many matters as "delegates of the Apostolic See" in their own dioceses. The Roman curia and the college of cardinals were reformed, not so much by abolishing offices and procedures, but by appointing persons of integrity to the offices and insisting on their responsible performance.

The missionary activity of the church in the sixteenth and seventeenth centuries, following upon the discovery and exploration of "new worlds," opened up extensive areas for the development of canon law. Spanish and Portuguese missionaries went to America, Africa and Asia right along with the explorers and exploiters. Franciscans, Dominicans, Carmelites, Jesuits and other religious communities supplied the missionary spirit and personnel. They encountered new problems and sought new disciplinary answers; e.g., about administering baptism, holy communion, ordination of the native peoples, the toleration of slavery, the resolution of jurisdictional disputes, and the adaptation of rites to local cultures. These discussions were vital concerns of the canonists of the day.

In 1622 Pope Gregory XV established the Roman Congregation for the Propagation of the Faith in order to foster and coordinate this new missionary activity, as well as to reassert papal claims to jurisdiction over the territories (which the Spanish and Portuguese kings had assumed). The *Propaganda* became a powerful influence in the whole missionary movement. For example, its leaders pressed for the creation of an indigenous Christianity in mission lands as early as 1659. It also served as the interface between traditional canonical discipline and special provisions for the missions.

Two important canonical collections must be mentioned from this long period of "decline and reform":

1) the *Corpus Iuris Canonici* (Body of Canon Law) is the name given to a compendium of Gratian's *Decree,* the Decretals of Gregory IX, and four subsequent collections of decretals, first published as a single work in Paris in the year 1500 by John Chappuis and Vitale de Thebis. It was corrected and revised under the direction of Pope Gregory XIII in 1582. The *Corpus* is of supreme importance historically: It is the main source for regulations issued before the Council of Trent, and it remained the church's guiding book of rules, along with the *Canones et Decreta Concilii Tridentini,* until the promulgation of the first Code of Canon Law in 1917.

2) An important collection which was made under papal authority but never published is called the *Liber Septimus* (after the six books of the *Corpus*) or the *Decretales Clementis VIII* (after the pope, 1592–1605, who was supposed to issue it). It was begun in the 1580s as an attempt to gather together the decrees of the councils of Florence, Lateran V, and Trent as well as the papal decrees issued after the last book of the *Corpus.* It would have been a very valuable source!

Canonical writing in the first half of this long (fourteenth to eighteenth century) period tended to be limited to special questions which reflected the problems of the time; e.g., on schism, heresy, benefices, elections, taxes, papal versus conciliar authority. Later, however, in what is sometimes called the "golden age" of canonical studies, several outstanding authors composed comprehensive works of lasting influence: John Paul Lancelotti of Perugia composed *Institutiones Iuris Canonici* in 1563. (He almost had his work promulgated as official by the pope!) Henry

Pirhing, S.J., of Dillingen, wrote *Universum Ius Canonicum . . . Explicatum* (All of Canon Law Explained), 1674–78. Anacletus Reiffenstuel, O.S.F., of Freising, wrote *Universum Ius Canonicum*, published from 1700–14. Francis Schmalzgruber, S.J., of Ingolstadt, published *Ius Ecclesiasticum Universum* in 1717.

F. *The Church in the Modern World*

The church truly struggled to find its place in the world of enlightenment rationalism, absolutist monarchies, the French Revolution and the new liberalism, and the modern secular state. The papacy negotiated endlessly with kings and generals and presidents in order to defend and promote the interests of the church, but the presuppositions of a commonly shared Christendom were long gone. The emerging governments wanted either to be entirely separate from churches or to manipulate them for their own purposes.

The Roman Catholic Church no longer held the kind of power, wealth and privilege which it once possessed. In the late nineteenth century it even lost the papal states (central Italy). The popes, bishops and people fought hard, in the context of modern state regimes, for enough freedom and leverage for the church to continue its work of witness and worship. They suffered heavy losses in the process, e.g., the exile, imprisonment or death of thousands of priests and nuns, the suppression of religious communities, and the confiscation of vast amounts of church property. It was a tumultuous time of radical political and cultural changes.

One set of canonical issues was closely entwined with this ongoing church-state struggle. Its most common label is the debate between the Ultramontanists (those fostering a strong, centralized papal government for the church) and the Gallicans and Febronians (those arguing for the rights and freedoms of the churches of France and Germany, respectively, and for episcopal authority). Gallicanism began earlier, and had roots in the conciliarism of the reform councils of Constance and Basel. It was tinted with the bright shades of French nationalism.

Febronianism (after the pseudonym used by Bishop Johann Nikolaus von Hontheim when he wrote *De statu ecclesiae et legitima potestate Romani Pontificis* in 1763) was the outgrowth of a very respectable canonical tradition. Zeger-Bernard van Espen, Kaspar Barthel and Christoph Neller were three of its major authors and teachers. They hearkened back to the early church, before the exaggerated papal claims of the Pseudo-Isidorian Decrees and the Gregorian Reform, and asked for a return to its constitution, one in which bishops were recognized as the successors of the apostles. Bishops hold authority by divine right, and were not vicars or delegates of the pope. Gathered together with the pope in general council, the bishops were the true representatives of the body of the church. The pope was the center of unity, but not Universal Bishop with unfettered jurisdiction.

The canonists of the Roman curia and others (Jesuits in the forefront), countered these theories, and strongly asserted the prerogatives of the Petrine office and warned of the dangers of national churches. Eventually the Ultramontanists won out, not so much by force of canonical and theological argument, but as a result of many other factors, e.g., the practical realization that national churches were no match for strong governments, and that a sovereign papacy was a great advantage, the popular appeal of the papal office, and effective diplomatic negotiations with national leaders (like the concordat with Napoleon in 1801). The First Vatican Council in 1870, with its formal declaration of papal supremacy (*Pastor aeternus*), effectively ended the debate.

Apart from the heated Gallican-Febronian controversy, the canonical waters of this period were relatively calm, nearly stagnant. There was no conciliar legislation because no other general councils were held; the First Vatican was the only one held since Trent, more than three centuries earlier. Papal decrees continued to be issued on various matters of discipline. The many concordats between the Holy See and civil governments added canonical regulations applicable in nations affected. For example, the concordat with Napoleon allowed the French ruler to name bishops, but assured that the state would pay the salaries of the clergy in compensation for confiscated church property. This pact was the prototype for several subsequent agreements in the nineteenth century.

Canon law had become formalistic and repetitive. Its study in seminaries and religious houses of studies was shallow and ahistorical. In important areas (e.g., sacraments, penalties, clerical obligations) its teaching was combined with that of moral theology, and neither discipline benefited from the marriage. Manuals of canon law multiplied, and were largely duplications of one another. Authors settled disputed issues by counting the authorities on both sides, rather than by intrinsic arguments.

There were a few outstanding canonical writers, and they broke some new ground, especially with important historical studies. These names stand out: Prosper Lambertini (1675–1758, also known as Pope Benedict XIV, 1740–58), Frederick Maassen (1823–1900), John Frederick von Schulte (1827–1914), Francis Xavier Wernz, S.J. (1842–1914), George Phillips (1804–72), Ferdinand Walter (1794–1879), Paul Hinschius (1835–98), and Ulrich Stutz (1868–1914).

G. The Codification of Canon Law

The papacy had come a long way from the humiliating imprisonment of Pius VII by Napoleon (1809–14) to the relatively exalted situation of Pius X (1903–14). The popes of the Catholic restoration had succeeded in gaining respect and authority for a renewed papal office. They never changed their defensive posture or shed their siege mentality in relationship to the modern world, but they managed to centralize and concentrate their authority within the church as well as their respect outside it. The Ultramontanist triumph left the papal office a virtually absolute monarchy.

Pius X was one of the great reform popes, but his mode of reform was conservative, restorationist, and "from the top down." No sooner was he elected than he began the reorganization of canon law.

Bishops and canonists for decades had sought a new collection of canons. The last official collection was that of John XXII in 1317. Little was added when the *Corpus Iuris Canonici* was put together in 1500 and again in 1582. The *Liber Septimus*, attempted after the Council of Trent, was never issued. The sheer number of extant laws was vast; they had grown like mushrooms in the ensuing centuries. They were not systematically arranged; often they were listed in chronological order. Some of the documents in the collections were not laws at all, some were contradictory, some had been abrogated or fallen into desuetude, many were written in a diffuse and obscure prose. The canons had grown into a large thicket in which living and dead branches intertwined, making passage exceedingly difficult even for the skilled canonist. In preparation for the First Vatican Council a group of French bishops had written to Rome: "We are drowning in laws."

In March, 1904, Pius X set in motion the "truly difficult task" (*arduum sane munus*) of "collecting the laws of the universal church, in a clear and concise order, and adapting them to the conditions of our time." To direct the effort he chose a curial canonist who had taught at the University of Paris, Pietro Gasparri (1852–1934), a man of extraordinary talent, energy and persistence. Gasparri worked with commissions of consultors for ten years at the prodigious task of organizing, sifting and reformulating the canons. It was more a work of legal drafting than legislating. Although the work was carried on in secret, it began and ended with a consultation of all the bishops and Catholic universities of the world.

A key decision, made at the outset, was the choice to make a code rather than a collection. All previous compilations of canons had been in the form of collections of documents; the original words, pastoral situation, date, and issuing authority were retained. The canonical rule remained in its historical context. *Codification* is an exercise in conceptual juridical abstraction. It strives to reduce the rules to terse and abstract formulations, and arrange them in a carefully constructed system. It is strong on clarity, brevity, consistency and order, but the rules are entirely set apart from the social and historical context which gave rise to them. (The Uniform Commercial Code is a good example of a contemporary law code in the United States.)

Codification was in vogue in Europe in the nineteenth century. Napoleon used the code style in 1804 to erase the memory of the *ancien regime* in France. Germany, Switzerland and Italy were using the codification process. Gasparri and his coworkers admired it and adopted it.

The reformulation of the canons and the final consultation were completed by the end of 1914, but Pius X had died and World War I broke out, so it was decided to wait until Pentecost, 1917, to promulgate the first Code of Canon Law. Pope Benedict XV, with that single legislative act "made it all his own," and swept aside all previous canonical enactments. The Code actually took effect one year later, Pentecost, 1918; a year's *vacatio legis* was given for the church to get used to its new set of rules.

The new Code was hailed as a great success. It was handy, well-ordered and accessible (just 2,414 canons), and canonists took to it with relish. They promptly began to prepare commentaries on it and restructured their courses in accord with it.

The Code furthered the centralization of authority at both papal and episcopal levels, and reinforced an extreme uniformity of practice in the church. But it also brought relative order out of the chaotic state of canon law at the beginning of the twentieth century. The promulgation of the Code marked the opening of a new canonical epoch.

In the following decades the Code served as a book of answers, sometimes even as a catechism. It began to get "out of date" in a fast-changing world. Many changes were made in the rules, but they were not inserted into the Code. Once again, the rules outside the rulebook began to outnumber those within it. More basically, the pastoral restructuring needed for effective ministry in the modern world was not forthcoming. But canonists didn't notice. It took the visionary Pope John XXIII to see that the canons needed *aggiornamento* (updating).

Reform Movements and Canon Law

By way of a reprise of this historical overview of canon law, it might be helpful to recall the reform periods in the church's history and the role that the canons played in them.

1. The Gelasian Renaissance (492–529), beginning with the papacy of Gelasius I (492–96), out of which came the collections of canons of Dionysius Exiguus, the *Dionysiana*.

2. The Carolingian Reform (750–850), named for the emperor Charlemagne, in which the collection *Dacheriana* (compiled from the *Dionysiana-Hadriana* and the *Hispana*) aided in the renewal.

3. The Gregorian Reform (1059–1122), in which the monk Hildebrand, Gregory VII (1073–85) used earlier collections of canons and stimulated further collections with his own *Dictatus Papae*.

4. The Conciliar Solution (1409–1449) to the constitutional crisis of the Great Western Schism was based on the canonical theories and courageous actions of ecumenical councils.

5. The Tridentine Reform or the Catholic counter-reformation (1534–1605) focused on the reform decrees of the Council of Trent (1545–63).

6. The Conservative Reform of Pius X (1903–14) in which the first codification of canons played a great part.

7. To these historical movements of reform, the present one might be added: inaugurated in 1959 by John XXIII, centered in the Second Vatican Council (1962–65), carried on by Paul VI and John Paul II, and including the 1983 Code of Canon Law.

Bibliography on the History of Canon Law

MAJOR STUDIES:

Histoire du Droit et des Institutions de l'Eglise en Occident, eds. Gabriel Le Bras and Jean Gaudemet, sixteen volumes (Paris: Sirey [later Cujas], 1955–1981).

Willibald Plochl, *Geschichte des Kirchenrechts*, five volumes (Wien: Herold, 1953–1969).

Hans Feine, *Kirchliche Rechtsgeschichte: Die katholische Kirche* (5th ed., Köln: Bohlau, 1972).

(History of Medieval Canon Law, eds. Wilfried Hartmann and Kenneth Pennington, in three volumes, to be published in Washington by The Catholic University of America Press, is eagerly awaited.)

SHORTER STUDIES:

A. Van Hove, *Prolegomena ad Codicem Iuris Canonici* (Malines: Dessain, 1945).

Alphons Stickler, *Historia Iuris Canonici Latini* (Turin: Salesianum, 1950).

Ivo Zeiger, *Historia Iuris Canonici* (Rome: Gregorianum, 1947).

Bertrand Kurtscheid, *Historia Iuris Canonici* (Rome: Catholic Book Agency, 1951).

FOR STUDIES OF INDIVIDUAL PERIODS AND TOPICS:

Dictionnaire de Droit Canonique, ed. R. Naz, seven volumes (Paris: Letouzey et Ane, 1935–1965).

Handbook of Church History [later, *History of the Church*], eds. Hubert Jedin and John Dolan, ten volumes (New York: Herder & Herder [later, Seabury, Crossroads], 1965–81).

ESSAYS IN ENGLISH:

G. May, A. Stickler, K. Morsdorf, L. Bender, "Ecclesiastical Law," *Sacramentum Mundi*, vol. 2 (New York: Herder & Herder, 1968) 142–167.

C. Vogel, H. Fuhrmann, C. Munier, L. Boyle, A. De Sousa Costa, P. Leisching, R. Metz, "Canon Law, History of" *New Catholic Encyclopedia*, vol. 3 (New York: McGraw-Hill, 1967) 34–50.

J. Lynch, "Canon Law," *The New Dictionary of Theology*, eds. J. Komonchak, M.Collins, D. Lane (Wilmington: Glazier, 1987) 149–156.

P. Huizing, "Canon Law," *Encyclopaedia Britannica*, 15th ed., 1974.

J. Taylor, "Canon Law in the Age of the Fathers," *Australasian Catholic Record* 56:2(1977) 151–168.

A. Cicognani, *Canon Law* (Philadelphia: Dolphin, 1935) 131–412.

Canonical Sources, Forms, and Distinctions

Sources

What are the sources of the rules which make up the church's canonical system? Where did those who compiled the various collections find the canons they included? This list summarizes the most common sources for the canons:

1. *The Sacred Scriptures.* Both New and Old Testament authors were cited as the highest authorities in matters of church discipline.

2. *Natural Law.* Those structures or values which are considered to be of the very essence of things, e.g., monogamy in marriage, truth in speech, were and are often called upon as bases for rules.

3. *Custom.* Long-standing practices within the earliest church communities, e.g., Sunday observance, the celebration of Easter, were taken to be normative. Custom is still a source of norms.

4. *Councils.* The periodic gatherings of the leaders of local churches, called synods or councils, often deliberated and settled matters of discipline, e.g., rebaptism or reordination. Ecumenical councils, like the Second Vatican Council, are a major source of ecclesiastical regulations.

5. *Fathers of the Church.* The writings of many authors in the early centuries were revered and taken to be authoritative, e.g., *Didache*, Irenaeus, Cyprian, Basil, *Constitutiones Apostolorum*, John Chrysostom, Ambrose, Jerome, Augustine.

6. *Popes.* The letters and responses sent by the Bishop of Rome were received with special respect and gradually evolved (in the early fifth century) into decretals with the force of general regulations.

7. *Bishops.* When leading bishops made pastoral judgments or rules for their dioceses, they were often imitated and applied elsewhere.

8. *Rules of Religious Orders.* The constitutions or rules evolved within religious communities, e.g., Benedictines, Franciscans, Dominicans, influenced other religious groups and, eventually, the general rules of the church.

9. *Civil Law.* The enactments of the Roman emperors and of later kings and legislatures on matters which affect religion have often been accepted as authoritative by the church.

10. *Concordats.* Formal international agreements between the Holy See and national governments are a modern source for canonical regulations.

Canon law is a complex tapestry woven from these diverse strands and threads.

Literary Forms

Strange as it might seem, canon law and the Code of Canon Law in particular, contain different literary forms. Not everything in the canons is law, not everything is statutory. It is necessary, from the very outset, to be attentive to the literary form which one encounters in the canons, just as it is, for example, in the sacred scriptures. The Old and New Testaments include many different literary forms, e.g., poetry, letter, history, parable, sermon, apocalyptic, prophecy, proverb. In order to understand the writing, one must first ask what kind of writing it is. It is the same in canon law. Although the canons look very much alike, they contain several different kinds of writing. It is important to recognize the literary form before trying to interpret the meaning of the canon.

Doctrinal Statements. Often canons are statements of the teachings of the church, rather than rules of behavior. Sometimes the formulations of doctrine are expressions of the church's faith, parts of its creed, e.g., the descriptions of the sacraments of baptism, eucharist and penance (cc. 849, 897, 959). At other times the doctrinal canons are theological opinions or moral values, e.g., the purposes of marriage (c. 1055), the nature of the evangelical counsels (c. 575) or of the contemplative life (c. 674). Occasionally, they declare philosophical theories, like the canon on Catholic education (c. 795). In all these instances the canons are doctrinal statements, intended to give the background or context for rules of action, but containing no sense of legal precept themselves.

Norms of Action. Within this broad category, there are diverse forms:

1. *Exhortations:* schools should be valued (c. 796), the faithful should join approved associations (c. 298), clerics should give superfluous income to charity (c. 282).
2. *Admonitions:* use discretion in the use of the media (c. 666), refrain from everything alien to the clerical state (c. 285), avoid dangerous companions (c. 277).
3. *Directives:* maintain communion (c. 210), show pastoral care for your people (c. 383), see that the word of God is proclaimed (c. 529).
4. *Precepts:* record the marriage (c. 1121), hear the finance council (c. 1277), take possession of the diocese (c. 382).
5. *Prohibitions:* do not damage another's good name (c.220), clerics are forbidden to assume public office (c. 285), do not sell church property without permission (c. 1291).
6. *Penalties:* a confessor who breaks the seal of confession is excommunicated (c. 1388), a priest who strikes a bishop is interdicted and suspended (c. 1370).
7. *Procedures:* a censure cannot be imposed unless the accused has been warned (c. 1347), the respondent must be notified of the trial (c. 1507).
8. *Constitutional elements:* those incorporated into Christ by baptism share his priestly, prophetic and royal offices (c. 204), the pope and the bishops hold supreme authority in the church (cc. 331, 336).

A threshold question in canonical investigation is: What kind of writing is this? Before one attempts to discern the meaning and possible obligation of a passage or a canon, its literary form must be clarified. That guides all further understanding.

Distinctions

1. **Universal, Particular.** Canon law is divided into universal or general or common norms as opposed to particular or proper or special norms depending on whether they apply to the whole Latin church, in all parts of the world, or just to some part of it. Particular laws are those which apply only to a determined area or group of people, like the church in one nation or one diocese. Proper law usually refers to the constitutions and other rules of a religious community, its own norms. Special law is that which governs a process, like the election of the

pope, the canonization of a saint, the operations of an office of the Roman Curia, or a particular kind of judicial trial.

2. **Prescriptive, Penal.** Canons are prescriptive, either preceptive or prohibitive, if they command those subject to them to do or refrain from doing something. They are penal if they attach a specific or generic penalty to the violation of the canon.

3. **Divine, Human.** Canons are said to embody divine law if they are drawn directly from God's revelation or from the natural law, God's creation. The vast majority of canons are human law ("merely ecclesiastical law," c. 11) that is, enactments of the church's own authority and, consequently, alterable.

4. **Invalid, Illicit.** Some rules are invalidating, which means that actions placed in violation of them are null and void, of no juridic effect. Some are incapacitating, meaning that the person is juridically unable to place the action, and the attempt brings the same result, a nullity. Such radical limitations must be expressly stated (c. 10). The violation of most prescriptive canons results in an illicit action, one that is unlawful, but still valid and effective.

5. **Constitutive.** Some canons are constitutive, that is, they define the very essence of a juridical institute or act, e.g., people for a parish (c. 515), water for baptism (c. 849), consecration for a bishop (c. 375). These cannot be dispensed from, because to do so would be to change the nature of the thing (c. 86).

6. **Normalcy, Emergency.** Most non-constitutive canons are intended to oblige "most of the time" (*ut in pluribus*), that is, in the common contingency, in ordinary circumstances. They may not oblige in emergencies or in extreme situations, depending on their seriousness.

7. **Substantial Observance.** Some canons admit of substantial rather than complete and total observance, meaning that occasional nonobservance does not constitute a violation. For example, those who regularly and habitually pray the liturgy of the hours (c. 276.2.3), abstain from meat on Fridays (c. 1251), and participate in mass and refrain from work on Sundays and holy days (c. 1247), may occasionally excuse themselves from the observance of these rules for a good reason without violating the general obligation.

8. **External, Internal Forum.** Almost all canonical matters pertain to the external forum, that is, the arena of the church's public governance wherein the power of governance is normally exercised (c. 130). There also exists the internal forum or the forum of conscience, also called the *forum Dei*, the forum of God, because it is the arena of one's personal relationship, graced or sinful, with God. Sacramental confession and absolution pertain to the internal forum, and therefore are surrounded with the strictest secrecy (cc. 993, 994, 1388). In rare instances the power of governance is exercised in the internal forum (cc. 1079, 1080, 1357).

The Code of Canon Law

The key and controlling document in the canon law of the Western church is the Code of Canon Law which was promulgated by Pope John Paul II in 1983. The official Latin text was published in a single volume of about three hundred pages. It contains 1,752 canons. An annotated and well-indexed version is also available from its Vatican publisher. The Code has been translated into many modern languages.

Background

It was Pope John XXIII who set things in motion. There was no talk of a revised Code when, on January 25, 1959, just a few months after his election, Pope John announced his vision of a three-part enterprise for his papacy: 1) a synod for the diocese of Rome, 2) an ecumenical council, and 3) a modernization (*aggiornamento*) of the Code of Canon Law.

Pope John created a Commission for the Revision (actually, *recognitio*, a rethinking) of the Code in 1963, not long after the beginning of the Second Vatican Council, and a short time before his own death. Pope Paul VI set the commission to work just as the Council drew to a close in November, 1965. He told them that their task was more than the updating of a fifty year old document (the 1917 Code). They were to reorganize the church's discipline and to accommodate it to the teachings of the council. They were also to reform the church's canonical style, to give it a "new way of thinking" (*novus habitus mentis*), responsive to new needs. Pope Paul implied that the old canonical style of formalism, legalistic hair-splitting and secular juridicism had to be transcended.

Principles of Revision

One of the commission's first actions was to draft a set of principles to guide their work of rethinking the Code. These were approved by the Synod of Bishops held in 1967. They endure as valuable guidelines for contemporary canonists. They are presented here in summary form:

35

1. The Code is to define and protect the rights and obligations of the faithful in relation to one another and to the church. Its norms are to help the faithful, in the course of their Christian lives, share in whatever assistance toward salvation the church offers them.

2. The external and internal forums should be coordinated and not in conflict with one another.

3. Pastoral care is to be fostered above all, and to that end both the legislation and its application are to be characterized by charity, moderation, humanity and equity as well as justice. Exhortation and persuasion are to be preferred to an insistence on rights.

4. Bishops are to have the authority to dispense from the general laws of the church.

5. The principle of subsidiarity is to be more effectively applied, especially because the office of bishop is of divine law. Where unity of discipline is not required, decentralization should prevail, especially in the form of particular legislation and a healthy autonomy of executive authority.

6. The rights of persons are to be defined and safeguarded, since all the Christian faithful are fundamentally equal and their offices and duties so diverse. Then the exercise of authority will appear more clearly as service, and it will be more effective and free from abuse.

7. Subjective rights are to be protected by suitable procedures. The administration of justice must be improved, and the various functions of church authority, namely, legislative, administrative and judicial, are to be clearly distinguished.

8. Portions of the People of God are to be determined territorially for purposes of governance, but other criteria may also be used to describe communities of the faithful.

9. Penalties are sometimes necessary, but they are to be imposed in the external forum and after judgment; those imposed by the law itself are to be reduced to a minimum.

10. The new Code is to be restructured to reflect its accommodation to a new mentality and different needs.

The preface to the Code affirms that the drafters were, in point of fact, guided by these principles. That is not always obvious in the results of their labors.

Promulgation of the Revised Code

In 1968 the commission organized itself into about a dozen working groups, composed mostly of canonists who served as consultors (over two hundred persons in all). They came together in Rome on a regular schedule, and corresponded between meetings. When a preliminary draft of their section of canons was ready, they circulated it to all the bishops (and Catholic universities) of the world for reaction. Then they weighed the responses, and modified the draft.

A final draft of the entire Code was ready in 1980, and it was circulated to the cardinals who made up the commission. They came together in October, 1981, made some emendations, and approved the product. In April, 1982, the draft was presented to Pope John Paul II, who spent several months with a small group of advisors reviewing and adjusting it. On January 25, 1983, exactly twenty-four years after Pope John XXIII announced the project, the pope promulgated the Code of Canon Law, and declared that it would go into effect on the First Sunday of Advent, November 27, 1983.

Relationship to the Council

It is of the highest importance to recognize the relationship of the 1983 Code of Canon Law to the Second Vatican Council. This relationship is a key to the proper understanding of the canons of the Code. The Code's connections to the Council are multiple and strong:

1. In the creative vision of Pope John XXIII the two were closely linked. He said that the council would suggest the reforms to be introduced into the legislation of the church.

2. The fathers (i.e., the bishops) of the council were quite conscious of the canonical revision which was to follow their own deliberations. They left the specification of many disciplinary matters to that subsequent drafting process. They thought of the Code as as instrument for carrying out the decisions of the council.

3. Pope Paul VI explicitly stated that the Commission for Revision would formulate in concrete terms the deliberations of the ecumenical council.

4. The Commission for Revision and the consultors who drafted the Code referred to the documents of the council continuously and conscientiously during the course of their work.

5. Pope John Paul II made the connection between the Code and council repeatedly, both during the drafting process and at the point of formal promulgation. He said that the Code depends on the previous work of the council, reflects its theology, and manifests its spirit.

6. The canons of the Code themselves reveal its close dependent relationship on the council. They employ very frequently the concepts and language of the conciliar decrees. Those documents are cited many hundreds of times in the footnotes to the canons.

The conclusion to draw from these firm and undeniable bonds between council and Code is that the council governs the Code, and not the other way around. To understand the canons properly, one must seek their meaning in their sources, the documents of the council. Those conciliar teachings rule and guide the interpretation of the canons.

It is true to say that the Code of Canon Law is the fruit of the Second Vatican Council, the council's "final document." This means that the canons of the Code must be read in the light of the constitutions and decrees of council which gave rise to them.

Organization of the Code

The Code of Canon Law features a new and improved internal organization, in response to principle number ten (above). In the past, canonical collections and codes borrowed their organizational design from secular or civil law patterns, with categories derived from Roman law. For example, the 1917 Code was divided into five sections (called "books"): General Norms, Persons, Things, Procedures, Crimes and Punishments. By contrast, the organization of the present Code of Canon Law is based on the theology of the church of the Second Vatican Council. It prominently employs the "People of God" language and the threefold division of the church's mission and ministry into teaching, sanctifying and ruling. (The Latin word used for this threefold role is *munus*, which can mean service, office, function, duty or work. "Function" seems to be the best translation here.) This triad is another way of describing the classical messianic roles of Christ: prophet, priest and king.

The Code of Canon Law is divided into seven sections (also called "books"). This is a brief summary of their contents:

1. **General Norms.** The first book contains the building blocks for the whole canonical system. These canons define the terms, persons, instruments and powers which are employed in the rest of the Code and outside it as well. These are very basic concepts, most of them drawn from the long canonical tradition and its Roman law roots.

2. **The People of God.** This is the central, largest and most important part of the Code. It reveals the constitution of the church. Members and their rights and duties are set forth first, then the ordained ministry (the clergy), and the associations of the faithful. The hierarchy is described: pope, college of bishops, dioceses, their officials and their groupings. Parishes, pastors and other pastoral roles are outlined, and religious institutes and societies of apostolic life are described.

3. **The Teaching Function.** The various persons responsible for preaching, catechesis, missionary action and Catholic schools are all set forth here. This book is mostly new and directly from the documents of the Second Vatican Council. It closes with rules on the prior censorship of books.

4. **The Sanctifying Function.** This is the second longest and most important book of the Code. It contains the canonical discipline of the sacraments and other acts of divine worship, as well as that for churches, altars, cemeteries, and days of feast and fast.

5. **Temporal Goods of the Church.** Here, in the Code's shortest book, are found the rules for the acquisition, disposition and administration of the church's monies, lands and buildings, as well as the rules on wills and bequests.

6. **Sanctions in the Church.** Those acts which are considered crimes in the church and the appropriate punishments for them are outlined here.

7. **Procedures.** This last book treats of the judicial processes used for trials in church courts, as well as some specialized administrative procedures, like those for administrative recourse or for the removal of a pastor.

The Code consists of 1,752 canons, very different in style, content, weight and application. Together they represent the controlling center of the church's whole canonical system.

Status of the Code

The Code of Canon Law, promulgated on January 25, 1983, has the "force of law" for the entire Latin church. It is the *ius vigens*, the canonical collection with unique juridical effect. This Code is the operative center of the church's system of canonical regulations. It does not contain all of the norms, or even the majority of them, but all the others are to accord with those in the Code.

The Code replaces all previous collections, i.e., the 1917 Code, the decrees of the Council of Trent, the Corpus Iuris Canonici, etc. It supplants them, abrogates them (c. 6). However, those previous collections, and the many other rules enacted apart from them do retain value. They are the *ius vetus*, the "old law," and, as such, are important witnesses to the canonical tradition. The present canons, when substantially similar to their predecessors (as is very often the case) are to be understood as the old ones were (c.6.2). Hence, the former collections of canons remain as sources of interpretation even though they now lack all juridical authority.

Scope of the Code

In its introductory canons (cc. 1–6) the Code states its own limits:

1. It only applies to the Latin or Western church, not to the Eastern or Oriental churches in union with Rome, e.g., the Byzantine, Armenian, Chaldean, Antiochene, or Alexandrian churches (c. 1).

2. It does not, for the most part, regulate liturgical matters (c. 2). This limitation is especially important to recognize. The rules which guide the church's liturgical life, the celebration of the sacraments and other acts of public worship, are usually not found in the Code. The Code is only a secondary source for a very limited number of liturgical norms. Sacramental and liturgical norms are found in the introductory sections of the ritual books or *ordines* for the various sacraments, for example, the General Instruction on the Roman Missal, the Rite of Christian Initiation of Adults, the Orders of Penance, Marriage and Anointing of the Sick. Not only are these liturgical books the more complete and appropriate sources for the norms of worship, but in them the rules are properly set within a rich context of theological and pastoral explanations. Go to them for liturgical and sacramental guidance rather than to the Code.

3. The canonical rules which apply in individual nations which result from special agreements between their governments and the Holy See, agreements called "concordats," are not found in the Code (c. 3).

4. Some acquired rights and privileges, which are not contrary to the canons of the Code, remain in effect (c. 4).

5. Some customs, either not contrary to the provisions of the Code or of ancient vintage, may also remain in effect (c. 5).

6. All sorts of special or particular rules, e.g., norms for the canonization of saints, procedures used within Roman congregations, national guidelines, diocesan rules, the constitutions and norms of religious institutes, etc., are not found in the Code (6.1.2). These various particular rules are to be in keeping with the canons of the Code, not in conflict with them.

A CANONICAL CONSTITUTION
OF THE CHURCH

Pope Paul VI, in his initial charge to the Commission for Revision of the Code in November, 1965, suggested that they might try to formulate a constitution for the church. He had in mind a "fundamental law" (*lex ecclesiae fundamentalis*) which would set forth the basic structures of the church, and which would form the basis for the codes of discipline for the Latin church and the Oriental churches.

The commission did compose such a constitutional statement, and first circulated it for reactions in 1969. It received mixed reviews. A second draft was sent around in 1971, and it fared no better. Work continued, and at least two more versions were made in collaboration with representatives of the Oriental churches, in 1976 and 1980.

Many serious objections were raised against this constitutional initiative: some felt that it would obscure the fact that Christ and his Spirit are the true basis of the church, that the sacred scriptures are its real constitution, and that it would be an obstacle to ecumenical progress. Finally, the project was abandoned, but many of the canons in the *Lex Ecclesiae Fundamentalis* were transferred into the Code, e.g., the list of rights and obligations of the Christian faithful (cc. 208–223).

The following summary of the 1980 draft is presented here, not because it has any juridical authority, but because it offers an overview of the fundamental principles of the external structures of the church. It was subtitled: "The Fundamental Canonical Law of the Universal Catholic Church." To reiterate: it was never promulgated. (References are to the canons of the draft.)

Title I: The Church

There is one church of Christ, the new People of God gathered by the Holy Spirit, and that church subsists in the Catholic Church (1). The universal church is a body of churches, made up of particular churches, portions of God's people, with their own bishop and presbyterate, called

45

together by the Spirit through the gospel and the eucharist. Some of these particular churches are gathered into ritual churches, with their own discipline, and others are joined into provinces and regions. The pilgrim church on earth shares the lot of humankind, and always seeks its own reform and faithfulness to its calling. It also strives that all be one in Christ, while respecting the varieties of customs, disciplines and formulations of doctrine (2).

Chapter I:
All the Christian Faithful

ARTICLE 1: CALL AND INCORPORATION OF PERSONS IN THE CHURCH

The church recognizes the dignity of the human person and the duties and rights which flow from it (3). All must seek the truth, and are called to the church of Christ when they recognize it, but always freely. They have a right to be received into the church (4). Persons are incorporated into the church by baptism, which establishes them as subjects of duties and rights, as long as they remain in communion (5). Those who are joined to Christ by bonds of faith, sacraments and church governance are fully in the Catholic communion (6). Those members of other, separated churches, who are baptized and believe in Christ, are recognized as sisters and brothers in the Lord; however, they are not bound by the laws of the Catholic Church (7). Catechumens are joined to the church, which cherishes them as its own (8).

ARTICLE 2: FUNDAMENTAL RIGHTS AND DUTIES OF THE FAITHFUL

(This list of rights and obligations, canons 9 through 24 in the draft, is substantially the same as canons 208–223 of the Code. They are summarized below in the chapter, "The People of God.")

ARTICLE 3: DIVERSE STATES OF THE CHRISTIAN FAITHFUL

Some of the faithful are, by ordination, sacred ministers, others laity. From among both, some are consecrated to God and the saving mission of the church by profession of the evangelical counsels (25). Sacred ministers are bound to nourish the people of God, so that together all might fulfill the commandment of love (26). Those who publicly profess the evangelical counsels work for the kingdom of God according to their calling (27). Laity, by reason of their baptism, are configured to Christ and share in the church's saving mission and functions. They give witness to Christ by directing temporal affairs according to God's plan (28).

Chapter II:
Hierarchical Structures of the Church

ARTICLE 1: THE POPE AND THE COLLEGE OF BISHOPS

The Lord Jesus willed that the apostles, with Peter as their head, be the pastors of his church. The bishop of Rome, successor of Peter, is the head of the college of bishops. He has supreme and full authority in the church. The bishops, successors of the apostles, by their sacramental consecration and ecclesial communion, make up a college, which also has supreme and full authority in the church (29).

The pope obtains office by election, along with episcopal consecration (30). The pope also has authority over all of the particular churches, so that he can strengthen the proper authority of the bishops in those churches. The pope is in communion with the other bishops and with the universal church (31). The bishops assist the pope in his role as supreme pastor; one way they do that is in the synod of bishops, a gathering of bishops from various regions. The cardinals and other persons and institutions also assist the pope according to the needs of the times (32).

Bishops, by their consecration, receive sanctifying, teaching and ruling functions, but they must exercise them in communion with the rest of the college. They also share in the solicitude for all of the churches which make up the universal church (34). The college of bishops exercises its authority solemnly in ecumenical council, otherwise by the united collegial action of bishops throughout the world (35). The pope convokes councils, presides over them, sets their agenda, and approves their decrees (36).

ARTICLE 2: PATRIARCHS AND MAJOR ARCHBISHOPS

In the Oriental churches, the patriarchs enjoy authority over clergy and people, including the nomination of bishops, in accordance with ancient traditions and decrees of ecumenical councils (40). Major archbishops in the Oriental churches have similar authority (41).

ARTICLE 3: INDIVIDUAL BISHOPS

Individual bishops who have been entrusted with the care of particular churches lead them as vicars and legates of Christ, and as pastors they nourish their people, exercising the functions of teaching, sanctifying and ruling. This pastoral authority, which they receive by episcopal consecration, is made operative by their canonical mission, which implies apostolic communion (43). All bishops, by Christ's command, are obliged to be solicitous for the universal church, hence they must be concerned about the unity and spread of the faith, commmon discipline, and assistance for needy churches (44).

ARTICLE 4: PRESBYTERS AND DEACONS

Presbyters share in the priesthood of Christ with their bishops, and they are ministers of Christ, deputed by ordination to announce the word of God, to offer sacrifice, and to forgive sins. Presbyters share in the ministry of Christ by means of sacred ordination and the mission which they receive from bishops. They nourish the communities entrusted to them, and give aid and counsel to bishops in caring for the people of God (46). Presbyters together with the bishop form one presbyterium, dedicated to the service of a particular church under the bishop's direction; they are related to one another in a close sacramental fraternity (47).

Deacons, strengthened by the grace of orders, assist bishops and presbyters, and serve the people of God in ministries of liturgy, word and charity (48).

Chapter III:
The Mission of the Church

The church, which is a spiritual community of faithful people, established on earth as a hierarchically ordered society, is directed to the spread of the kingdom of God, with the aid of the Holy Spirit. The church has its proper mission in the religious sphere, and from that mission it can offer light and energy to the human community so that it might be structured in accord with God's law (49). The church recognizes the autonomy, laws and values of the temporal order, so long as they respect the Creator's design. The faithful, in keeping with their vocations, are to see to it that temporal affairs are ordered in accord with God's plan. The church is not tied to any one form of human culture or any political, economic or social system, and it can bond together diverse human communities (50).

The church acknowledges and defends religious liberty for all persons; they are to be free from all coercion to lead their religious lives, privately and publicly, according to their consciences (51). The church has a right to its own freedom and independence, so that it can fulfill its own saving mission; it claims the right to live in civil society according to the norms of Christian faith (52). This religious liberty is the fundamental principle of the church's relationship with the state (53). The church takes its place in the community of nations, and strives to work with them for justice and peace in the world (54).

Title II: The Functions of the Church

The church has a threefold function: to teach all nations, to sanctify those who believe in Christ, and to govern God's people. The three come together in the eucharist, and they are all directed to the praise of God and the sanctification of humankind (55). Sacred ministers, i.e., bishops, presbyters and deacons, have a leading role in these functions, but all of the faithful, since they share in Christ's priestly, prophetical and kingly functions in virtue of their baptism and confirmation, also have their own role in fulfilling these three functions (56).

Chapter I:
The Teaching Function of the Church

The church has the right to preach the gospel to all nations, to safeguard and announce revealed truth, and to state moral principles in the social sphere (57). The pope and the college of bishops enjoy infallibility when they define matters of faith or morals as divinely revealed (58). What the church's teaching authority proposes as divinely revealed is to be believed with divine and Catholic faith (59). What that authority declares non-definitively deserves religious respect (60). Bishops are authentic teachers of the faith, and their teaching also deserves religious respect (61). The body of bishops has the responsibility for announcing the gospel to the whole world; individual bishops are to preach it to the people entrusted to them (62). Presbyters and deacons also have the duty to preach the gospel (63), and all the faithful are to see that the gospel message is spread (64). The church has the right to give religious and moral instruction, and to sponsor schools (65).

Chapter II:
The Sanctifying Function of the Church

The church fulfills its sanctifying function by imparting to all the means to holiness entrusted to it, especially in celebrations of the liturgy (66). Bishops exercise the sanctifying function first of all; they are dispensers of God's mysteries and moderators of the liturgical life of the particular church entrusted to them. Presbyters are consecrated to the celebration of divine worship and the sanctification of the people, and deacons share in worship as well.

The faithful also share in this sanctifying function, especially when they participate actively in the liturgy (67). The sacraments are the chief means of sanctification; the church's highest authority defines and regulates the celebration of the sacraments (68). Prayer, especially the divine office, penance, works of charity, and the veneration of the Blessed Virgin and other saints, are also means of sanctification (69–70).

Chapter III:
The Ruling Function of the Church

The church has been charged to rule the faithful in the name of Christ the Shepherd, so that they might truly live as his disciples and gain their salvation. The church has all the authority, i.e., legislative, executive and judicial, required to accomplish this spiritual governance of the faithful, but it must be used only to build up the people of God in truth and holiness (71). The pope and the college of bishops have full and supreme authority in the universal church (72). Laws made by this supreme authority oblige the faithful for whom they are given (73). The supreme authority exercises executive authority in the administrative governance of the faithful by issuing decrees and instructions, usually through the congregations of the Roman Curia (74). The supreme authority normally exercises judicial authority through tribunals, and any one of the faithful may appeal a case to the pope at any time (75).

A bishop of a particular church has all the authority he needs to exercise his pastoral functions (76). The bishop exercises legislative authority personally, but he can exercise executive and judicial authority either personally or through vicars (77). Bishops sometimes exercise legislative authority collegially in synods, particular councils and episcopal conferences (78). Presbyters and deacons cooperate with bishops in the exercise of this governing function in particular churches, especially in councils and other offices (79). Likewise the faithful may be called upon to share in the bishop's governing function in various offices (80).

The church has the right to care for the spiritual governance of the faithful and its own hierarchical order without interference from any other authority. It must be free to select and prepare its ministers, to name and transfer its bishops, and to communicate freely with the Holy See and with the faithful (81). The church sponsors and organizes works of charity and mercy for the needy and sick as well as other kinds of mutual assistance. And the church has the right to acquire and administer temporal property to be used for worship, the support of its ministers, and its charitable and apostolic efforts (82).

Final Norms

The canons of this fundamental law have force in the universal church for all the faithful (83). They prevail over all other church laws and decrees; all contrary laws and customs lack force. Other laws are to be interpreted and applied in accord with these canons (84). Only the pope can declare null laws which are contrary to these canons, but tribunals should not uphold laws which are shown to be contrary to them (85). Only the supreme authority can abrogate these norms (86).

Critique of the Fundamental Law Draft

The foregoing "fundamental law of the church" was never promulgated. It has no authority as canon law. It is offered here as an example of a serious attempt to describe the basic canonical structure of the Roman Catholic Church, an attempt to draw up a constitution for the church. This attempt was made by high authority, and drew heavily on the documents of the Second Vatican Council.

No reasons were given for not issuing the fundamental law, but it does seem to have serious shortcomings. For example, it fails to convey the basic vision of the universal church as a communion of particular churches, and it ignores completely the primary reality of the church, namely, local congregations of the faithful, i.e., parishes and similar communities. The draft scarcely alludes to such collegial bodies as the synod of bishops, conferences of bishops, pastoral councils and priests' councils. It is so preoccupied with the expression of hierarchical authority that sometimes it seems to identify the church with the hierarchy instead of the faithful, e.g., c. 71, "the church is charged to rule the Christian faithful." However, in spite of these shortcomings, the "Fundamental Law of the Church" may be the best try ever made at a constitutional statement for the church.

RIORDAN HIGH SCHOOL LIBRARY
175 PHELAN AVENUE
SAN FRANCISCO, CALIFORNIA 94112

THE PEOPLE OF GOD

Book Two of the Code

The Christian Faithful

The people are the church. The baptized and believing people, who are in communion with Christ and with one another, constitute the church in the world. They are God's children, the Holy Spirit dwells in them, their goal is God's kingdom. The Christian faithful are, quite properly, the first and foremost subject in this book, "The People of God."

Members

The church is made up of human persons (cc. 96 & 205). Persons are incorporated into the church by two factors: baptism and communion. In the sacrament of baptism men and women are reborn as God's children, configured to Christ, and enter the church (c. 849). Being "in communion" with the church is a very ancient way of expressing that one belongs to and is accepted as a member. The concept is derived from the holy eucharist, that is, being admitted to partake, along with one's fellow Christians, of the Lord's Supper, holy communion. That has always marked the final stage of initiation into the church community, and the sign of being a member in good standing. But there are many other signs and mutual acknowledgements of communion in addition to sharing in the eucharist. It implies a whole network of ties and linkages. "Full communion" includes three elements: the profession of a common faith, sharing in sacramental celebrations, and the acceptance of the church's governance (c. 205).

Persons who are baptized and in commmunion with the Roman Catholic Church are the subjects of rights and obligations in this community. In other words, they have juridic personhood, official standing in the church's system of rules (c. 96).

All Christians (not just Catholic Christians) are described as "Christ's Faithful" (*Christifideles*) in the Code. (However, the term is frequently used to refer to Catholics.) All baptized Christians are incorporated into Christ and belong to the People of God. All share in Christ's prophetic, priestly and royal roles, and all are called to exercise the mission which God has assigned the church to fulfill in the world (c. 204.1). This "Great

Church" of all baptized Christians subsists in the Roman Catholic Church, which is governed by the successors of Peter and the apostles, the pope and the college of bishops (c. 204.2). In other words, the Roman Catholic Church is one embodiment of the greater gathering made up of all those baptized into Christ.

Within the Catholic Church the faithful are described canonically as either lay persons (*laici*) or as ordained ministers (*ministri sacri*) (c. 207.1). That is, those who are "in orders," who belong to the diaconate, presbyterate or episcopate, are distinguished from the vast majority of the lay members of the church. From both groups, the laity and the clergy, some persons choose to profess the evangelical counsels, consecrate themselves to God and foster the mission of the church in special ways (c. 207.2). They are called "religious" (*religiosi/ae*). All religious are either lay persons or ordained ministers. In sum, there are three basic canonical categories of church members: laity, ordained ministers, and religious.

The Bill of Rights and Obligations

For the first time in the history of canon law, this Code presents a list of the rights and obligations of all of the church's members, lay persons as well as ministers (cc. 208–223). This "bill of rights" is truly of constitutional proportions. That is, because of their placement in the Code, their unique history and intrinsic importance, and because the legislator has so designated them, these rights and duties are of foundational and primary significance.

The *rights* can be summarized as follows:

1. All of the Christian faithful are truly equal in their dignity and activity in cooperating to build up the Body of Christ. (c. 208).

2. All the Christian faithful have the right to evangelize the nations (c. 211).

3. The Christian faithful have the right to make their needs and desires known to their bishops (c. 212.2).

4. The Christian faithful have the right to make their opinions regarding the good of the church known to their bishops and to other church members (c. 212.3).

5. The Christian faithful have the right to receive the word of God and the sacraments (c. 213).

6. The Christian faithful have the right to worship God in their own rite and to follow their own form of spirituality (c. 214).

7. The Christian faithful have the right to assemble as well as to found and direct associations for charitable or religious purposes (c. 215).

8. The Christian faithful have the right to initiate, promote and sustain apostolic activities (c. 216).

9. The Christian faithful have the right to a Christian education (c. 217).

10. Those engaged in the theological disciplines enjoy freedom of inquiry and expression (c. 218).

11. The Christian faithful enjoy freedom from all pressure in choosing their state of life (c. 219).

12. No one may damage the reputation of others nor invade their privacy (c. 220).

13. The Christian faithful have the right to vindicate and defend their rights in a church court (c. 221.1).

14. The Christian faithful have the right, if summoned to judgment in the church, to be judged according to canon law, applied with equity (c. 221.2).

15. The Christian faithful have the right not to be punished except in accord with canon law (c. 221.3).

In the exercise of these rights the faithful are to be mindful of the common good of the church, the rights of others, and their duties toward others (c. 223.1). Church authorities may regulate the exercise of these rights, on account of the common good (c. 223.2).

The following *obligations* are enumerated:

1. The Christian faithful are obliged to maintain communion with the church (c. 209.1).

2. The Christian faithful are to fulfill their canonical duties toward the universal church and their particular church (c. 209.2).

3. The Christian faithful are to strive to lead holy lives and to promote the growth and holiness of the church (c. 210).

4. The Christian faithful have the duty to see that the message of salvation reaches all humankind (c. 211.)

5. The Christian faithful are obliged to follow what the bishops declare as teachers of the faith or determine as leaders of the church (c. 212.1).

6. The Christian faithful are obliged to express their opinions about the good of the church to their bishops and fellow church members (c. 212.3).

7. The Christian faithful are obliged to contribute to the needs of the church for worship, apostolic and charitable works, and the support of its ministers (c. 222.1).

8. The Christian faithful are obliged to promote social justice and to assist the poor from their own resources (c. 222.2).

These rights and obligations, in the years which have intervened since the Code was promulgated, remain largely unknown. The rights have not been widely recognized and the means for vindicating or defending them are, for the most part, still lacking. They represent an unrealized goal of the Code.

Lay Rights and Duties

After its major "Bill of Rights," the Code presents a shorter list of rights and responsibilities specific to lay members of the church (c. 224–231). They fall into two categories:

1. The rights and duties proper to the lay state, e.g., active share in the apostolate (c. 225.1), special role in the temporal order, i.e., "the marketplace" (c. 225.2), parental prerogatives (c. 226), and political responsibilities (c. 227).

2. Rights and duties related to knowledge of the teachings of the church, e.g., learning and teaching the theological disciplines (c. 229), and the ability to serve the church in certain offices, functions and advisory roles (cc. 228 & 230), to be adequately prepared for such roles, and to be decently remunerated for performing them (c. 231).

Associations of the Faithful (Cc. 298–329)

The Code affirms the right and freedom of association of the Christian faithful (c. 215). For many centuries multitudes of associations have existed within the church for various purposes: charitable, social, liturgical, apostolic, doctrinal or spiritual. They have used many names, e.g., guilds, confraternities, societies, third orders, sodalities, pious unions, etc. (The "third orders" were affiliated with religious communities (c. 303); the male religious groups were traditionally referred to as first orders, their female counterpart communities as second orders, and the lay affiliate groups as third orders.)

Associations of the faithful resemble religious communities in some ways, but they are really quite different. They are purely voluntary. They may include ordained ministers or professed religious, but they are mainly lay organizations. Their members do not take vows of poverty, chastity and obedience, and they do not live in common. They are simply members of the church who have freely chosen to band together for some religious or religion-related purpose. Some examples are: Confraternity of Christian Doctrine, Christian Life Communities (formerly Sodalities of Our Lady), Secular Franciscans (formerly the Third Order of St. Francis).

The canons seek to order and regulate this plethora of church-related voluntary associations. The canonical issues in regard to these associations, in addition to the fundamental rights to assemble and associate, have to do with the extent that they are related to the hierarchy of the church. For example, an association may be entirely Catholic in its membership, purpose, activities and spirit, but it may not use the name "Catholic" unless it has permission from church authority to do so (c. 300). Besides the use of the title "Catholic," the canons describe various levels of official recognition, juridical standing, autonomy and accountability to church authorities. In this regard there are at least four degrees or categories of associations:

1. *Non-canonical;* an association which has no recognition, no juridical standing or canonical personality, needs no review of its statutes, and has no obligation to report to or be subject to visitation by church authorities;

2. *Private;* initiated and directed by the faithful, recognized after a review of its statutes, but without juridic personality (i.e., the association itself is not a subject of canonical rights and obligations; however, its members may jointly contract for rights and obligations, and own property), it is subject to the vigilance and visitation of ecclesiastical

authority (cc. 299, 305, 310, 322, 323). All canonical associations must have statutes which spell out their purpose, headquarters, conditions for membership, and policy-making bodies (c. 304). All private associations, in addition to being recognized, can also be praised or recommended by church authority; this does not change their juridic status (cc. 298, 299).

3. *Private and possessing juridic personality* (cc. 113–123) which is given by church authority; a recognized association, the subject of canonical rights and obligations, and subject to vigilance and visitation by church authority (c. 305).

4. *Public;* established by ecclesiastical authority, and given juridic personality and a canonical mission at the same time; the association must have its statutes approved, and function under the direction of church authority (cc. 312–315), which authority names or confirms the moderator of the association, and can remove that person and appoint a caretaker (c. 317–318); the association must render an annual accounting of its properties and funds (c. 319), and it can be suppressed by church authority (c. 320).

Sacred Ministers (Cc. 232–293)

Canon law refers to deacons, presbyters and bishops as sacred ministers or clerics. Ordained ministers, although they are firmly situated among and within (not separate from or above) the people of God, are distinguished canonically from lay persons and even lay ministers.

The three ordained ministries are envisioned as corporate groups, i.e., classes, grades or ranks (*ordines*). That is, the symbolic laying on of hands at ordination means the admission to an *ordo*, the diaconate, presbyterate or episcopate. It signifies the entrance or initiation into a "holy order" of sacred ministers. This corporate concept tempers any notion of ordination as personal privilege. All ministry is service (the meaning of *ministrare*, and of the Greek, *diakonein*), and ordination means inscription into one of the serving classes.

The canonical tradition abhors a ministerial loner, i.e., an unattached or free-floating cleric. Hence, every ordained minister must be connected, tied in to a particular church (diocese) or religious institute. The canonical terms for this linkage are incardination (from the Latin *cardo*, hinge, hence it means hinged on, like a door on a jamb) or inscription (c. 265). This attachment canonically anchors and identifies every ordained minister.

Ordained ministers are also called "clerics," members of the clerical caste or class, the clergy. The term comes from the Greek word *kleros*, which means lot or portion or share. It refers to those who have the Lord for their inheritance, like the priestly tribe of Israel, the Levites (Dt 18). The same expression was used when Matthias was chosen by lot to receive Judas' share in ministry (Acts 1,15–26). The clerical state is a juridical category in canon law. It is entered by ordination to the diaconate (*diakonia*, service, a suitable name for the entry point to a life of service; c. 266.1). It carries with it certain prerogatives and obligations (cc. 273–289), and it can be lost or one can be deprived of it (cc. 290–293), even though the order itself is permanent.

Sacramental ordination, then, carries with it three distinct canonical effects. The ordained person is simultaneously inducted into:

(1) the order of diaconate, presbyterate or episcopate;
(2) the diocese or religious community as a cleric, by incardination;
(3) the clerical state, by means of diaconal ordination.

The Code's section on Sacred Ministers (cc. 232–293) does not offer a full, well-rounded picture of the life and ministry of the ordained. The major responsibilities of these key ministerial personnel must be sought elsewhere, for example, in the sections on pastors, on preaching, on the sacraments, on the administration of church property, and so on. These canons on Sacred Ministers outline only the basic structures of the clerical state. Four specific issues are treated in the four chapters of this section: 1) the formation of ministers (the focus here is exclusively on preparation for the priesthood in diocesan or regional seminaries), 2) the process of entrance into the clerical state and transfers within it, 3) the obligations and rights of sacred ministers, and 4) the loss of the clerical state.

Formation of Clerics (Cc. 232–264)

Under this title one would expect to find the norms for the preparation of deacons, presbyters and bishops, since all three of these groups are sacred ministers or clerics. Such is not the case. The entire chapter treats of the formation of men for the presbyterate, with the exception of one canon on the formation of permanent deacons (c. 236). There is no guidance in canon law for the preparation of bishops.

These canons give the basic norms for the establishment, support and administration of diocesan or regional seminaries. They include explicit directions for the various components of the seminary program: spiritual, academic and pastoral. The canons detail the authority structure in the seminary (bishop, rector, director of studies, spiritual director), and the qualifications for instructors. Many of the canons are taken from the decree of the Second Vatican Council on priestly formation, *Optatam totius*. This document should be consulted for further background.

In 1970, after the council and before the revised Code, the Congregation for Catholic Education issued more detailed norms for priestly formation, *The Basic Plan for Priestly Formation*. Each national conference of bishops was to formulate and issue a national program for priestly formation based on the *Basic Plan*. The National Conference of Catholic Bishops issued the *Program for Priestly Formation* for the church in the United States in 1971. Revised editions were published in 1976 and 1982. Many other bishops' conferences took similar actions. The *Basic Plan* and the national programs provide more detailed and appropriately adapted guidelines for priestly preparation than do these canons of the Code.

Incardination and Transfer of Clerics (Cc. 265–272)

Every sacred minister must be accountable to the church through the affiliation called incardination. Each deacon, presbyter or bishop must be incardinated into a particular church (diocese) or religious institute (c. 265). This occurs canonically at the ordination to the diaconate (c. 266).

Deacons and presbyters may transfer their affiliation from one jurisdiction to another, but only under the conditions which are carefully prescribed in canons 267–272. The process requires that excardination (disaffiliation) from one diocese or religious community be simultaneous with incardination into another. The cleric is never to be unattached or "headless" (acephalous).

Obligations and Rights of Clerics (Cc. 273–289)

To serve the church as an ordained minister carries with it serious implications. Prominent among them are obedience to church authority and personal exemplarity of life. This dedicated service has also traditionally implied certain prerogatives. These canons, ancient and modern, outline the norms for clerical life.

Clerical duties and obligations:

1. Ordained ministers oblige themselves to obey the legitimate directions of the pope, their bishop or religious superior, and to undertake and fulfill the assignments they are given (cc. 273–274).

2. Ordained ministers are not holier than lay persons, but they are held to special modes of Christian striving because of their dedication to the service of God's people. The canons outline the forms of this exemplary lifestyle:

   (a) They are to pursue holiness by fulfilling the duties of their pastoral ministry, by nourishing themselves from the scriptures and the eucharist, by praying the liturgy of the hours, and by giving time to mental prayer (c. 276).

   (b) They are to observe continence and celibacy (c. 277). Continence means refraining from genital sexual activity, and celibacy means remaining unmarried. The canon, therefore, obliges clerics (except married deacons) not to marry or have sexual relations. (Cf. cc. 1037 and 1041.3 on prerequisites for ordination, and cc. 1394 and 1395 on penalties for violations.)

   (c) They are to cultivate a simplicity of life and avoid any appearance of luxury (c. 282).

3. Sacred ministers are to continue their education, in order to deepen their understanding and improve their pastoral skills (c. 279).

4. They are to maintain residence in the diocese or place of assignment (c. 283.1).

5. They are to wear ecclesiastical attire in keeping with local norms and customs (c. 284).

6. Sacred ministers are to avoid activities unbecoming to the clerical state, and specifically they are not to assume public offices which involve the exercise of civil power (c. 285); they are not to conduct a business or trade (c. 286), and they are not to take active roles in political parties or labor unions (c. 287.2).

7. Sacred ministers are to foster peace and harmony based on justice (c. 287.1).

   Clerical rights and prerogatives:

1. Ordained ministers can obtain ecclesiastical offices which require the power of orders or the power of governance (c. 274.1).

2. They have a right to a decent remuneration, one which will provide for their needs in ill-health and old age (c. 281), and they have the right to an appropriate time for annual vacation (c. 283.2).

3. Ordained ministers may be exempt from military service and other public civil offices and duties, depending on local civil law (c. 289).

Loss of the Clerical State (Cc. 290–293)

Loss of the clerical state means that an ordained minister is deprived of all ecclesiastical offices and functions, the obligations (except that of celibacy) and rights of sacred ministers, and it means that he reverts to the juridical status of a lay person in the church. A dispensation from the obligation of celibacy is a separate matter, but it too can be granted by the pope.

A person loses the status of cleric in one of three ways:

1. by an official declaration that his ordination was invalid, i.e., null and void;

2. by a dismissal imposed as a penalty for a specific and serious canonical crime, e.g., attempted marriage, certain sexual offenses involving minors, solicitation in confession (cf. cc. 1364.2, 1367, 1370.1, 1387, 1394.1, 1395.1 & 2).

3. by the administrative action of the Holy See, that is, a rescript granted at the request of the cleric himself or by someone else, e.g., his bishop or religious superior.

All three of these procedures must include due process, for example, ample opportunity for fair hearing.

The canons do not provide for resignation or renunciation of ministerial status.

Hierarchical Structures

The Roman Catholic Church is a hierarchical church. "Hierarchy" comes from the Greek words *hieros*, sacred, and *arche*, rule or power. However, the term does not imply domination, for Jesus himself forbade that any of his disciples should "lord it over" others; among them leaders are to serve the others (Mt 20,25–28; Mk 10,42–45; Lk 22,25–27). The Second Vatican Council reiterated that those who have been given hierarchical authority are the servants of their brothers and sisters (*Lumen Gentium*, 18). This part of the book on the People of God sets forth the ordered structure of the church's communities and offices.

Highest Authority: Pope and College of Bishops

The Roman Catholic Bishop of Rome is probably the best known and most prestigious religious leader in the world. Within the church the pope speaks and acts with apparently unlimited authority. This style of papal activity gives the impression that the papacy is an absolute monarchy, that the Roman Catholic Church is headed by an elected king. This perception, while understandable, is seriously mistaken. The highest authority in the Roman Catholic Church is collegiate, not monarchical. The college of bishops, with the pope at its head, is the subject of supreme authority in the church.

The analogy, of course, is that of the twelve apostles with Peter in their midst, all chosen by Jesus. Just as they formed a single collective body or college, so do the bishops, the successors of the apostles, together with the Roman pontiff, the successor of Peter (c. 330). The concept of collegiate responsibility for the church at the highest level is key because of its biblical warrant and because it reflects the nature of the universal church as a communion of churches (*communio ecclesiarum*). The bishops of those local churches share with the Bishop of Rome in a common pastoral solicitude for the entire church. They all participate, as a college, in teaching and governing the church.

Roman Pontiff

In the Code, the preferred title for the pope is "Roman Pontiff." Pontiff (from *pons*, bridge, and *facere*, to make, meant one who bridged the chasm between the gods and humankind) is the ancient term used for the priest in the Roman Empire; the *Pontifex Maximus* was the high priest in pagan Rome. The title was applied to bishops in the early church, and gradually its use was reserved to the Bishop of Rome. The other canonical title for the pope is "Supreme Pontiff" (*Summus Pontifex*). The name most commonly used, "pope," comes from the Greek *pappas* and Latin *papa*, father, and is the source for the more formal title, "Holy Father."

The pope of Rome is one of Catholicism's most compelling symbols. Within the communion of the churches, which is the universal church, the papal office serves as a unique sign, center and guarantor of unity. The successor of Peter is charged to nourish, support, encourage and unify his fellow faithful Christians. (Jesus ordered Peter to feed his flock and strengthen his disciples. Jn 21,15–17; Lk 22,32.) But the canons of the Code say little of these central pastoral responsibilities. Instead, they accord to the Roman pontiff an extraordinary panoply of juridical powers and responsibilities. The canons define papal authority, primacy, and a plethora of prerogatives.

Authority. The originating identity of the pope is the Bishop of the church at Rome. In virtue of that sacramental office, he is the successor of Peter, the head of the college of bishops, and the pastor of the universal church on earth. Canon 331 describes his authority as ordinary (comes with the office), supreme (there is none higher), full (complete), immediate (may relate directly to any person in the church without intermediaries), universal (extending to all parts of the church), and states that he may exercise it freely.

This statement of papal authority makes it sound absolute, but in fact it is not. It is limited by many factors: the revealed word of God, the Christian tradition, the nature and purposes of the church, the role of the papal office, the natural law, the collegial relationship with other bishops, and so on. So, even though the canonical description of the pope's power is maximal, perhaps even slightly exaggerated, that authority in reality is certainly not untrammeled.

Primacy. Canon 333 summarizes the relationship of the pope to the churches of the Roman Catholic communion. He is much more than a first among equals. That is, in addition to possessing supreme authority over the universal church, he also has authority in each and every one of the particular churches which make up the universal church. His authority does not replace or nullify that of the local bishop in his diocese, but it complements it. It is intended to affirm and preserve the bishop's authority. Primacy gives the pope the power to intervene in the life of the local church when exceptional circumstances make it necessary. In this sense it implies a "reserve power" to be used in emergency situations.

In virtue of his headship of the college of bishops there is a presumption that the pope always acts in communion with all of the other bishops (c. 333.2). And, since he is the highest authority, the "court of last resort," there is no appeal from his decision, no "going over his head" (cc. 333.3, 1372, 1629.1). He is subject to no one's judgment (c. 1404).

Prerogatives. The canons say that the pope:

——possesses infallible teaching authority, is the supreme pastor and teacher of all the faithful (c. 749);

——supervises the sacred liturgy (c. 838), defines what is valid and licit in sacramental celebrations (c. 841, "supreme church authority");

——is the supreme judge for the whole Catholic world (c. 1442), any case may be appealed to him at any time (c. 1417.1);

——is the supreme administrator and steward of all the church's temporal goods (c. 1273);

——has the right to send legates to particular churches and to sovereign nations (c. 362);

——receives the obedience of all clerics (c. 273) and religious (c. 590.2);

——convokes and controls ecumenical councils (c. 338);

——reviews the decrees of particular councils and episcopal conferences before they can be promulgated (cc. 446, 455);

——appoints or confirms all bishops (c. 377.1);

——receives a report on the state of each diocese from the bishop every five years (c. 399.1);

——can limit the authority of bishops by reserving certain matters to himself (c. 381.1);

——reserves to himself dispensations from clerical celibacy (c. 291), from non-consummated marriages (c. 1142), from irregularities for sacred orders (c. 1047), and certain marriage impediments (c. 1078);

——establishes feast days or days of penance for the whole church (c. 1244, "supreme ecclesiastical authority");

——approves religious communities (c. 589) and any changes in their constitutions (c. 587.2); confirms the dismissal of their members (c.

700); can exempt religious institutes from the authority of local bishops (c. 591).

These canonical powers and prerogatives (and there are many more than those listed here) have accrued to the papacy over centuries. Together they represent a dramatically aggrandized office, a centralization of authority which is truly remarkable. One reason is that the pope functions as the principal rule-making authority, the supreme legislator. One result is that the the pope is viewed as the "universal bishop." The Christian lives of ordinary Catholics all over the world are influenced much more by the pope than by their own bishop.

The pope obtains his office by means of two events: 1) his ordination as a bishop, and 2) his acceptance of his election by the college of cardinals (c. 332.1). The custom has been for the pope to serve for life, but he can resign the office if he chooses to do so (c. 332.2).

Obviously, the pope requires many assistants to carry out his many duties. Bishops, cardinals and many other persons and offices provide such assistance. The various groups which make up the Roman curia are discussed below. It is important to note that these assistants carry out their specific tasks, within their canonical limits, in the name of and by the authority of the pope (c. 334). The lines and limits of that authorization are sometimes difficult to discern and, as in any bureaucracy, lesser officials tend to expand their authority.

College of Bishops

The college of bishops, which is the successor body to the college of the apostles, is the subject of supreme and full power in the universal church (c. 336). This means that the college holds complete and preeminent authority within the church, juridic and moral authority as well as pastoral solicitude. The college is an organic, animated reality, not a mere category of office-holders. It is the best expression of the communion of the churches, which constitutes the universal church. The college of bishops embodies the strong bonds of faith, love, sacrament, and order which tie the Catholic Church together.

Bishops belong to the college in virtue of their episcopal ordination, in which they receive the fullness of the sacrament of orders, and their communion with the other members of the college and the pope (c. 336). The Bishop of Rome is a member of the college, but he is also its head, operative center, and usual spokesperson.

The college of bishops constitutes the highest teaching authority (*magisterium*) of the church. It has the duty of proclaiming the gospel with respect to the universal church (c. 756). The college possesses infallible teaching authority, both when gathered in an ecumenical council and when dispersed throughout the world, as long as its members agree on what is to be definitively held as true church doctrine (c. 749.2). When not defining doctrine, the college still exercises authentic teaching authority (c. 752).

The decrees and constitutions issued by the college (such as those issued by the Second Vatican Council) are to be observed by all the Christian faithful (c. 754). The college of bishops is to promote and direct the participation of Catholics in the ecumenical movement, whose purpose is to restore Christian unity (c. 755.1). Also, it is the responsibility of the college to direct and coordinate the missionary effort of the church, which is part of its very nature (cc. 781 & 782.1).

The college of bishops acts as a body most dramatically and effectively when it is gathered in ecumenical council; then it exercises its authority in a solemn manner. But it acts with equal authority when its members throughout the world take united action, as long as that action is initiated or accepted by the pope (c. 337).

Ecumenical councils are not frequent events; only twenty-one have taken place in the history of the church. Since there are now over three thousand members of the college of bishops, gathering them in council is both cumbersome and expensive. However, councils are vivid symbols of the unity and universality of the church, and have marked crucial turning points in the church's journey through history.

All of the members of the college of bishops have the right and the duty to take part in such general councils (c. 339.1). Canonically the pope now has almost complete control over councils: he alone can call one, he presides, he alone can suspend or dissolve a council, and he must approve its decrees (cc. 338–341). But councils sometimes take on a dynamic life of their own, under the impetus of the Holy Spirit, and the results are not always predictable or programmable.

Synod of Bishops

The word "synod" comes from the Greek, *synodos*, meaning a coming together, a meeting. It is one of the terms, along with "council," used for meetings of leaders of the church from the very earliest times.

The international synod of bishops is a representative gathering of the bishops of the world, in contrast to the total membership of the college of bishops which convenes at an ecumenical council. The representative bishops to a synod are, for the most part, elected by the national conferences of bishops all over the world. Most of the synods held since the

Second Vatican Council have consisted of about two hundred bishops (and ten superiors of religious communities). The meetings have been held in Rome about every three years, for three or four weeks each, and have treated topics such as evangelization, catechetics, the family, reconciliation, the laity, and the ministerial priesthood.

The Code gives a threefold purpose for the synod of bishops: 1) to foster close ties between the bishops and the pope, 2) to advise the pope on matters of faith, morals and church discipline, and 3) to consider the activities of the church in the world (c. 342).

The synod of bishops is a modern revival of a very ancient practice. Such deliberative gatherings of bishops, patterned on the Council of Jerusalem depicted in Acts 15, often met in the early centuries of the church's life. Over the years, as the church grew and the papal office assumed more and more authority, this synodal activity waned. It was reinstituted at the Second Vatican Council because the bishops and the pope saw the value of meeting more frequently and in smaller numbers between the relatively rare ecumenical councils.

The synod, although it is clearly representative of the college of bishops, does not act with the supreme and full authority of the college. It usually considers topics and gives opinions about them, but does not decide questions or issue decrees. The pope can ask the synod to act deliberatively, that is, to decide matters authoritatively (c. 343), but thus far he has not. The synod is viewed as advisory to the pope.

In fact, the synod is completely under the control of the pope. He convenes it when and where he wishes, he ratifies the selection of the bishops who attend, he picks the topics and sets the agenda, he presides, and he concludes or dissolves the meetings (c. 344).

Synods can take various forms, i.e., general or special, ordinary or extraordinary, and the "mix" of member bishops selected for each form differs somewhat (cc. 345–346). Those who head the offices of the Roman curia are usually included. The synod has a permanent secretariat, with a general secretary and a council of bishops, which has certain limited functions between synods (c. 348). The more complete rules governing the synod of bishops can be found in the *Canon Law Digest*, 6, 388–393, and 7, 323–327, 338–341.

College of Cardinals

The college of cardinals is the group of bishops that elects the pope. Beyond that critical function, the title of cardinal (from the Latin, *cardo*, hinge) is largely honorific, even though it is considered the highest dignity in the Western church after the papal office. (Patriarchs of the eastern ritual churches are included in the college of cardinals, but their historic and canonical authority is different and greater than that of cardinals.)

This special college assists the pope collectively when called together for that purpose (which rarely happens), and individually by serving in the various offices of the Roman curia and in special assignments (cc. 349, 356, 358). There are usually about one hundred and thirty cardinals. Only those under eighty years of age may vote in the papal elections.

The college of cardinals has a history as rich and colorful as the brilliant red silk robes which go with the prestigious title. Certain influential clerics in and around Rome in the early Middle Ages were called cardinals. They served as counselors of the pope, like a cabinet or senate. Their meetings were (and are, cf. c. 353) called "consistories" (from *consistere*, to stand with). Important decisions on matters of policy were commonly taken "in consistory." The role of these "princes of the church" was so great in medieval times that some authors considered the college of cardinals to be of divine institution; in fact, the successors of the apostles.

In the eleventh century the college was entrusted with the duty of electing the new pope. Their electoral meetings became known as "conclaves" (from *cum clave*, with a key) when, in the year 1271, in order to force them to make a choice after a delay of three years, the people locked them in their meeting place until they decided on a candidate. The cardinals are still locked in for these prayerful deliberations in order to avoid any outside influences on their decision.

Cardinals are freely chosen by the pope (c. 351), and assigned to one of three ranks (of mostly historical significance) in the college (c. 350). Those chosen are usually archbishops of major archdioceses throughout the world or prominent members of the Roman curia. Individually, they are often quite influential in church affairs, even though they do not enjoy much canonical authority as cardinals, except that of being the papal electors. They do have the privilege of hearing confessions anywhere in the world (c. 967.1) and of being personally exempt from the authority of local bishops (c. 357.2).

The canons of the Code on cardinals are surprisingly detailed, but the norms which govern the college when the papal throne is vacant and when it comes together to elect a new pope are found in exquisite detail (down to the folding of the ballots!) in *Canon Law Digest*, 8, 133–169.

The Roman Curia

The Roman curia is the collective name for the complex of secretariats, congregations, tribunals, councils and offices which assist the pope in the exercise of his pastoral office of service to the churches which make up the Roman Catholic communion (c. 360).

The name "curia" is derived from *curare*, to take care of, and in Roman times the *curia* was the building where the senate met. In the Middle Ages the papal court came to be called the *Curia Romana*.

The curia today is the large administrative apparatus which carries on the ordinary business of the church's central office. Its agencies are headed by cardinals, and staffed by many hundreds of bureaucrats, most of whom are bishops and priests.

Within the curia, the Secretary of State is the coordinating office with authority over both the church's internal and external affairs. There are nine congregations (the name congregation refers to the committee of cardinals and bishops which heads each office), each with responsibility for an area of the church's life, e.g., doctrine, bishops, worship and sacraments, evangelization, clergy, religious, and so on. There are also three judicial bodies, that is, tribunals or courts, several councils for various causes; e.g., for laypersons, the family, justice and peace, Christian unity, migrants, etc., and offices for the administration of funds and properties.

The Code often uses the terms "Apostolic See" or "Holy See" to refer to the papal office. (The word "see" comes from the Latin *sedes*, seat, and it means the seat or place of authority, as Americans refer to the county seat or a seat in Congress.) These two terms include both the Roman pontiff and the institutions of the Roman curia (c. 361). This can cause some confusion when it comes to canonical rule-making. The curial agencies are administrative (except for the tribunals, which are judicial) and, although they act in the name of and by the authority of the pope, they do not have legislative authority. They issue instructions, declarations, directories, responses and the like, but they cannot enact laws or issue general decrees without the specific approval of the pope.

The Roman curia has been reorganized three times in this century, in 1908, 1967 and 1989. The regulations which currently govern its activities can be found in *Acta Apostolicae Sedis*, 80, 841–912. Each agency of the curia also has its own internal rules. The names and addresses of the agencies and the names of the officials of each can be found in a directory called the *Annuario Pontificio*, published each year by the Vatican Press.

Legates of the Roman Pontiff

The pope, as the highest authority of the church, has the right to send permanent representatives to the particular churches in various nations and to the governments of those nations as well (c. 362 & 363). These diplomats are not the pope's personal emissaries nor the agents of Vatican City State. They are the official representatives of the head of the Roman Catholic Church. They are recognized as such in international law. It is a unique prerogative of the Catholic Church.

This system of permanent diplomatic representatives began in the Middle Ages, and developed when the pope was a major player in European politics. The papacy had territorial responsibility for the area of central Italy known as the papal states up until 1870. Today the Holy See has diplomatic relations with about one hundred and twenty countries, and maintains legates to the churches in several more. The Holy See also sends delegates or observers to international bodies, such as the United Nations, the European Community and the Organization of American States, and to many international meetings and conferences.

The papal legate who has official relations with both the church and the government of a country is called a "nuncio" (from *nuntius*, messenger). One who relates only to the church and is not officially recognized by the civil government is called a "delegate."

With regard to the local churches (dioceses), the legates strive to strengthen the bonds of unity with the Holy See; they report on the condition of the local churches, advise their bishops and the conference of bishops, suggest candidates for new bishops, and promote peace and ecumenism (c. 364).

With regard to the governments of states, the papal legates foster relations between the state and the Holy See, and, in consultation with the bishops of the country, try to work out issues of church-state relations, e.g., the church's freedom to found schools, maintain buildings and property, support clergy, etc. (c. 365).

The special canonical regulations for legates of the Roman pontiff are found in *Canon Law Digest*, 7, 277–284.

Dioceses and Bishops

Dioceses

Catholics experience church at different levels. We are most conscious of our own parish, base community, or the local band of believers with whom we worship and associate. But we are also aware of the church in our city or county, the surrounding parishes. And we know that we are part of a diocese, headed by a bishop. We also think of the Catholic Church in our country as having a certain identity and various activities, a national church. And, finally, we are very much aware of belonging to a worldwide church, one headed by the pope of Rome.

In canon law, the diocese is the primary reality of church. The Code uses the term "particular church" to refer to the diocesan church. It is this level of church which is viewed as basic, complete, fully realized. The Roman Catholic Church fully exists in each diocesan church, and the universal church is made up of diocesan churches (c. 368). Canonically, the Roman Catholic Church is a communion of diocesan churches. There are about 2500 dioceses and archdioceses in the world, about 190 in the United States.

The word "diocese" comes from the Greek *dioikesis*, which etymologically refers to the management of a household, but in the Roman Empire was used to name administrative jurisdictions, like those headed by magistrates or legates. The church gradually began to use the term, and by the Middle Ages it meant the local church headed by a bishop.

The canons define a diocese as a portion of the People of God. This is of fundamental importance. The believing people are the primary reality, then those who minister to them. The people are entrusted to a bishop for their pastoral care. In providing that care, the bishop is assisted by the presbyterate, the college of presbyters. Three forces gather the people, their bishops and priests into a church: the Holy Spirit, the gospel, and the eucharist. Thus gathered, they constitute an embodiment of the one, holy, catholic and apostolic church of Christ. This is the canonical vision of the diocesan church (c. 369).

In mission areas and elsewhere, particular churches are sometimes called by other names: territorial prelature, apostolic vicariate, apostolic administration, etc. (cc.369, 370, 371). They are equivalent to dioceses in canon law.

Dioceses are, as a rule, territorial. That is, the diocese has clear geographical boundaries, and the "portion of the People of God" is the people living in that territory (c. 372.1). In exceptional situations, a particular church can be established on another basis, e.g., language, national origin, etc. (c. 372.2).

Only the highest authority in the church, i.e., the pope, can formally establish a diocese. When he does so, the diocesan church becomes a juridic person, that is, it is a canonical subject of rights and obligations (c. 373).

Bishops

It is customary to categorize the Christian churches according to their form of polity into episcopal, presbyteral or congregational, depending on where authority is lodged, with bishops, elders or with the members of the local congregation. In terms of its church order, the Roman Catholic Church is an episcopal church. Canonically, it is very clear that the bishop is the chief pastoral leader and key authority figure in the churches which make up the Catholic communion.

The title "bishop" comes from the Greek *episkopos*, which means overseer or superintendent. The term was used to refer to church leaders several times in the New Testament. For that reason, and because subsequently bishops came to play the central role in the local churches, the episcopal office is considered to be of divine origin.

Bishops are successors of the apostles by divine institution; they are made such by the Holy Spirit who is given to them. They are pastors in the church, teachers of doctrine, priests of sacred worship, and ministers of governance (c. 375.1). Bishops receive these offices in their episcopal ordination, and they can exercise them only if they remain in communion with the College of Bishops and its head, the pope (c. 375.2).

A candidate for the office of bishop should be (c. 378):
1. a good Christian, with virtue (faith, morals, piety, zeal, wisdom, prudence), talent, and a good reputation;
2. a priest, ordained at least five years, and at least thirty-five years of age;
3. a holder of a graduate degree in scripture, theology or canon law, or at least well qualified in these disciplines.

(It is interesting to compare this list of requirements with that given in the First Letter to Timothy, 3, 1–7.) The Holy See makes the final judgment about the worthiness of candidates.

Bishops are called "diocesan" when a diocese has been entrusted to them. All other bishops, e.g., auxiliaries, retired, etc., are called "titular," that is, they have been given a nominal see, one which no longer exists, as a symbol of their relationship to a "portion of the People of God" (c. 376). It is a reminder that ordained ministers have always been viewed in relationship to a community of people whom they served.

The pope either appoints bishops or confirms those who have been elected (c. 377.1). (The first bishop in the United States, John Carroll, was elected by his fellow-presbyters in 1789. In some parts of the world bishops are still elected.)

There are four distinct steps to becoming a bishop: selection or designation, conferral of the office, episcopal ordination or consecration, and the formal taking possession of the office.

A pool or list of names, compiled in secret by the bishops of each province (group of dioceses) and periodically updated, of those priests who are thought suitable for the episcopacy, is sent to the Holy See and maintained there in the Congregation of Bishops (c. 377.2).

When a diocesan bishop dies or retires, the papal legate gathers the suggestions of neighboring bishops, and of the head of the bishops' conference, for a likely successor. In the process the apostolic legate is to hear from some of the members of the diocesan college of consultors (cf. c. 502), and he may also ask the opinions of other priests and laypersons. The legate sends a slate of three names to the Holy See along with his own preference (c. 377.3). The whole procedure is secret. The considerable influence of the papal legate is obvious. Other members of the hierarchy also intervene in this selection process.

When the bishop of a diocese desires an auxiliary (assistant) bishop, he sends a list of three suitable names to the Holy See (c. 377.4). More detailed rules for this selection or nomination process can be found in *Canon Law Digest*, 7, 366–373.

Bishops serve the church primarily by ministering within their local churches, but they also share collegially certain responsibilities for the larger church. As agents of the communion of the churches, they participate in activities at the state, provincial, regional, national conference levels, and in the universal college of bishops. The following sections focus on the powers and obligations of bishops within their dioceses.

Diocesan Bishops

A priest, once named a diocesan bishop, must be ordained a bishop (unless he was already a bishop), and then publicly "take possession" of the diocese by presenting his letter of appointment from the Holy See to the college of consultors (the group of presbyters initially responsible for the diocese between bishops). This should take place within a liturgical ceremony in the cathedral church. Only then can the new bishop exercise authority in the diocese (cc. 379, 382).

A diocesan bishop is given great authority because he has great responsibilities. His authority is described in a remarkably open-ended way: all he needs to get the job done. A diocesan bishop has all the ordinary (goes with the office), proper (exercised in his own name, not vicarious), and immediate (directly to everyone in the diocese) power which is required for the exercise of his pastoral office. The only exceptions are those cases reserved to higher authority (c. 381.1). The bishop exercises this authority in his own name, not as the vicar of the pope. Christ and his Holy Spirit are its source; it comes to him through the sacrament of orders.

The canons delineate the facets of the bishop's office by listing those for whom he must have pastoral care, and then by stating his major responsibilities as teacher, sanctifier and ruler.

Pastor. The bishop is to care about all those within the boundaries of the diocese, not only the Catholics who come to mass on Sunday. He is to reach out to all the Catholic faithful, regardless of age, nationality, condition or rite, including shut-ins and fallen-aways. He is to reach out in love to those who are not Catholics, members of other churches as well as non-Christians (c. 383). The bishop must have special concern for the diocesan presbyterate, the college of priests who are his helpers in ministry. He is to look out for them, listen to their advice, and see that they fulfill their duties (c. 384).

Teacher. The diocesan bishop is to propose and explain the truths of the faith to the faithful. He is to preach frequently himself, and he is to oversee the entire ministry of the word, from liturgical preaching to catechetical instruction. His concern is both the integrity of the faith and the freedom of those who study its truths (cc. 386, 756.2, 763, 775.1, 802, 806).

Sanctifier. The bishop is to promote the holiness of the Christian faithful, according to the vocation of each. He is to be an example to them in charity, humility and simplicity of life. The bishop is the principal dispenser of the mysteries of God, the promoter and guardian of the liturgical life of the diocese. He is to seek to have the faithful grow in grace through the celebration of the sacraments (cc. 387, 835.1). The bishop must celebrate mass for the people every Sunday and holy day, and he is to preside at the eucharist frequently in the cathedral or another church of the diocese (cc. 388, 389).

Ruler. The bishop possesses legislative, executive and judicial power, with which to govern the diocese (c. 391.1). There is no separation of powers in the Catholic Church, in either the episcopal or papal offices; instead, in those key positions the three kinds of authority are united. However, the bishop can (and usually does) delegate much of his authority. He cannot delegate his law-making power, but he can act through vicars in both executive and judicial matters (c. 391.2). The bishop is to promote the common discipline of the church, and to be watchful lest abuses creep in, especially relating to preaching, worship and the administration of property (c. 392). The bishop is the representative of the diocese in juridical matters (c. 393). The obedience owed to the bishop by the ordained ministers of the diocese is a key element of his ruling function (cc. 273, 274).

In addition to these major clusters of responsibilities, the diocesan bishop is to coordinate the various apostolates of the diocese, and to administer its property. He is to foster apostolic activities, e.g., schools, hospitals, agencies of charity, evangelization, etc., and both encourage and assist the faithful to take part in these works of the apostolate (c. 394, 678.1, 782). The bishop is responsible not only for the funds, lands and buildings which belong to the diocese itself, but he also must oversee the properties of the juridic persons subject to his authority, e.g., the parishes and other institutions within the diocese (cc. 1276, 1287).

The diocesan bishop has three more traditional duties:
1. He must be present to his diocese. He is obliged to reside within the diocese for at least eleven months of the year, and to be actively involved in his ministry (c. 395).
2. He must visit the parishes and other institutions of the diocese. At least once every five years he is to conduct a pastoral visitation (cc. 396–398); it is his chance to hear the people, and to evaluate the state of the congregations and their ministers.
3. He must report to the pope on the state of the diocese every five years. This, too, is a serious, detailed matter, and involves visits to the Holy See (cc. 399–400).

This overloaded leader has one final responsibility, and that is to lay his burden down. When he reaches the age of seventy-five years or when he can no longer fulfill his duties, he is requested to submit his resignation to the pope (c. 401). As bishop emeritus he has a right to a residence in the diocese and to decent support (c. 402).

The pastoral role of bishops is set forth in the *Directory on the Pastoral Ministry of Bishops*, Washington: USCC, 1974. Their canonical responsibilities are spelled out in T. Green, *A Manual for Bishops: Rights and Responsibilities of Diocesan Bishops* (Washington: USCC, 1983).

Auxiliary Bishops

There are three categories of titular bishops who are appointed to assist or partially replace diocesan bishops:

1. Auxiliary (from *auxiliaris*, giving help, assisting) bishops are appointed, upon the request of the diocesan bishop, to help him, when the pastoral needs of the diocese call for it (c. 403.1).

2. Auxiliary bishops with special faculties are imposed on a diocesan bishop in response to some difficulty or deficiency in the diocese or with the diocesan bishop himself, e.g., financial crisis, ill health, abuses of discipline, etc. (c. 403.2).

3. Coadjutor (from *adjutor*, a helper or deputy) bishops are auxiliary bishops with special faculties whose appointment also gives them the right to succeed the diocesan bishop when he dies, retires or becomes incapacitated (c. 430.3). The coadjutor becomes the diocesan bishop immediately upon the vacancy of the see (c. 409.1).

The latter two categories of assistant bishops are also vicars general (cc. 406.1, 479), and aid the diocesan bishop with the entire governance of the diocese, not just in one or another area of pastoral responsibility. They take his place when he is absent or incapacitated (405.2), and they must be consulted on all important matters (c. 407.1).

All auxiliary or assistant bishops have real canonical authority in the diocese, either as vicars general or episcopal vicars (c. 479); they are primary consultors to the diocesan bishop, and are to work in harmony with him (c. 407.2 & 3). Of course, all of them are sacramentally ordained and full members of the college of bishops.

There are hundreds of auxiliary bishops in the world, and the vast majority are of the first category, that is, requested by diocesan bishops who needed some help with their episcopal tasks. The auxiliaries are usually assigned some specific areas of responsibility, either geographic regions of the diocese or areas of the apostolate, in addition to liturgical and ceremonial roles, e.g., administering the sacrament of confirmation, attending funerals and meetings.

Impeded or Vacant Sees

Transfers of authority are delicate matters. The canonical system abhors vacuums, ambiguities and conflicts in such transitions. The canons make special provision for supplying leadership when the diocesan bishop is completely prevented from fulfilling his pastoral duties, and when the see becomes vacant.

The first situation occurs when the bishop is imprisoned, exiled or incapacitated, e.g., by an accident or stroke, to the extent that he cannot communicate with the people of the diocese, even by letter (c. 412). The diocesan see is said to be impeded. In this situation, the coadjutor bishop, if there is one, assumes governance of the diocese. But coadjutors are rare, so the governance devolves upon the persons designated by the diocesan bishop on a list of names, which might include an auxiliary bishop, a vicar general or episcopal vicar, or other priests. When the diocesan bishop first takes possession of the diocese he draws up an ordered list of such persons for this purpose. The list is kept by the chancellor of the diocese, and also by the metropolitan (the archbishop of the province), who has a supervisory role. The list is to be updated every three years (c. 413.1). If no such list exists at the time of impedance, then the diocesan college of consultors (c. 502) selects a priest to govern (413.2).

A diocese is considered vacant when the bishop dies, has his resignation accepted, is transferred, or is deprived of the office (c. 416). If there was a coadjutor bishop, he immediately succeeds when the see becomes vacant. Otherwise, an administrator of the diocese is designated until a new bishop is appointed and takes possession. In the case of a bishop being transferred to another diocese, the bishop remains as administrator of the old diocese until he takes possession of the new one (c. 418.2). In the other instances of vacancy (namely, death, resignation or deprivation), the college of consultors (c. 502) is required to elect a diocesan administrator within eight days of learning that the see is vacant (c. 421). The administrator must be a priest, at least thirty-five years old, and should be outstanding in doctrine and prudence (c. 425). The administrator, from the time of his election, has the authority and responsibilities of a diocesan bishop (cc. 427, 429), but there are certain limitations on his powers and initiatives (cc. 427.1, 428).

Groupings of Dioceses and Bishops

Each diocesan church, a portion of the People of God, is a single part of the communion of churches which is the Roman Catholic Church. It is both fitting and necessary that neighboring dioceses relate to one another. The churches must communicate and plan together so that they can cooperate in their common mission and witness. In addition, the bishops of the dioceses, members of the college of bishops, share a solicitude and responsibility for the wider church. They also need to meet, weigh common policies, and collaborate.

The canons allow for groupings and meetings of churches (provinces and councils, both plenary and provincial) and of bishops (provincial meetings and national conferences).

Provinces, Metropolitans

Neighboring dioceses are gathered into groupings called ecclesiastical provinces, in order to promote their common pastoral activity and to foster the relations among their bishops (c. 431.1). There are usually between three and ten dioceses in a province, sometimes those within the boundaries of a state or two or three adjoining states. They are grouped around a larger or older city, where the diocese is called an archdiocese (the prefix "arch," from the Greek, means chief or principal) and the archbishop is called the metropolitan of the province (c. 435). (Metropolitan comes from *meter*, mother, and *polis*, city, the mother or parent city. The other dioceses in the province are called "suffragans," from the Latin *suffragium*, a vote, because their bishops used to be the electors of the metropolitan.)

The metropolitan exercises some vigilance and supervision within the province, but has very little authority over the other churches or their bishops (c. 436). The bishops of the province are not required to meet, and seldom do, at least formally. As a provincial group they have a very modest canonical role (cc. 377.2, 952.1, 1264).

In the Middle Ages provinces were a vigorous and effective "middle level" of church governance. Their authority and influence have been eroded, from above and below, so that now they are largely irrelevant. Archbishops enjoy the prestige of the larger and older churches, and sometimes they exercise personal leadership within the province, but they have only marginally greater canonical authority than other diocesan bishops.

Provincial and Plenary Councils

A large part of the reason why provincial governance has almost vanished in the church is the demise of local councils. The canons provide for representative meetings of neighboring churches, provincial or plenary (at the level of the conference of bishops, that is, national), but they are not held. This most ancient and honorable form of church deliberation is in danger of becoming a mere memory.

One reason these "particular councils" (their generic name) have fallen into disuse is that the church has moved from synodal forms of decision-making and governance toward more administrative or executive styles. Another is the control which the Holy See exercises over the conciliar process (e.g., cc. 439, 446). Still another reason is the success of the more modern conferences of bishops.

At any rate, the Code contains clear guidelines for both provincial and plenary councils: who calls them, who is to be invited, who sets the agenda, what is their authority, and a broad mandate, namely, to provide for the pastoral needs of the People of God in the territory (cc. 439–446). The decision to hold a council is a discretionary judgment (cc. 439–440).

Perhaps a time will come when councils will once again become occasions for the churches to experience the Spirit's vitality.

Conferences of Bishops

National conferences of bishops are the modern deliberative assemblies of the bishops (not the churches) of individual countries. The bishops, both diocesan and auxiliary, gathered in these conferences jointly exercise certain pastoral functions on behalf of the faithful of the nation; they try to adapt the church's apostolates to the time and place so as to enhance the church's service to humankind (c. 447). The conferences are permanent institutions (not just annual meetings), with officers, an executive council, commissions, and staff (cc. 451–3, 457–8). They are an exercise of the bishops' collegial responsibility for the church in the nation, another manifestation of the communion of the churches.

Canonically, bishops' conferences are quite new, stemming from the Second Vatican Council. They have their roots in the ancient conciliar tradition, and more recently in the various national assemblies of bishops in Europe in the nineteenth century and in the United States after the First World War. At the council the bishops expressed the need to have an effective policy-setting mechanism at the national level. The conferences were officially established in canon law to meet this need.

The juridical rule-making authority of conferences is quite limited. They can make regulations which are binding on the churches of the nation only in specifically designated matters, by a vote of two-thirds of the members, and those decisions are subject to review by the Holy See (c. 455). But the most important activities of the bishops' conferences are exercises of their teaching office (c. 753), and efforts of planning, support, encouragement and coordination of the apostolate. In these vital areas the conferences make very substantial contributions to the churches and the nations of the world.

National conferences of bishops are encouraged to communicate with one another, but when cooperation reaches the point of action or program, the Holy See must be consulted (c. 459).

Internal Organization of Dioceses

The diocesan church, which is a portion of the People of God served by a bishop who is assisted by a presbyterate, is the paradigm of a particular church in the Roman Catholic communion of churches. For that reason, the canons offer detailed descriptions of the various organs and offices which help this church to function. Some are instruments of collegial action, i.e., diocesan synod, presbyteral council, college of consultors, pastoral council, finance council, and others are administrative aids to the bishop, i.e., vicars general and episcopal, chancellor, moderator of the curia, finance officer.

[Note: Those who assist the diocesan bishop in judicial matters (as over against executive or administrative affairs), the officers of the diocesan court, are treated in Book Seven of the code, Processes, beginning with canon 1419. They are briefly explained below in the chapter on Processes.]

Most of these diocesan offices and organs are presented in the Code as mandatory, but the way that they are actually deployed and utilized in dioceses varies greatly. In small dioceses, several offices may be held by one person; in large dioceses, the roles may be multiple, and their effective coordination may be channeled through vicariates, secretariats, or cabinet-like departments. The canonical requirements appear quite rigid and fixed, but their arrangement is very flexible in practice.

Consultative Bodies

The canonical concept of consultation implies much more than a passive hearing of the opinions of persons or groups which one is required to consult. The notion is based on the conviction that there is genuine wisdom, God's wisdom, in the community, and the leader must strive earnestly to learn it. The group to be consulted must be brought together, not called by phone or polled by mail. They must be fully informed of the issue, not kept in the dark about the rules or facts. There should be full and free discussion, not a perfunctory exchange. Those consulted are obliged to give their opinions sincerely. If there is unanimity or solid consensus, the leader should not act contrary to it. If the leader feels compelled to act contrary to the consensus of the consultors, he or she should give the reasons, preferably in writing (cf. c. 127).

Diocesan Synod. The largest and most broadly representative of the consultative bodies is the diocesan synod. It is described as a group of priests and other faithful which offers assistance to the diocesan bishop for the good of the whole diocesan community (c. 460). But a synod is not envisioned as a permanent body; rather it is an event which is celebrated when circumstances warrant (c. 461). Regrettably, synods are rarely held.

Gathering the representatives of the local church in a synod is a practice which goes back to the early centuries of the church's existence. In times of reform, the synod was the occasion for announcing and enforcing the reform decrees. The Fourth Lateran Council (1215) and the Council of Trent (1563) ruled that diocesan synods were to be held every year. The 1917 Code required them at least every ten years, but they seldom occurred.

Only the diocesan bishop can convoke a synod, and he must first consult the presbyteral council before doing so (c. 461). He also presides (c. 462). Certain persons must be invited to a synod, and many others may be (c. 463). "Free discussion" is to characterize the exchange within a synod (c. 465). All members of the synod have consultative votes, but the bishop is the sole legislator, if canonical rule-making is part of the agenda (c. 466). The outcome of a diocesan synod is to be communicated to the metropolitan of the province and to the conference of bishops (c. 467).

Most of the dioceses which have celebrated synods since the Second Vatican Council have used them as listening, planning, and animating events for the diocesan community. They can be occasions to unify and energize the local church for its mission.

Presbyteral Council. A consultative group of priests is to exist in every diocese. It is described as a sort of senate to the bishop and at the same time representative of the entire presbyterium. The purposes of the presbyteral council are to help the bishop in governing the diocese and to promote the pastoral welfare of that portion of the People of God (c. 495).

The presbyteral council is another creature of the Second Vatican Council. It was intended to breathe new life into the old chapters of canons and diocesan consultors. And it was to give expression to the diocesan presbyterate, the college of priests which shares in the pastoral leadership of the diocese with the bishop (cc. 369, 384) and of which the bishop is also a member, linked by ties which are sacramental, fraternal and amicable.

About half of the members of the council should be elected by the presbyters of the diocese (secular and religious), others can be *ex officio*, and still others named by the bishop. The aim is to make the group roughly representative of the regions and ministries of the diocese (cc. 497–499). Members are to serve for designated terms, so that the membership is gradually renewed (c. 501.1).

The bishop is obliged to consult the presbyteral council on matters of greater importance, and on certain specific decisions (cf. cc. 461, 515, 531, 536, 1215, 1263, 1742), but the group should be a primary source of counsel for him on all issues related to the welfare and ministries of the diocesan church. The bishop convenes the council, presides over it and sets its agenda (c. 500).

College of Consultors. This small group of priests is appointed by the diocesan bishop from among the members of the presbyteral council for a narrow range of very specific responsibilities (c. 502). The college plays a key role when the diocesan see is impeded or vacant (cc. 421, 272, 413, 419, 422, 485, 501), and in major decisions related to finances (cc. 494, 1277, 1292).

The college of consultors has from six to twelve members, and serves for a five-year term. The bishop presides over meetings of the consultors (c. 502).

Pastoral Council. This consultative body is the most representative of the permanent councils. It reflects the diocesan church, and is composed of laypersons especially, and also of religious and clergy. Its purpose is to advise the bishop about pastoral tasks, to investigate, to weigh, and to suggest courses of action regarding them (cc. 511, 512).

The pastoral council springs right out of the Second Vatican Council. It embodies the themes of the active participation of the laity, their co-responsibility for the church's mission, and the need for collaboration in ministry.

A diocesan pastoral council is highly desirable for every diocese, and its members should be chosen or elected so that the people of the diocese are fairly represented, by regions, by social groups, by employment, and by apostolic involvements (c. 512). Its members are to serve for designated periods of time (c. 513). The bishop is to call the council, preside over it, listen to it, and make public its recommendations (c. 514).

Finance Council. Each diocesan bishop is to establish a council to assist him with the financial management of the diocese. Its members, lay or clerical, are to be skilled in financial affairs and civil law, and persons of outstanding integrity. They serve for terms of five years (c. 492).

The finance council has very specific duties, chief among which are the preparation of the annual budget for the diocese and the approval of the financial report at the end of the year (c. 493; cf. also cc. 423, 494, 1263, 1277, 1281, 1287, 1292, 1305, 1310).

Offices of the Diocesan Curia

The curia consists of those institutions and persons who assist the bishop in the governance of the entire diocese, especially by directing pastoral activity, by caring for the administration of the diocese, and by exercising judicial authority (c. 469). "Curia" (for the meaning of the word, see the Roman curia above) is simply a global term which refers to the officials who help the bishop run the diocese. Often other names are used for this leadership group, like chancery staff, cabinet, or pastoral team.

The curia is a flexible concept. It may and should include those who have diocesan leadership roles, and who should be talking to each other, e.g., directors of divisions or departments or offices, like the superintendent of schools, the director of charities or family services, the personnel director, etc. It is not limited to the offices named in the canons which follow (cc. 475–494; cf. also, 1419–1437), but it should include many of them.

The diocesan bishop appoints all of these officials (c. 470), and he can remove them. They are to promise to fulfill their offices faithfully, and to observe secrecy if and when it is required of them (c. 471). The official documents (curial acts), for example, letters of appointment, are to be signed and notarized (c. 474).

The coordination of the diocesan administration is the bishop's responsibility, and canon 473 suggests some alternative ways of accomplishing it, depending on the size and complexity of the diocesan structures.

Vicar General. A vicar is one who takes the place of another (from *vicarius*, one who takes another's place, a substitute). In canon law, a vicar is one who acts in place of another or with another's authority. A diocesan bishop acts on his own or "proper" authority; a vicar general acts with the bishop's authority, in his stead. "General" here means not limited to some specific area of the diocese, but for the entire diocese. The bishop is to appoint a vicar general (usually just one) to assist him with the governance of the diocese (c. 475).

The vicar general has the same executive authority in the diocese as the bishop. That is, he can perform all the same administrative actions, except those which are reserved to the bishop alone (c. 479). Note that the vicar general acts only in the executive or administrative area; he does not share in the bishop's legislative or judicial authority, much less in his teaching or sanctifying roles. Still, canonically it is the most powerful office in the diocesan church after that of the bishop.

The vicar general must be a priest, at least thirty years old, learned in canon law or theology, and have sound doctrine, integrity, prudence and pastoral experience (c. 478). The vicar general is to report to the bishop, and never to act against the policies or wishes of the bishop (c. 480).

Episcopal Vicar. The vicar general has executive authority in the entire diocese; episcopal vicars have the same authority in particular areas of the diocesan church. They may be appointed by the bishop for parts of the territory (e.g., a vicariate), or for areas of the apostolate (e.g., for parishes, for personnel), or for specific groups of the faithful (e.g., an ethnic minority or immigrant group—c. 476). Within their areas of responsibility they act with the bishop's authority (c. 479.2). The qualifications, appointment and removal, and coordination with the bishop are the same for episcopal vicars as for vicars general (cc. 478, 480, 481).

Chancellor. The chancellor's duty is to collect, arrange and keep the documents of the diocesan curia (c. 482.1). He or she also acts as a notary, establishing the authenticity of church documents by means of a signature (c. 483).

The name comes from the Latin, *cancellarius*, an usher or gatekeeper in a Roman court whose place was *ad cancellos*, at the bars or grating which separated the judge from the public. The *cancellarius* became the secretary for the judge, and then the keeper of the court records.

The office of chancellor in many dioceses (especially in the United States) is much more than that of archivist and notary. The chancellor is often the "executive officer" or "general manager" of the diocesan administration, fortified with the authority of a vicar general or with delegated power. The chancellor need not be a cleric, but must be of good character and above reproach (c. 483.2).

Finance Officer. The bishop is to appoint a finance officer or comptroller to administer the assets of the diocese, and to oversee authorized expenditures (c. 494.3). The finance officer, who may be a layperson or a cleric, is to be skilled in financial affairs and outstandingly honest (c. 494.1). He or she reports to the bishop and the finance council, works with the budget approved by the council, and makes a year-end financial report to the council. The finance officer has a renewable five-year term of office (c. 494).

Moderator of the Curia. Like that of the finance officer, this position is a new one canonically. It is one response to the important concern for coordination within the administration of a diocese. The bishop may name someone, preferably a vicar general or episcopal vicar, to coordinate the exercise of administrative responsibilities, and to see that the other officials of the curia do their jobs (c. 473.2 & 3). The person with these unenviable tasks is called the moderator of the curia.

Parishes and Pastors

The parish is where the vast majority of Catholics experience church. It is the place of primary and usual contact. The faithful know one another as members of a parish; they celebrate the sacraments together in the parish church, share in common projects and identify themselves as parishioners. The local congregation is a true church, one of those linked and bonded in the communion of churches called the diocesan church. The parish is a subdivision of the diocese (c. 374), but in reality it is much more than that.

The canons define a parish as a community of the Christian faithful. That community, clearly described and stably established, is entrusted by the bishop to a pastor for its pastoral care (c. 515.1). The key words are "a community of believers." A community implies a dynamic interaction among its members; it conveys more cohesion and interdependence than the static expression, "a portion of the People of God," which is used to define a diocese.

"Parish" stems from the Greek *paroikia*, a neighborhood or district. In the earliest centuries it designated the church headed by a bishop, but somewhere between the fourth and sixth centuries it came to be used as the name for the smaller, local churches within the diocese, cared for by a presbyter. In the feudal period the parish became "privatized," that is, owned by the local lord who entrusted its care and its income to a priest, as his job and sustenance. Only recently has canon law returned to the more authentic vision of the parish as a community of believing people.

Catholic parishes are usually territorial, i.e., membership in them is based upon residence within the parish boundaries. But parishes can also be personal, i.e., with membership based on language, nationality, affiliation with a college or university, military service, or other criterion (c. 518). There are about 20,000 Catholic parishes in the United States.

The diocesan bishop establishes parishes, and it is within his authority to alter or combine them, or even to suppress them, but only after consulting the presbyteral council. The parish is a juridic person, that is, a subject of rights and obligations, and able to own property (c. 515).

Usually, each parish has a presbyter as pastor, but when circumstances require, parish ministerial personnel can be differently configured, e.g., several parishes may be entrusted to one pastor, several priests as a team may jointly provide pastoral care for one or several parishes, or a deacon or layperson(s) may be entrusted with the pastoral care of a parish (c. 517). (In the latter case, a nearby priest is appointed to supervise the pastoral care.) Communities not established as parishes can be considered quasi-parishes or provided for in some other way (c. 516).

Parish councils, made up of parish members and those who minister in the parish, exist to help promote the pastoral activity of the parish. They have a consultative role, and are subject to the pastor. The councils are required, if the diocesan bishop so decides (c. 536).

Each parish is also to have a finance council to aid the pastor in the administration of parish property and finances (c. 537).

Pastors

What the bishop is to the diocese, the pastor is to the parish. The pastor's role includes broad teaching, sanctifying and governing responsibilities, but on a human scale. A good pastor knows the people of the parish by name, visits their homes, cares about them and for them at the turning points of their Christian lives. In the Catholic Church, as in other Christian churches, the pastor is the mainstay of ministry.

The title of "pastor" comes from the Latin word for shepherd, which is one of the descriptions Jesus used of himself:

I am the good shepherd. I know my sheep and my sheep know me . . . ; for these sheep I will give my life. (Jn. 10, 14–15).

The term "pastor" has been used for the central ministerial role since New Testament times.

A pastor cares for the community entrusted to him, fulfilling the duties of teaching, sanctifying and governing. The pastor does so under the authority of the diocesan bishop, with whom he shares the ministry of Christ. His sacramental connection with the bishop in holy orders is one expression of the communion of the parish community with the diocesan church. The pastor is charged to cooperate with other presbyters, deacons and laypersons in carrying out his ministry to the parish community (c. 519).

Teaching. The pastor must see to it that God's word is proclaimed to all the people in the parish, not only by teaching and preaching to the Catholic faithful, but to everyone by every possible means, from catechetical formation to evangelical outreach and works of social justice. Announcing God's saving word is the pastor's chief charge (cc. 528.1, 757, 762–772, 776–777, 217).

Sanctifying. The pastor is to make the eucharist the life-giving and nourishing center of the parochial congregation; he is to promote both family prayer and active participation in the liturgy (c. 528.2). The pastor baptizes new members of the community, reconciles the penitent, anoints the sick, assists at weddings and buries the dead, in addition to celebrating mass for the people of the parish every Sunday and holy day (cc. 530, 534, 914, 968, 986, 1001, 1063, 1108, 1177). Carefully prepared and prayerful sacramental celebrations are the core of the pastor's sanctifying role within the parish community, but the role also implies a broader dimension of spiritual leadership (cc. 213, 214).

Governing. "Pastoring" implies knowing the persons and families of the parish, supporting, comforting, and sometimes even correcting them. It also means looking out for the poor, the afflicted, the lonely and the migrant (c. 529.1). The pastor is to promote the active participation of the laity in the church's mission, striving to have the people of the parish share vitally in their local communion, and at the same time to feel themselves a vigorous part of the diocesan communion, eager to cooperate with the bishop and the presbyterium (c. 529.2). The pastor is also the juridical representative of the parish, and the administrator of the parish property (cc. 532, 1220, 1279, 1281–1288). He is responsible for keeping and preserving the parish sacramental records and archives (c. 535).

Even though, as stated above, the pastoral role in a parish may be divided or shared in various ways, only an ordained presbyter can qualify for the official title of pastor of a parish. The presbyter must also be of sound doctrinal and moral probity, zealous, and personally suited to the parish in question (c. 521).

The diocesan bishop confers the office of pastor (c. 523), but only after consultation with the dean or vicar of the area in which the parish is located and, if need be, with other presbyters and laypersons (c. 524). If the parish is entrusted to a religious community, the religious superior presents the candidate for pastor to the bishop, and the bishop names him pastor (cc. 520, 682).

The pastor should enjoy stability in office; it is necessary for the community's sake as well as his own. He can be named for an indefinite term, but the more common practice is to have a term of six years, renewable for six more (c. 522). The pastor is obliged to maintain residence within, and be present to, the parish community, at least for eleven months of the year. Usually this means living in the parish house (rectory), and taking no more than a month's vacation (c. 533). Pastors lose their office by the expiration of their term, transfer, removal or resignation. They, like bishops, are requested to submit their resignations at the age of seventy-five (c. 538). (Reasons and procedures for the removal of pastors are stated in canons 1740–1741.)

Vacant or Impeded Parishes

When a parish is without a pastor or if the pastor is prevented from exercising his pastoral functions, e.g., due to an accident, ill-health, imprisonment or exile, the diocesan bishop appoints an administrator who has the rights and duties of a pastor (cc. 539–540). The title of "parish administrator," therefore, is given canonically only to the priest who temporarily replaces a pastor. It is often used unofficially for those who lead parish communities on a permanent basis in the absence of a presbyter-pastor.

Parochial Vicars

"Parochial vicar" is the canonical name for the ordained presbyter (c. 546) who is appointed to help the pastor; less officially he is sometimes called the assistant or associate pastor or curate. (For the meaning of the term "vicar," see Vicar General.) The vicar shares the pastor's concern for the parish community, and collaborates with him, under his authority, in ministry to it (cc. 545.1, 548.3). The vicar's role can be variously structured: he may assist the pastor in the entire pastoral care of the whole parish, or be responsible for certain ministries or geographical areas or groups of people within the parish, or even exercise specific kinds of ministry, e.g., counselling, catechesis, liturgical coordination, in more than one parish at the same time (cc. 545.2, 548.1 & 2).

Vicars are appointed by the diocesan bishop, who should first consult the pastor and the dean or episcopal vicar of the area (c. 547). Vicars are obliged to reside in the parish, as the pastor is, and they are entitled to the same amount of vacation time (c. 550). Vicars do not enjoy the same stability in office as pastors, however, and may be removed by the bishop for any good reason (c. 552).

Deans

Deans, who are sometimes called "vicars forane" or archpriests, are priests appointed by the bishop to exercise a limited oversight function over the parishes and ministers in geographical areas of the diocese. The regions are called deaneries or vicariates (cc. 374.2, 553–554).

The name "dean" comes from the Latin *decanus*, a chief of ten, one set over ten soldiers or monks. "Forane" comes from *foras*, out-of-doors, outside of, and means an outlying or remote area. So deans or vicars forane are representatives of the bishop in certain outlying areas of the diocese.

The dean visits the parishes of his region, attempts to coordinate pastoral activities among them, sees that the church buildings are well maintained and liturgical regulations obeyed, and observes that the clergy are doing their jobs. He is to care especially for presbyters who are in difficult situations, troubled or sick, and to arrange for the burial of pastors. The dean looks to the welfare of the parish when a pastor is sick or dies, lest records or property go astray (c. 555).

Chaplains

Chaplains are priests to whom the pastoral care of some community or special group of the faithful is entrusted (c. 564). (The name derives from "chapel"; one who is in charge of or conducts services in a chapel.) Chaplains are appointed for hospitals, prisons, military bases, sailing ships, large religious houses, migrant and refugee groups (cc. 567–569). Although they are not, strictly speaking, pastors, the chaplain's role is analogous to that of a pastor, only more restricted in scope. Chaplains are given the authority they need to fulfill their pastoral duties, e.g., to preach the word of God, celebrate the liturgy, and hear the confessions of the people for whom they care (cc. 566–567). Chaplains are appointed and can be removed by the diocesan bishop or other appropriate authority (cc. 565, 569, 572).

Consecrated and Apostolic Life

Religious

Christ's faithful people are distinguished canonically into laypersons, sacred ministers, and religious. "Religious" is the name commonly used for those members of the church who are consecrated to God and the church's salvific mission through the profession of the evangelical counsels of poverty, chastity and obedience (c. 207.2).

Historically, religious life has been one of the church's vital signs. Men and women, gifted by God, have pointed out to their followers new ways of making the Christian journey, new ways of working for God's kingdom. Religious groups have manifested the impulses of the Holy Spirit by which the church has been enlivened, enriched and sometimes reformed. Religious communities are not unique to the Catholic Church, but they are one of its distinctive features and strengths. They are not part of the church's hierarchical structure, but pertain to its life and striving for holiness (c. 207.2).

Canonically, groups of religious men and women are distinguished into three categories:

1. *Institutes of Consecrated Life.* The members of religious institutes take public vows as their way of professing the evangelical counsels, and they live a common life, i.e., a life "in community" (c. 607.2). Institutes of consecrated life include the religious orders and communities, both men's and women's, of the classic traditions: Benedictines, Franciscans, Augustinians, Carmelites, Dominicans, Jesuits and others.

2. *Societies of Apostolic Life.* The members of these societies are committed to an area of the apostolate or mission of the church, to the common life, and to a life of charity, but not through the profession of public vows (although many profess the evangelical counsels in some other form, e.g., promise, pledge or consecration—c. 731). Societies of Apostolic Life include many of the more modern missionary groups

93

such as Missionaries of Africa, Oratorians, Vincentians, Daughters of Charity, Society of the Precious Blood, Paulists, Pallottines, Columbans and Maryknoll.

3. *Secular Institutes.* The members of these groups are not religious; their form of consecrated life is characterized by secularity, i.e., working for the sanctification of the world from within it, while engaging in secular pursuits. They do profess the evangelical counsels in some form, and some do live a common life, but others live with their families in the world (cc. 710-714). Secular Institutes are a twentieth-century innovation; they are relatively small and few in number.

The first two of these three categories are really quite similar, at least when viewed from the outside. They are considered together in this book simply as "religious communities," their members are referred to as women or men "religious." However, the differences between institutes of consecrated life and societies of apostolic life in spirit and tradition are often significant. Canonically, the tendency to homogenize or blur the differences between religious groups must be resisted; their distinctive orientations and traditions must be respected (c. 577-578).

The hierarchy of the church claims the right to regulate the practice of the consecrated life by means of canonical approval (c. 576). This has often served to strengthen and protect wholesome religious traditions, but it has also contributed to tensions between charismatic and structural elements in the church.

Religious Communities

Basic Distinctions. Religious communities are gender-identified, of women or of men. However, the canonical norms are the same for both kinds of communities (c. 606). Communities are recognized by church authority as either lay or clerical. They are lay if their proper role does not require the exercise of sacred orders, clerical if their basic purpose presumes the exercise of orders (c. 588). Communities are diocesan or pontifical depending upon whether they were established or approved by a diocesan bishop or by the pope (c. 589).

External Control. The establishment of religious communities, the approval of their constitutions and any changes in them, their mergers and their suppression, are subject to the authority of the church's hierarchy, either episcopal or papal (cc. 579, 582-584, 593-595). Communities are subject to the pope, and their individual members are to obey him (c.

590). He can exempt religious orders from the authority of diocesan bishops (c. 591). The superiors of the communities are to submit regular status reports to the Congregation for Religious in Rome (c. 592).

Autonomy and Authority. Each religious community possesses a precious heritage which it is to cherish: the vision and intent of the founder regarding the nature, purposes and spirit of the group, and its own healthy traditions. In other words, its own communal identity (c. 578). Each community has its own autonomy of life and governance by which it preserves its own identity and appropriate discipline (c. 586). The community draws up its own constitution in which it spells out its heritage, governance structures, membership and formation criteria, and its own understanding of the evangelical counsels. In addition to this fundamental document, the community also draws up secondary or supplemental codes or rules of life, which are more easily changed (c. 587). The elected superiors and deliberative assemblies of the communities have authority to direct their activities and govern their members (c. 596).

Consecrated Lives. Those who join religious communities pledge to follow Christ by living the evangelical counsels of chastity, poverty and obedience, which are gifts from the Lord and observed with the aid of his grace (cc. 573.2, 575). The counsel of chastity entails consistent sexual continence in a celibate, i.e., unmarried, state (Mt 19,12; 1 Cor 7, 32–35; c. 599). Poverty implies being poor both in spirit and in fact, being dependent and limited in using and disposing of material goods (Mt 6,20; 8,20; 2 Cor 8,9; c. 600). The counsel of obedience means submission to the directives of one's religious superiors (Jn 4,34; 5.30; c. 601). The common life of the religious community is to be familial and mutually supportive of the members in fulfilling their vocations (Acts 4,32; c. 602).

Structures and Governance

Religious Houses. Religious communities are organized according to houses, that is, dwelling places where members live together or at least to which they are attached by assignment. Houses are formally established by the appropriate community authority, and members are obliged to reside in the house to which they are assigned. Each house has a superior. The diocesan bishop must approve the establishment of a religious house in the diocese, and that approval carries with it certain other prerogatives, e.g., the right to an oratory where the eucharist is reserved, the right to exercise the apostolic works proper to the community, the right to establish their own lay association (cc. 608–611, 665, 733, 312).

Superiors. Houses are grouped together into provinces under a superior known as a provincial. The supreme moderator (or superior general) holds authority over all of the provinces, houses and members of the entire community. These two levels of superiors, provincials and supreme moderators, are called major superiors; they and their vicars are to exercise governance over the community in accord with the community's own rules (cc. 596, 617, 620–622). These superiors are elected by the members of the community for specific terms of office (cc. 624–625). The superiors have real authority with regard to the members of the community, but they are to exercise it in a spirit of service (c. 618). They are to build a community of sisters or brothers in Christ, caring pastorally for their needs (c. 619). Superiors are to visit the houses under their charge and attend to the members individually (c. 628). However, they are obliged to respect the personal autonomy of individual members, and must never intrude on their freedom of conscience (c. 630).

Councils. Provincial superiors and supreme moderators are required to have a council, made up of several members of the community, to assist them in the governance of the community. These provincial and general councils advise the superior and enable some members to share in the direction of the community. The councils are advisory, but there are many instances in which the superior either must consult the council before acting or obtain the consent of the council in order to act (c. 627).

Chapters. Chapters are collegial assemblies, representative of the entire community; they are the highest authority in the community. These gatherings, which are carefully structured and regulated, are usually held every three to six years, and are signal events in the lives of communities. In chapter, the delegates recall the identity and traditions of the community and strive to renew it in light of that heritage, they elect the supreme moderator (superior general), they deliberate major questions, and issue norms to guide the community in the future (cc. 631–633). Most communities also hold provincial chapters for the same purposes.

The name "chapter" comes from the Latin, *capitulum*, a diminutive form of *caput*, head. It came to mean a heading, a division of a writing, a chapter of a book. In the early Middle Ages monks came together daily to listen to the reading of a chapter of their rule. The meetings, which also took up other matters, were called chapters.

Property. Communities and their provinces are juridic persons, hence they may own and administer their own property. They are to do so while avoiding any appearance of wealth, and in such a way as to express their version of poverty. Each community and province is to have a finance officer who is accountable to the superior and council. The norms for the administration of church property (Book Five of the Code) must be observed (cc. 634–640, 741.1).

Admission and Formation. No one may be admitted to a religious community without suitable preparation (c. 597.2). The stages of this preparation are:

1. *Pre-novitiate.* A preliminary period of affiliation or association with the community.
2. *Novitiate.* Qualified and suitable candidates are admitted to a structured process of vocational discernment and spiritual formation while living within the community, for at least one year (cc. 641–653, 735).
3. *Temporary profession.* After novitiate, candidates are incorporated into the community by assuming the observance of the evangelical counsels, usually for three years. During this time they continue their spiritual and apostolic formation within the community (cc. 654–657, 659–660).
4. *Perpetual profession.* Upon the expiration of temporary vows, if they request it and are judged worthy, the religious are admitted to permanent profession, the final step in community membership (cc. 657–658). (Cf. "Directives on Formation in Religious Institutes," March 13, 1990, *Origins* 19:42(3–19–90)677–699.)

Separation. A member can be separated from a religious community in three ways:

1. *Transfer.* A person can transfer from one religious community to another, but only with the permission of the authorities of each, and after completing a three-year period of probation (cc. 684–685, 744).
2. *Departure.* Professed religious may leave their communities:
    (a) temporarily, by means of an indult (concession) of exclaustration, i.e., permission to live outside the cloister, given by the supreme moderator for a period of up to three years (cc. 686–687, 745);
    (b) permanently, by means of an indult of departure, which carries with it a dispensation from vows, given by the supreme moderator and the appropriate hierarchical authority (cc. 691-693, 743).
3. *Dismissal.* Permanently professed members of religious communities may be dismissed on three grounds:
    (a) one who publicly leaves the Catholic faith or who attempts marriage is dismissed *ipso facto* by the canons (c. 694);

(b) one who commits murder, abortion, other violent crimes, or a cleric who lives in concubinage or other scandalous sexual arrangement, must be dismissed, and the major superior initiates action to that end (c. 695);

(c) one who has committed other very serious and publicly established offenses against the church or consecrated life may be dismissed, but only after repeated warnings, opportunities to be heard, referral to the supreme moderator and confirmation by hierarchical authority (cc. 696–701).

Obligations and Rights

The church has great expectations of religious men and women because of the public witness of their consecrated lives. Their supreme rule of life is the following of Christ (c. 662). They are to devote themselves to prayer, the holy eucharist, reading the scriptures, the liturgy of the hours, meditation and conversion of heart (cc. 663–664). They are to pursue their own ongoing spiritual and theological formation (c. 661).

In addition to these serious spiritual obligations, religious are held to a duty of residence in observance of their commitment to community life (c. 665). They are to make appropriate disposition of their material property, in keeping with the rule of their community (c. 668, 741.2). What they acquire by their personal work accrues to their community (c. 668.3). They are to obey their superiors, accept the tasks assigned them, and keep themselves free for the service required of them (cc. 601, 618, 671, 738). Religious are also required to wear the habit or insignia of their community (c. 669), and they are bound by some of the same obligations as sacred ministers, including that of continent celibacy (cc. 672, 739, 277, 285, 286, 287, 289).

In return, religious have a right to expect that their community will sustain and support them, physically and spiritually, so that they can live out their calling (c. 670, 737). This includes the time and resources necessary for their own continued development (c. 661). Religious also have both vote and voice in the selection of their superiors and the policies of their communities (cc. 626, 631, 633).

Apostolate

Apostolate is the term which the Second Vatican Council and the Code use to describe what active (as over against contemplative) religious communities are engaged in. Globally, apostolate signifies all the activity of the church directed toward the attainment of the goal of spreading the kingdom of Christ everywhere, of causing everyone to share in Christ's saving redemption. Within that large purpose, each religious community has its own characteristic services, ministries and works to perform; these constitute the corporate apostolates of the community, e.g., evangelization, teaching, parish ministry, care for the poor or the sick (c. 676). However, the primary apostolate of all religious consists in the witness given by their consecrated lives (c. 673).

Apostolic action belongs to the very nature of active religious communities; their apostolic spirit and their religious spirit suffuse one another. Their apostolic activities proceed from their union with God and are carried on in communion with the church (c. 675). Communities are to retain the mission and works proper to them, but they are also to accommodate them to contemporary needs (c. 677).

It is in the apostolate that religious communities and diocesan bishops must relate to one another, for the pastoral welfare of the people. Religious communities enjoy autonomy of life and governance (c. 586), but religious are subject to the authority of the bishop in four areas: the care of souls, public worship, the works of the apostolate, and specific tasks or offices which the bishop assigns to them (c. 678, 681–682). Consultation, coordination and cooperation between religious communities and bishops are required in these areas of apostolic activity (cc. 678.3, 680–682, 394). Religious should enter into written agreements when assuming and assigning responsibilities in a diocese (c. 681.2). In addition, the bishop has a limited oversight of the churches, oratories, schools and other works carried on by religious in the diocese (c. 683).

Conferences of Major Superiors

The major superiors (provincials and generals) of religious communities associate in conferences for purposes of collaboration, both in achieving the goals of their individual communities and in cooperating with bishops (c. 708). These conferences are voluntary associations, regulated by the Holy See (c. 709). In the United States there exist the Leadership Conference of Women Religious and the Conference of Major Superiors of Men. In Canada the women and men together belong to the Canadian Religious Conference. There are also men's and women's Unions of Superiors General in Rome.

THE
TEACHING
FUNCTION

Book Three of the Code

Christ clearly and solemnly ordered his followers to proclaim the gospel to all nations and to teach them all that he commanded (Mt 28,19–20; Mk 16,15; Lk 24,47). The church has always heeded Christ's charge. Spreading the good news of God's mercy and salvation has always been a central part of the church's mission. However, the Catholic reaction to the Protestant Reformation caused this central ministry to be downplayed somewhat; for a long time sacramental ministry was emphasized to the partial detriment of the teaching function. The Second Vatican Council returned the church's prophetic task to its proper primacy, and this is reflected here in the Code. The canons on the teaching office, greatly expanded and renewed, are placed immediately after the book on The People of God, and ahead of the treatment of The Sanctifying Function.

This proclamatory function belongs to the entire church, not only to the hierarchy or the clergy. Gone are the days when the church was neatly divided into the "teaching church" (*ecclesia docens*) and the "learning church" (*ecclesia discens*). The council and the Code affirm that the teaching and preaching role falls to the People of God, to the whole church. However, the canons of the Code assign specific responsibilities to designated groups of people within the church. That is the principal purpose of the canons of Book Three.

Two of the functions included in the teaching office are essential, that is, they belong to the very nature of the church. They are the ministry of the word and missionary action. Without them, the church would not be the church. These two tasks are at the heart of the teaching function. By comparison, the rest of the matters in this book are either of an introductory nature or of secondary importance.

Introduction

The church has the duty and right to preach the gospel to all nations. This includes the right to teach about moral principles, social justice and human rights. Christ the Lord entrusted revealed truth to the church to safeguard, contemplate, announce and explain, with the help of the Holy Spirit (c. 747). Everyone is obliged to seek the truth about God and the church and, when they find the truth, to embrace it. However, no one can ever be forced to accept the Catholic faith (c. 748).

The inerrancy in fundamental truths, which was promised to the church, is here articulated in relation to two offices. The pope and the college of bishops possess infallible teaching authority when, and only when, speaking as teachers of the faithful, they define that some truth of faith or morals must be held as a doctrine of faith (c. 749). They do so very rarely.

The canons describe four levels of teaching together with the response appropriate to each:

1. That which is found in the scriptures or in tradition and is taught by the magisterium as divinely revealed must be believed with divine and catholic faith (c. 750).

2. That which is taught authoritatively, but not definitively, by the magisterium on faith or morals deserves a religious respect of intellect and will (c. 752).

3. That which is taught by bishops, individually or in conference or particular council, for the faithful entrusted to their care, is to be received with a sense of religious respect (c. 753).

4. Constitutions and decrees (such as those from the Second Vatican Council) which church authorities issue to propound doctrine or proscribe errors, are to be observed (c. 754).

The term "magisterium" comes from the Latin, *magister*, meaning master, director or teacher. "Magistrate" and "mastery" come from the same root. In the church, magisterium came to mean teaching authority, and gradually its meaning narrowed to refer to the pastoral teaching office of bishops, the teaching function of the hierarchy.

Three offenses against the faith are described in the canons:

1. **Heresy** is the obstinate denial or doubt of a truth which is to be believed with divine and catholic faith;
2. **Apostasy** is the total repudiation of the Christian faith;
3. **Schism** is the refusal of submission to the pope or of communion with the members of the church (cc. 751, 1364).

The ecumenical movement is the impetus to restore unity among all Christians. The church is bound by the will of Christ to promote that unity (Jn 17,21). The college of bishops and the Holy See are to direct the participation of Catholics in the ecumenical movement, and the bishops are to do the same in the churches entrusted to them (c. 755).

Ministry of the Divine Word

Everyone in the church has a part to play in this preeminent ministry. The canons assign special roles to six groups:

1. The pope and the college of bishops have the duty to proclaim the gospel with regard to the universal church (c. 756.1).
2. Individual bishops are moderators of the ministry of the word in the churches entrusted to them (cc. 756.2, 386).
3. Presbyters, especially those with pastoral offices, are to proclaim the gospel of God (cc. 757, 528).
4. Deacons are to serve the People of God in the ministry of the word (c.757).
5. Religious, because of their consecrated lives, give testimony to the gospel, and may be enlisted to help in its proclamation (c. 758).
6. Laypersons, in virtue of their baptism and confirmation, are witnesses to the gospel message by word and the example of their Christian lives; they, too, can be invited to exercise the ministry of the word (c. 759).

In the ministry of the word the mystery of Christ is to be set forth in its entirety, based on the scriptures, tradition, liturgy, the magisterium, and the life of the church (c. 760). Every available means is to be used to proclaim Christian teaching. Preaching and catechetical formation are primary, but schools, conferences, meetings, public statements, and the media are all to be employed (c. 761).

Preaching

From earliest times the church has sought to exercise some control over those who preach in its name. Here, alongside exhortations for frequent preaching, those controls are stated in terms of rights, faculties and permissions to preach.

Ordained ministers are to take preaching the gospel of God very seriously, since it is among their principal duties. After all, it is the word of the living God which gathers God's people together (c. 762). Bishops have the right to preach everywhere (c. 763). Presbyters and deacons have the faculty to preach everywhere, with at least the presumed permission of the person in charge of the church (c. 764). Preaching to religious in their own oratories requires the permission of their superior (c. 765). Laypersons can be permitted to preach in church in cases of necessity or usefulness (c. 766).

The homily at mass is the preeminent form of preaching; it is a part of the liturgy itself, and is reserved to presbyters and deacons. A homily is an exposition of mysteries of faith and norms for Christian living from the sacred texts of the liturgical year. Homilies are to be preached at all masses on Sundays and holy days, and should also be given on other days as well. The pastor is to see that these norms regarding the homily are observed (c. 767).

Preachers of the divine word are to tell the faithful what is to be believed and done for God's glory and their salvation. They are also to impart the teachings of the church on social issues, such as the dignity and freedom of the human person, the unity and stability of the family, the just distribution of material goods, and the quest for peace (c.768). Christian teaching is to be accommodated to the conditions of its hearers and adapted to the needs of the times (c. 769).

Bishops and pastors are to strive to project the word of God to those who lack ordinary pastoral care because of their situation, e.g., shut-ins, migrants, travelers, military, etc. They are also to see that the gospel message reaches the non-believers who live in their area (c. 771, 383, 528). (On homilies, see *Fulfilled in Your Hearing: The Homily in the Sunday Assembly*, USCC, 1982.)

Catechetical Instruction

Catechesis is that form of the ministry of the word directed toward those who have been evangelized, that is, who have heard the gospel and responded in faith. (The word "catechesis" comes from the Greek *katechein*, to instruct or teach.) Catechetical instruction aims at rendering that faith lively, explicit and operative. In other words, it is the local community's effort to make disciples out of believers, to nurture them in Christian living, and help them develop and mature in faith. The entire community is responsible for this ongoing process, especially those charged with pastoral leadership, and parents in regard to their own children (cc. 773–774).

The bishop is to facilitate and oversee the catechetical effort in the diocese, making sure that guidelines and materials are available, and that catechists are properly trained (cc. 775, 780).

The pastor has a central, coordinating responsibility to provide for the catechetical formation of adults, young people and children in the parish. For assistance in this complex task he can call upon other clerics, religious, catechists and other laypersons, all of whom are admonished to be generous with their help (c. 776).

A canon provides pastors with a checklist of special catechetical moments and needs:

1. on the occasion of all sacramental celebrations;
2. children at first communion, penance and confirmation;
3. further formation of children after their first communion;
4. catechesis suitable for those handicapped in mind or body;
5. development in faith for young people and adults (c. 777).

Religious are to see to it that catechetical formation is given to those served by their churches, schools, missions and other apostolates (c. 778). (For a fuller treatment of catechetics, see Pope John Paul II's apostolic exhortation, *Catechesis in Our Time*, USCC, 1979.)

Missionary Action

The church is missionary by its very nature, and evangelization is a fundamental duty of the people of God. Therefore, every one of the Christian faithful has a role in the missionary effort (c. 781).

The pope and the college of bishops direct and coordinate the church's missionary effort (in large part through the Congregation for the Evangelization of Peoples). Individual bishops share the concern for this missionary work, and they are to foster it in their dioceses (c. 782, 791). Those bishops in mission territories are to supervise and coordinate the activity of missionaries in their dioceses (c. 790). Religious men and women, because of their consecration to the church, are to engage in missionary activity (c. 783).

Missionary activity aims at implanting the church where it has not yet taken root. It means sending heralds of the gospel among peoples who have not heard it, until young churches are fully established and able to mount their own evangelization efforts (c. 786).

Missionaries are those persons who are sent to engage in missionary work; they may be native or foreign, presbyters, deacons, religious or laypersons (c. 784). Catechists are laypersons, well instructed and known to be good Christians, who assist missionaries by teaching the gospel, leading liturgical celebrations and promoting works of charity (c. 785).

Missionaries strive to establish sincere dialogue with non-Christians by means of their words and the witness of their lives; they try to open ways for them to come to an understanding of the gospel. They teach the truths of the faith to those who seem ready to accept the gospel message, so that they can be baptized, if and when they request it (c. 787).

Those who show a willingness to embrace the Christian faith are to be enrolled in the catechumenate (from the Greek *katechoumenoi*, the instructed). The catechumens are initiated into the mystery of salvation and introduced to the life and apostolate of the People of God (c. 788). After baptism, the new Christians continue to grow in their understanding of the gospel truths and their own Christian duties; they come to love Christ and his church (c. 789).

(For a larger treatment of missionary activity, consult the apostolic exhortation of Pope Paul VI, *Evangelization in the Modern World*, USCC, 1975. For an understanding of the catechumenate, see the *Rite for Christian Initiation of Adults*, Congregation for Divine Worship, 1972. The Study Edition published by the NCCB in 1988 is especially helpful.)

Catholic Education

Parents have the duty and the right to educate their children. This includes the right and obligation to choose the most suitable means for the Catholic education of their offspring. The state should assist parents in providing for this religious formation (c. 793). Parental prerogatives loom large in this section of the Code. It refers to Catholic schools as well as other means of education, e.g., public and private schools and programs of religious instruction.

The church has the duty and right to educate people, because of its divinely-given mission to help them attain the fullness of their Christian lives. The church seeks to vindicate its right against sometimes hostile governments. Pastors have the responsibility to see that all of the faithful can enjoy some form of Catholic education (c. 794).

Schools. Primary and secondary schools, both Catholic and non-Catholic, are the subject here and, once again, parents are in the forefront. They should esteem the schools which are available for their children, and cooperate closely with the teachers in support of the educational effort (c. 796). Parents should send their children to schools where Catholic education is provided, if they can. If they are unable to do so, they are still obliged to provide for their children's Catholic education (c. 798).

Parents should be free to select the school they prefer for their children; they should not be penalized by the state for exercising that freedom of choice (c. 797). The faithful should strive to see that the state provides in some way for the religious and moral formation of children, always in keeping with their parents' consciences (c. 799).

The church has the right to found and run schools of whatever kind, and the faithful should support them, according to their abilities (c. 800). If schools which impart good Christian education are not available, the bishop should see to their establishment (c. 802). Religious communities, whose mission is education, are encouraged to devote themselves to Catholic education (c. 801).

Church authorities can exercise control over schools in several ways:

1. Only those schools officially recognized by church authority are considered to be Catholic; they cannot use the title "Catholic" without permission (c. 803).
2. Catholic religious instruction in any school, Catholic or not, is subject to the authority and vigilance of the bishop (c.804).
3. The diocesan bishop has the right to appoint and dismiss religion teachers (c. 805).
4. The bishop can regulate all Catholic schools in the diocese, and he has the right of vigilance and visitation of them (c. 806).

Catholic Colleges and Universities. The church, in exercise of its teaching office, claims the right to found and operate institutions of higher learning (c. 807). The bishops' conferences are to see to the establishment and distribution of such schools in their territories (c. 809). Bishops are to provide, in particular, for the establishment of faculties or chairs of theology in Catholic universities (c. 811). Bishops are also to provide for the pastoral care of college students by means of parishes or other forms of campus ministry (c. 813).

The Code recognizes that these Catholic institutions of higher learning have legitimate autonomy. They are not simply extensions of the church, even though they are church-related. Canon law states that the school authorities make appointments of instructors in these schools in accord with their own statutes. However, there is concern that the teachers have "integrity of doctrine and probity of life" as well as academic competence (c. 810). Bishops are to be vigilant that the principles of Catholic doctrine are observed in colleges and universities, and those who teach theological disciplines should have a mandate from the bishop (cc. 810, 812).

[Note: Most Catholic colleges and universities in the United States and Canada were not canonically established. There is serious question about the applicability of canon 812 to those who teach in them.]

Ecclesiastical Universities and Faculties. The church sponsors a few schools of its own, mainly for the pursuit of theological disciplines (c. 815). They can only be established with the approval of the Holy See; their statutes and programs of study must also be approved (c. 816). In addition, they are subject to the same local vigilance and control as other Catholic institutions (c. 818). Only these schools can grant academic degrees with canonical effects, i.e., degrees required for certain church offices (c. 817). Dioceses and religious communities are encouraged to send students to these schools (c. 819). (For greater detail, see the apostolic constitution of Pope John Paul II *On Ecclesiastical Universities and Faculties*, USCC, 1979.)

Publication of Books

The canons impose on church leaders a duty of general vigilance over publications and other media of communications, in order to preserve the integrity of faith and morals of the faithful. Bishops can ask that Catholics submit their writings on faith or morals to their judgment, and they can criticize writings which they deem harmful (c. 823, 827.3).

Certain publications, however, are very closely related to the church's own teaching and worship, and the church tries to exercise greater control over them. It requires permission or approval to publish six different kinds of books:

1. books of the sacred scriptures (the Holy See or conference of bishops must approve; c. 825);
2. liturgical books (e.g., missals, rituals, breviaries) and prayer books (c. 826);
3. catechisms (c. 827.1);
4. textbooks on the theological disciplines for use in schools (c. 827.2);
5. publications displayed or distributed in churches (c. 827.4);
6. collections of decrees or official acts of a church authority, like a council or synod or chapter (c. 828).

These regulations apply, not only to books, but to any writings which are destined for public distribution. The person who grants the permission to publish is the bishop of the author or of the publisher (c. 824). The bishop may use a censor to evaluate the writing in relationship to the church's teachings, and then make his own prudent judgment (c. 830). New editions or translations of works require their own permissions (c. 829). Members of religious communities are also to seek the permission of their superiors to publish on matters of religion or morals (c. 832).

Profession of Faith

The canons require a public profession of faith on the occasion of the assumption of certain offices or duties. The formula is basically the traditional creed from the fourth-century councils of Nicaea and Constantinople. Those required to make the profession of faith are:

1. participants in councils and synods;
2. cardinals;
3. bishops and diocesan administrators;
4. vicars general, episcopal and judicial;
5. pastors;
6. seminary rectors and professors;
7. candidates for the diaconate;
8. Catholic university rectors and teachers of theology;
9. superiors of religious communities (c. 833).

THE SANCTIFYING FUNCTION

Book Four of the Code

To sanctify means to make holy, and to glorify the Holy One. The church's work of sanctification is focused on its public acts of worship of God, the sacred liturgy, and certain other devotional and penitential practices. This book of the Code, its second largest, is concerned with the regulation of the church's divine worship. The canons reflect the liturgical renewal inaugurated at the Second Vatican Council.

Most of the church's liturgical rules are not found in the Code, but in its ritual books. It is of prime importance to recognize that the ritual books are the best source for the church's rules of worship. Not only are the complete and detailed liturgical norms found in those sources, but in those books, especially in their introductions, the norms are set within a rich, intelligible context of theology and pastoral practice. The place to go for the church's rules of worship is to its ritual books. They will be noted at appropriate places in the course of this chapter. (Most are available in two collections: *Documents on the Liturgy, 1963–1979*, Collegeville: Liturgical Press, 1982, and *The Rites of the Catholic Church*, two vols., New York: Pueblo, 1976, 1980.)

This book of the Code begins with a general introduction about worship. The church fulfills its sanctifying function in a special way through the liturgy, which is the exercise of the priestly office of Jesus Christ. In the liturgy the entire Mystical Body of Christ, Head and members, offers public worship to God. This worship occurs when it is carried out in the name of the church, by persons deputed, and through acts approved by church authority (c. 834). All of the faithful are deputed for worship in virtue of their baptism. Liturgical books contain the acts of worship approved by church authority.

The whole church celebrates its liturgy, but some within it have special responsibilities. Bishops lead this sanctifying function; they are the promoters and moderators of the liturgical life of the churches entrusted to them. Presbyters share in the sanctifying office; they are consecrated for the celebration of worship. Deacons, too, have a part to play in divine

115

worship. The faithful share in the office of sanctification, especially by their active participation in liturgical celebrations (c. 835).

Christian worship is the exercise of the common priesthood of all the faithful. Ministers must arouse and illumine their faith, because worship depends on belief (c. 836). Liturgical actions belong to the whole church, God's holy people; they manifest and affect the whole body of the church, hence they are not private actions. They are to be celebrated with the active participation of the faithful (c. 837).

The supervision of the church's liturgy pertains to the Holy See, which publishes the liturgical books, and to the diocesan bishops. Conferences of bishops are to prepare and publish translations of the liturgical books for their regions (c. 838). Prayer and works of penance and charity also belong to the church's sanctifying function (c. 839).

Sacraments

General Rules

There are many canons (325 of them) on the sacraments because the sacraments are the principal elements of Roman Catholic worship, and because various abuses in the past have generated a lot of regulations. The canons tend to focus on essentials, on those things minimally necessary for sacramental administration, on the requirements for validity and liceity. They do not even attempt to describe the fullness of sacramental celebrations, with active participation, diverse ministerial roles, integrity of signs, and pastoral adaptations. Look to the ritual books for what is normal and desirable in sacramental worship.

Sacraments are the actions of Christ and the church, which express and strengthen faith, worship God, and effect the sanctification of humankind. The sacraments both establish and manifest ecclesial communion. Ministers and faithful should celebrate the sacraments with the greatest reverence and care (c. 840).

The church's highest authority, that is, the college of bishops and the pope, determines what is required for the validity of the sacraments; that same authority as well as the bishops' conferences and diocesan bishops determine what is for the liceity and order of sacramental celebrations (c. 841).

The official liturgical books govern the celebration of the sacraments, and no one is to change anything in them (c. 846). The canon refers to unauthorized alterations on private initiative; it does not suppress the many legitimate options and alternatives allowed by the liturgical books,

nor does it blur the distinction between liturgical rules which are preceptive and those which are directive or merely descriptive.

Baptism is the gate to the sacraments; one who has not been baptized
may not be admitted to the other sacraments. Full Christian initiation
consists of the sacraments of baptism, confirmation and eucharist; the
three are closely interrelated, and should be received in that sequence (c.
842). (Present pastoral practice often causes children to receive the sacraments in a disrupted sequence: baptism, penance, eucharist and
confirmation.)

The faithful have a right to the sacraments (c. 213). Therefore, ministers cannot refuse the sacraments to those who ask for them at appropriate
times and are properly disposed. It is the duty of pastors and the entire
community to prepare those who seek the sacraments by suitable evangelization and catechesis (c. 843).

The sacraments of baptism, confirmation and orders cannot be repeated. If, after careful investigation, there is prudent doubt whether one
of them was actually or validly conferred, then it is to be conferred conditionally (c. 845).

Catholic ministers may administer sacraments only to Catholics and,
Catholics may receive sacraments only from Catholic ministers (c. 844.1).
That is the general principle, but, at the present stage of ecumenical rela-
tions, there are five exceptions to the general rule:

1. In necessity, anyone may baptize (c. 861.2);
2. In necessity or for spiritual benefit, Catholics may receive penance,
   eucharist and anointing of the sick from non-Catholic ministers in
   whose churches these sacraments are valid, e.g., the Orthodox
   (c. 844.2);
3. Catholic ministers may administer those same sacraments to Eastern
   Christians (i.e., the Orthodox) or others similarly situated, if they ask
   and are properly disposed (c. 844.3);
4. In danger of death or grave necessity, Catholic ministers may administer these sacraments to others not in full communion, but who have
   faith in the sacraments and cannot approach a minister of their own
   community (c. 844.4);
5. Mixed marriages, with permission (cc. 1124–1127).

These very limited instances of sacramental sharing among Christians of
different church affiliations are called *communicatio in sacris*, sharing in
sacred things.

A minister is to ask nothing for the administration of sacraments
beyond the offerings officially established, and the poor are not to be

deprived of the sacraments on account of their poverty (c. 848). The bishops of each province are to determine the amount of mass offerings and "stole fees," i.e., the offerings on the occasion of other sacramental ministrations (cc. 952, 1264).

The sacred oils used in the administration of sacraments are olive or other vegetable oils, recently blessed or consecrated by a bishop (at the Mass of Chrism in Holy Week). The pastor is to seek the oils from his own bishop, as a sign of the communion among the parishes of the diocese and with the bishop (c. 847).

Baptism

Baptism causes men and women to be freed from sin, reborn as children of God, configured to Christ and incorporated into the church. It is necessary for salvation. Baptism is conferred by a washing with water accompanied by the required form of words, i.e., the trinitarian formula (c. 849).

Celebration. Adults prepare for baptism through the stages of the catechumenate. Parents and sponsors of infants to be baptized are similarly to be prepared by their pastor (cc. 851, 788). Baptism is conferred by immersion or by pouring of water which has been blessed (cc. 853–854). Baptism is ordinarily to be celebrated on Sunday or at the Easter Vigil, and in one's own parish church (cc. 856–857). The name given at baptism should not be offensive to Christian sensibilities (c. 855).

Minister. The ordinary minister of baptism is a bishop, presbyter or deacon, but it is a pastor's prerogative. Others may be deputed to baptize and, in necessity, any person with the right intention may baptize (cc. 861, 530). The minister is to baptize only within his own territory, unless he has permission to baptize elsewhere (c. 862). Those over fourteen years of age are to be referred to the diocesan bishop for baptism (c. 863).

Those to be Baptized. Every person not yet baptized is able to be baptized (c. 864). Adults, in order to be baptized, must be willing, sufficiently instructed, and proven in the Christian life through the catechumenate. If they are in danger of death, they may be baptized if they have shown an intention to be baptized and promise to observe the requirements of the Christian faith (c. 865). Adults are to be confirmed and share in the eucharist immediately after their baptism (c. 866).

Infants are to be baptized within the first weeks after their birth. If in danger of death, infants are to be baptized without delay (c. 867). The parents (or at least one of them) must consent to the infant's baptism, and there must be a founded hope that the infant will be brought up in the Catholic religion; if such a hope is lacking, baptism should be deferred. An infant in danger of death may licitly be baptized even if its parents are unwilling (c. 868).

If, after careful investigation, doubt remains about whether a person was baptized at all or baptized validly, baptism is to be conferred conditionally (e.g., "If you are not baptized, I baptize you . . ."). Those baptized in non-Catholic Christian churches are not to be baptized conditionally unless, after an examination of their baptism, there is a serious reason for doubting its validity (c. 869, 845).

Sponsors. The baptized is given a sponsor (godparent) to present the person for baptism and, after that, to help the baptized to lead a Christian life faithfully (c. 872). There may be one sponsor or one of each sex (c. 873). A sponsor should be chosen by the person to be baptized or the parents, over sixteen years old, a fully initiated Catholic who lives the faith, and not be a parent of the one to be baptized. One who belongs to a non-Catholic church may serve as a witness at a Catholic baptism, but not as a sponsor (c. 874).

Records. The pastor of the place where the baptism is celebrated must without delay record in the baptismal book: the names of the baptized, the minister, parents, sponsors, and witnesses, the date and place of the baptism and the date and place of birth (c. 877.1). This is the person's primary sacramental record in the church; notations of other sacraments are added to it (cc. 535.2, 895, 1054, 1122, 1123).

[See the *Rite for Christian Initiation of Adults* (1972) and *Rite for Baptism of Children* (1973) from the Congregation of Divine Worship, and the Instruction on the Baptism of Infants from the Congregation for the Doctrine of the Faith, Oct. 20, 1980 (*AAS* 72(1980)1137–1156).]

Confirmation

The sacrament of confirmation continues the baptized on the path of Christian initiation, enriches them with the gift of the Holy Spirit, and bonds them more perfectly to the church. It strengthens them to be witnesses to Christ by word and work (c. 879).

Celebration. Confirmation is conferred by anointing with chrism on the forehead, which is done by the imposition of the hand, and the prescribed words (c. 880). The word chrism comes from the Greek *chriein*, to anoint. It is made of oil and balsam, and is consecrated by the bishop. Confirmation should be celebrated in church and at mass (c. 881).

Minister. The bishop is the ordinary minister of the sacrament of confirmation, but presbyters who have the faculty in virtue of the canons or by special concession of the bishop can also confirm (c. 882). The canons give the faculty of confirming to presbyters:

1. who are equivalent to bishops, e.g., apostolic administrators;
2. who baptize or receive an adult (or young person over seven) into the church;
3. who confirm someone in danger of death (c. 883).

The bishop, although he is to confirm personally, may, if necessary, give the faculty of confirming to specific presbyters and, either he or they, for a serious reason, may associate other presbyters with them to confirm in individual instances (c. 884).

The bishop is obliged to see that confirmation is available to the people at reasonable times, and presbyters with the faculty to confirm are obliged to use it for the people (c. 885). Bishops may confirm both within and outside the diocese, but presbyters with the faculty may not confirm outside the diocese (except in danger of death—cc. 886–887).

Those to be Confirmed. All baptized persons who have not been confirmed are capable of receiving confirmation. Outside the danger of death, those who enjoy the use of reason must be suitably instructed, properly disposed, and able to renew their baptismal promises (c. 889). The faithful are obliged to receive confirmation; parents and pastors are to see that they are properly instructed and receive it at the appropriate time (c. 890).

The sacrament is to be conferred at about the age of discretion (around seven years of age), unless the conference of bishops sets another age, or there is danger of death or some other grave cause (c. 891). (In the United States in 1972, the conference of bishops permitted diocesan bishops to set a later age as normative, if they wished. The problem is that the further confirmation is distanced from baptism and from first communion, the less it is perceived as a sacrament of initiation.)

Sponsors. There should be a sponsor for the one to be confirmed. That person is to see that the one confirmed behaves as a true witness of Christ (c. 892). Preferably, the person's baptismal sponsor should take this role, but someone else could serve instead. The requirements are the same as for baptismal sponsors; see above or c. 874 (c.893).

Records. The pastor is to record the names of those confirmed, the minister, parents and sponsors, with the date and place, in the confirmation register, and he is to notify the pastors of the places of baptism so that the confirmation can be noted on their records of baptism (c. 895, 535.2).

(See the *Rite for Christian Initiation of Adults* (1972) and the *Rite of Confirmation* (1971) from the Congregation for Divine Worship.)

Eucharist

The most holy eucharist is the most august of all the sacraments; all the others are ordered to it. In the eucharist Christ the Lord himself is contained, offered and received. By it the church lives and grows. The eucharistic sacrifice is the summit and source of all Christian worship and life. It signifies and brings about the unity of God's people; it builds up the Body of Christ. It is the memorial of the death and resurrection of the Lord, the perpetuation of the sacrifice of the cross (c. 897). The faithful are to hold the eucharist in highest honor, actively participating in its celebration, receiving it frequently and devoutly, and worshiping it. Pastors are to instruct the faithful carefully about the eucharist (c. 898).

The holy eucharist, unique among the sacraments, exists in three forms or modes: 1) a liturgical celebration (*actio liturgica*), the sacrifice of the mass, 2) food and drink, holy communion, the body and blood of Christ, received under the species of bread and wine, and 3) the reserved species, an object of veneration. The following canons speak of all three.

Celebration. The celebration of the eucharist is the action of Christ and the church. In it Christ offers himself to God the Father, and gives himself as spiritual food to the faithful who join in his offering. He does this by means of the ministry of a priest. And he himself is substantially present under the species of bread and wine. In the eucharistic banquet the People of God are called together, and all, laity and clergy, participate according to their diverse liturgical roles. A presbyter presides, under the authority of the bishop. The celebration is to be carried out in such a way that it is fruitful for all who take part (c. 899).

Minister. The minister of the eucharistic celebration is solely an ordained priest (c. 900). He may apply mass, i.e., say it for someone's intention, for anyone, living or dead (c. 901). Those in charge of churches, e.g., pastors, are responsible for the priests who celebrate mass in them; they may ask for a letter of identification from the priest's bishop or religious superior (c. 903).

Priests are urged to celebrate mass frequently, even daily (c. 904); however, they are not to celebrate more than once each day, except when liturgical norms allow it or their bishop permits them to binate or trinate, i.e., to say two or three masses on the same day (c. 905). A priest is not to celebrate mass without the participation of at least some member of the faithful (c. 906). No one else in the celebration is to say the prayers or perform the actions which are proper to the priest (c. 907).

Priests are allowed to concelebrate, i.e., more than one celebrate mass together, unless the welfare of the faithful dictates otherwise (c. 902), but they are not to concelebrate with priests or ministers of churches which are not in full communion with the Catholic Church (c. 908).

Ordained ministers, i.e., bishops, presbyters, deacons, are the ordinary ministers of holy communion, but laypersons may be deputed to distribute communion as well, at or outside of mass (cc. 910, 230.3).

Viaticum is holy communion for those in danger of death. The term is Latin, from *via te cum*, "with you on the way," and it meant provisions for a journey. Here it means spiritual nourishment for the journey to the next life. The church takes special care that it is provided, and so makes it a responsibility of pastors, parochial vicars and chaplains to bring the eucharist to the sick. Other priests and ministers of holy communion also share this sacred duty (cc. 911, 921–922, 530, 566).

Participation. Any baptized person who is not prohibited by canon law can and must be admitted to holy communion (c. 912). This fundamental right to eucharistic communion is based on a person's ecclesial communion; taking communion demonstrates most vividly one's being in the communion of the church (cc. 205, 213, 843).

Children are to have adequate knowledge and careful preparation in order to be admitted to the eucharist. They should be able to receive the Body of the Lord with faith and devotion (c. 913). The parents of children who have reached the age of reason, as well as their pastors, should see that the children are prepared and admitted to communion as early as possible. The children should be given the opportunity to go to sacramental confession beforehand (c. 914).

The faithful are strongly encouraged to receive holy communion during the celebration of the eucharist (c. 918); they may receive twice in the same day, but the second time must be while participating in a eucharistic celebration (c. 917). All the faithful who have made their first communion are obliged to receive communion at least once a year, preferably at Easter time (c. 920). The faithful may participate in the eucharist and receive communion in any Catholic rite (c. 923).

Those who are to receive the eucharist are to abstain from food and drink, except for water or medicine, for one hour before holy communion. Those who are advanced in age or suffer from an infirmity may receive even though they have taken something during the preceding hour (c. 919).

Those in danger of death are to be nourished by holy communion in the form of Viaticum. It should not be delayed, and should be given while the person is fully conscious. Viaticum may be given repeatedly, but on separate days (cc. 921–922).

A person who is conscious of grave sin is not to celebrate mass or receive the Body of the Lord without first going to sacramental confession. If there is a grave need to celebrate or receive and no opportunity to confess, the person is to make an act of perfect contrition and include the intention of confessing as soon as possible (c. 916). Anyone who has been formally excommunicated or interdicted is not to be admitted to communion, nor is a person who obstinately persists in manifest grave sin (c.915).

Rites and Ceremonies. The eucharist is celebrated with bread and wine; the bread is to be of wheat, unleavened, and recently made, the wine of grapes, and unspoiled (c. 924, 926). Holy communion is given under the form of bread alone or under both species; in case of necessity it can be given under the form of wine alone (c. 925). The eucharist may be celebrated in Latin or in the language of the people (c. 928). Priests and deacons are to wear the vestments prescribed in the liturgical books (c. 929).

Time and Place. The celebration and distribution of the eucharist may take place on any day at any hour, except those times excluded by liturgical norms (c. 931). Celebration is to be at an altar and in a sacred place, unless necessity demands otherwise (c. 932). If there is a good reason, the bishop can permit mass to be celebrated in a non-Catholic church (c. 933).

Reservation and Veneration. The most holy eucharist must be reserved in cathedrals, parish churches and the oratories attached to religious houses (cc. 934, 608). The churches are to be open to the faithful for at least some time each day so that they can pray before the Blessed Sacrament (c. 937).

Someone must care for the reserved eucharist, and a priest should celebrate mass in the church or oratory of reservation at least twice a month (c. 934). Consecrated hosts are to be reserved in a special vessel, in sufficient quantity for the needs of the faithful; they are to be frequently renewed, and the old hosts consumed (c. 939). The eucharist is reserved in a tabernacle, which is to be firmly fixed and locked, and located in a prominent, well-decorated and prayerful place in the church (c. 938). A special lamp, indicative of the presence of Christ, is to burn at all times before the tabernacle (c. 940).

(The word tabernacle comes from the Latin *tabernaculum*, a tent, but this usage is derived from Moses' use of a tent as the dwelling of God in the midst of his people. Exodus 25-40.)

The eucharist is not to be kept on one's person nor carried on a journey, unless there is an urgent pastoral need to do so (c. 935).

There may be exposition of the Blessed Sacrament and benediction in those churches and oratories where the eucharist is reserved (cc. 941-943).

Offerings. A priest who celebrates mass may take an offering to apply the mass according to a definite intention (c. 945). Formerly the canons referred to these free-will offerings on the occasion of eucharistic celebrations as mass stipends. They are now called offerings in order to stress their voluntary nature, and to remove any hint of a purchase, a *quid pro quo*. The faithful who make an offering so that a mass may be applied for their intention contribute to the good of the church and its ministers (c. 946).

Separate and distinct masses are to be applied for the intentions for which individual offerings were accepted (c. 948), and a priest may retain the offering for only one mass each day, even if he celebrates more than one (c. 951). A priest may not accept more mass offerings than he can satisfy in a year's time (c. 953). He is to record the offerings he has accepted and satisfied (c. 955.4).

Mass offerings may be transmitted elsewhere so that they can be more promptly satisfied (cc. 954, 955.1). Those mass obligations not fulfilled within a year are to be given to the bishop or major religious superior (c. 956). Any appearance of commerce or traffic in mass offerings is to be strictly avoided (c.947).

The bishops of the province are to set the amount of mass offerings, and priests may not ask for a larger amount (c. 952). Bishops and religious superiors have the duty to see that mass obligations are fulfilled (c. 957), and they are to examine the mass offering books of their churches every year to that end (c. 958).

(Cf. the *General Instruction of the Roman Missal* (1975), *Rite of Holy Communion and Worship of the Eucharistic Mystery Outside Mass* (1973), *Directory on Children's Masses* (1973), all from the Congregation of Divine Worship, and *Pastoral Care of the Sick: Rites of Anointing and Viaticum*, Collegeville: Liturgical Press, 1983.)

Penance

In the sacrament of penance, the faithful confess their sins to the church's minister, express their sorrow for them and their intention to reform. They obtain from God forgiveness for their sins through the absolution of the minister, and they are reconciled with the church (c. 959). The whole church, as a priestly people, acts in this work of reconciliation. The church's preaching calls sinners to repentance and conversion, its prayer supports and strengthens them, and its ministry expresses the mercy of God, who alone can forgive sins.

Celebration. There are three distinct and well-developed forms of the sacrament of penance in the church's *Rite of Penance*, but the canons are focused on one, the reconciliation of individual penitents ("private confession"), with just three canons on the third form, general absolution. Consult the *Rite*.

Individual and integral confession and absolution is the ordinary way the faithful who are aware of serious sin are reconciled with God and with the church. The physical or moral impossibility of confessing in this way excuses one from doing so, and permits the use of other means of reconciliation (c. 960). Confessions are to be heard in churches or oratories, and confessionals or reconciliation chapels are to be made readily available for this purpose (c. 964). (The United States bishops consider it desirable that rooms for reconciliation be provided which offer the penitent the option of anonymous confession or face-to-face encounter with the priest.)

General absolution, without prior individual confession, can be given to a number of penitents at once only in imminent danger of death or in serious necessity, i.e., when there are insufficient confessors to hear the individuals within a suitable time, so that the penitents would be deprived of sacramental grace or holy communion for a long time. The diocesan bishop is to decide when these conditions are present (c. 961). The faithful who wish general absolution must be suitably disposed and intend to confess their serious sins individually as soon as they have the opportunity; they are to be instructed about this and the need for each one to make an act of contrition, before general absolution is granted (cc. 962–963).

Minister. Only a priest is the minister of the sacrament of penance (c. 965). However, for a priest to absolve someone validly he must have, in addition to the power received through ordination, the faculty to exercise that power over the penitent. He receives this faculty from the canons or from a concession by a church authority (c. 966).

The Council of Trent in 1551 described the priest's absolution as a judicial act (*actus judicialis*). The council linked that notion to the gospel references to binding or loosing, forgiving sins or retaining them (Mt 18,18; Jn 20,23). The concept of a judicial act is not central to the understanding of this sacrament of reconciliation, but it does help to explain the canonical structure of the sacrament. Just as a judge must have jurisdiction over those who come before him, must hear the evidence in the case, and then give a judgment and impose a sentence, so the priest is required to have a quasi-jurisdictional faculty, to listen to the confession, evaluate the penitent's disposition, grant absolution and impose a penance. Both the judge and the confessor have a designated place in which they normally render judgment. Canon 978 reminds the priest that he acts as a judge, a minister of divine justice, in hearing confessions. This concept of penance as a judicial act should not be overemphasized, because it tends to obscure the community's role in sacramental reconciliation, but it does help to understand the present discipline of penance.

The canons state that bishops and pastors have the faculty to hear confessions in virtue of their office (c. 968.1). Bishops (and other local ordinaries) grant the faculty to presbyters, both secular and religious (c. 969.1); it should be given in writing (c. 973). This is usually done when a presbyter is given his first assignment in a diocese.

Those who have the faculty of hearing confessions habitually from either source, in virtue of office or by concession from the ordinary of their place of incardination or domicile (canonical residence), can exercise that faculty everywhere in the world, i.e., it is not limited to the territory of the parish or diocese (c. 967.2). A bishop can revoke a presbyter's faculty to hear confessions, but he must have a serious reason for doing so (c. 974). The faculty is also lost by loss of office, excardination or change of domicile (c. 975).

There is a supplementary source for the faculty to hear confessions in certain exceptional circumstances. The church itself supplies the faculty to a presbyter in situations of common error or positive and probable doubt (c. 144). This can occur when members of the faithful assume that a presbyter is empowered to hear confessions, or when he himself is not sure whether he has the faculty or not, but has positive reasons for thinking that he does.

Superiors of clerical religious communities have the faculty to hear the confessions of members of their community and of those who live in their religious houses, and they can grant that faculty to any presbyter (cc. 968.2, 969.2, 967.3, 974.4).

When someone is in danger of death, any presbyter can validly and licitly absolve that person, whether the presbyter has the faculty to hear confessions or not (c. 976).

Those who have pastoral offices are obliged to hear the confessions of the faithful when they reasonably request, and to give them the opportunity for confession at times regularly scheduled for their convenience. Any confessor is obliged to hear a person's confession if that person is in urgent need, and, in danger of death, every priest is so obligated (c. 986).

The confessor functions as a healer, a minister of God's mercy, and one bent on the salvation of souls (c. 978). He is to be prudent and discreet in questioning penitents, and must never ask the identity of someone's partner in sin (c. 979). If the confessor has no doubt about the disposition of a penitent who asks for absolution, he is to grant absolution, not deny or delay it (c. 980).

The confessor assigns a suitable and salutary penance, which should be related to the penitent's own situation as well as to the sins confessed (c. 981).

A very special level of confidentiality surrounds sacramental confession, because in it the penitent reveals secrets of conscience to the confessor who is acting as God's minister. This sacramental seal is inviolable; the confessor must not betray the penitent, by word or in any other way, for any reason (c. 983, 1388). Nothing which the penitent reveals in order to receive absolution can be revealed, i.e., sins, circumstances, penance; the secrecy is total. Furthermore, even when there is no danger of revealing the identity of the penitent, the confessor is forbidden to use knowledge acquired from confession when it might harm the penitent. Those in positions of authority may not allow their governance to be influenced by their confessional knowledge of someone's sins (c. 984). Those in formative roles, such as novice directors or seminary rectors, are not to hear their students' confessions, unless students, on their own initiative, should ask them to (c. 985, 240).

A priest who, in the context of confession, solicits a penitent, male or female, for a sexual sin, is to be severely punished (c. 1387), and his absolution of his partner in a sexual sin is not valid, except in danger of death (c. 977).

Penitent. Penitents are not passive recipients of the sacrament of penance. They actively celebrate the sacrament with the confessor; their acts are part of the sacrament. The faithful are to dispose themselves for conversion of heart, a turn toward God, by a repudiation of their sins and a purpose of amendment (c. 987). After the confession of sins and acceptance of penance, the penitent prays for God's pardon, and expresses contrition and a resolution to begin a new life.

The faithful are obliged to confess, in kind and number, all of the serious sins they committed after baptism (c. 988). After reaching the age of discretion, the faithful are obliged to confess their serious sins at least once a year (c. 989). Even when personal repentance and God's pardon have already taken place, there remains the obligation to submit grave offenses to the power and ministry of the church ("the power of the keys," Mt 16,19) in the sacrament of reconciliation. The faithful are not bound to confess to a designated confessor; they are completely free to choose their confessor (c. 991).

(Consult the *Rite of Penance* (1973) from the Congregation of Divine Worship.)

Anointing of the Sick

In the sacrament of anointing the church commends to the suffering and glorified Lord the faithful who are seriously ill, so that he might alleviate their suffering and save them. The sacrament is conferred by anointing with oil accompanied by the words of the ritual (c. 998).

The sacrament of anointing of the sick was formerly known as "extreme unction" or "last anointing," and it was perceived as reserved for persons at the point of death. The Second Vatican Council restored the sacrament to its earlier purpose, namely prayer, support, and healing for those who are seriously ill. It is based on the passage in the Letter of James, 5, 14–15. In ministering to the sick sacramentally, the proper sequence to be followed is: confession, anointing, and Viaticum.

Celebration. Pastors and those who are close to sick persons, i.e., relatives, friends, care-givers, are to see to it that the sick are provided this sacrament at an appropriate time (c. 1001). The anointings are to be performed carefully, observing the words and order in the liturgical books (c. 1000). At least some small community of the faithful should be assembled to participate in celebrating the sacrament. Communal celebrations of the sacrament of anointing may be held for many sick persons at the same time (c. 1002). The bishop is to bless the oil used for anointing the sick, or a presbyter may do so in the very celebration of the sacrament (c. 999).

Minister. Every priest, and only a priest, validly administers the anointing of the sick. Those priests who have a pastoral office are charged with the duty and right of anointing those entrusted to their care. Other priests may also administer the sacrament. Priests are allowed to carry the blessed oil with them, so that they can anoint the sick in cases of necessity (c. 1003, 530.3).

Those to be Anointed. Anointing of the sick is to be administered to those of the faithful who, after attaining the use of reason, begin to be in danger due to sickness or old age. The appropriate time to celebrate the sacrament is at the beginning of serious illness. The sickness may be physical or psychological. The sacrament may be repeated whenever the person again becomes seriously ill after some recovery, or whenever his or her condition becomes more grave (c. 1004).

If there is doubt about whether the person has reached the use of reason, or is seriously ill, or has died, the sacrament is to be administered (c. 1005). (Sacraments are never given to those who are certainly dead.) It is to be conferred on persons who requested it, at least implicitly, when they were in control of their faculties (c. 1006), but not on those who obstinately persist in manifest grave sin (c. 1007).

(See the *Rite of Anointing* (1972) from the Congregation for Divine Worship or *Pastoral Care of the Sick: Rites of Anointing and Viaticum.* Liturgical Press, 1983.)

Orders

Some among the Christian faithful are made sacred ministers by means of the sacrament of orders. They are consecrated and deputed to nourish the people of God by performing the functions of teaching, sanctifying and governing, in the person of Christ (c. 1008). The three orders are episcopacy, presbyterate and diaconate; they are conferred by the imposition of hands of the ordaining bishop and the consecratory prayers prescribed in the liturgical books (c. 1009).

The term orders comes from the Latin *ordo*, meaning an order, rank, class, or band, like a company of soldiers. It is a collective noun, the name of a group. Ordination means being incorporated into a group or order, i.e., into the college of bishops or the presbyterium, as well as being commissioned for public ministry in the church.

Celebration. A large congregation should be present for ordinations; the people and those in orders are to be invited (c. 1011.2). Ordinations are to be celebrated within mass, preferably on a Sunday or holy day (c. 1010). They are to be held in the cathedral as a rule, but may be held in another church or oratory, for pastoral reasons (c. 1011.1).

Minister. The minister of ordination is a consecrated bishop (c.1012).

At the ordination or consecration (the terms are interchangeable) of a bishop, the principal celebrant is to have at least two other bishops with him as co-consecrators; it is most fitting that all the bishops present should consecrate the bishop-elect (c. 1014). This is one of the ancient signs of the communion of the churches. The ordaining bishop must have a mandate from the pope in order to consecrate another bishop (c. 1013, 1382).

In regard to ordinations to the diaconate or presbyterate, the diocesan bishop should ordain the candidates for the diocese. For deacons, the proper bishop is the one of the diocese where he has a domicile or in whose diocese he intends to serve; for diocesan presbyters, the proper bishop is the one of the diocese into which he was incardinated as a deacon (c. 1015, 1016). Major superiors of clerical religious communities issue dimissorial letters so that the deacon and presbyter candidates for their communities can be ordained (c. 1019). The diocesan bishop does the same when he himself cannot ordain the candidates for his diocese (c. 1016, 1018).

Dimissorial letters ask or depute a bishop to ordain candidates other than those of his diocese. The term comes from the Latin *dimittere*, to send forth, send away, release. Those who issue the dimissorial letters vouch for the suitability of the candidates for ordination (c. 1052). Hence, the letters cannot be sent until all the testimonials and documents required by the canons have been obtained, i.e., certification of previous sacraments and ministries, of studies completed, and of personal and spiritual qualifications (cc. 1020, 1050–1051). The dimissorial letters may be sent to any bishop of the same rite who is in communion with the Holy See (c. 1021).

Candidates. Only baptized males receive ordination validly (c. 1024). They must also have been confirmed (c. 1033), and they must be judged useful for the ministry of the church (c. 1025).

Disqualifications or impediments for orders are of two kinds: permanent (called irregularities) and temporary (called impediments—c. 1040).

The following are irregular for orders:

1. those who are insane or suffer a serious psychic defect;
2. apostates, schismatics and heretics;
3. those who have attempted marriage when already bound by marriage, orders or vows, or whose partners were in vows;

4. those who have committed murder or abortion or positively cooperated in either;
5. those who have mutilated themselves or others, or attempted suicide;
6. those who performed an act of orders while lacking the order or while prohibited from exercising the order (c. 1041).

The following are simply impeded from orders:

1. those who are married (except for the permanent diaconate);
2. those who hold offices forbidden to clerics (cc. 285–286);
3. those who are new in the Catholic faith (c. 1042).

Some of the foregoing conditions which prohibit the reception of orders also prohibit the exercise of orders already received (c. 1044). Irregularities and impediments to orders can be dispensed, some by bishops, some by the Holy See (c. 1047–1048). The faithful, if they know someone to have an impediment, are obliged to reveal it to the bishop or pastor before that person is ordained (c. 1043).

The qualifications and requirements for the orders of presbyterate or diaconate are the following:

1. admission to candidacy (c. 1034) and reception of the ministries of lector (reader) and acolyte (from the Greek *akolouthein*, to accompany or attend upon; c. 1035);
2. freedom from coercion (c. 1026), full instruction about the order and its obligations (c. 1028), a declaration of intent to devote oneself permanently to ministry and request for ordination (c. 1036);
3. preparation and probation (cc. 1027, 1025), six years study of philosophy and theology plus a diaconate internship (for the presbyterate; cc. 1032, 250);
4. integral faith, correct motivation, requisite knowledge, good reputation, sound morals, proven virtue, suitable physical and psychological qualities (c. 1029);
5. public assumption of the obligation of celibacy (except for married deacons; c. 1037); permanent vows, for those in religious life (c. 1019);
6. for the presbyterate, at least twenty-five years of age and six months as a deacon; for the transitional diaconate, twenty-three years of age and six months in the ministries of lector and acolyte; for the married permanent diaconate, thirty-five years of age and wife's consent; 1031);
7. a retreat of at least five days before ordination (c. 1039).

The bishop or major religious superior of the candidate judges his fulfillment of these qualifications and requirements (cc. 1025, 1029).

Records. The ordaining bishop gives a certificate of ordination to each of those ordained. A careful record of all ordinations is kept in the diocese in which the ordination took place and in the diocese or religious community to which the ordained persons belong (c. 1053). Notice of the ordination is also sent to the parish where the person was baptized, so that it can be entered in the baptismal register (cc. 1054, 535).

(See the *Roman Pontifical* for the *Ordination of Deacons, Priests and Bishops* (1968) and the *Rite of Institution of Readers and Acolytes* (1972). Also see Pope Paul VI's *General Norms for Restoring the Permanent Diaconate in the Latin Church* (1967) and *Norms for the Order of the Diaconate* (1972), Washington: USCC.)

Marriage

[Prefatory note: Canonically, marriage is a preoccupation for the Roman Catholic Church. The Code devotes one hundred and eleven canons to marriage, and many more to the procedures which govern marriage courts. Every Catholic diocese has a marriage court, and these courts, in the United States, process over 70,000 petitions regarding marital status each year. Church personnel in the hundreds and funds in the millions support this activity.

Why is marriage such a canonical preoccupation? Marriage is a sacrament, but the church's concern extends to non-sacramental marriages as well as sacramental ones. Marriage is a vitally important personal relationship and social institution, and both Jesus and Paul taught very explicitly about marriage in the New Testament. Still, most other Christian churches, even those with firm commitments to the sacredness of marriage, are not nearly as concerned about the discipline of marriage as the Catholic Church is.

The reason for the church's unusual preoccupation with marriage discipline lies in the unique historical involvement of the church with marriage. In the Middle Ages the church acquired juridical competence over the marriage of Christians in addition to its pastoral care for them. It made the rules regarding who could marry, and it adjudicated the disputes over who actually was married. Eventually it used a judicial process to evaluate these marriages.

The church has not been willing to relinquish this juridical role in relationship to marriage, since it is related to the church's witness to the sacredness of Christian marriage, and a change in its procedures might send a false signal about a diminished regard for the permanence of marriage.]

A man and a woman establish a partnership of the whole of their lives by means of a matrimonial covenant. The covenant is naturally ordered to the good of the spouses and to the procreation and education of children. Christ the Lord raised the marriage covenant between baptized persons to the dignity of a sacrament, and for this reason, a marriage contract cannot exist between baptized persons without it also being a sacrament (c. 1055). The essential properties of marriage are unity and indissolubility, which in Christian marriage have a special firmness because it is a sacrament (c. 1056).

Marriage is made by the consent of the two parties. Consent must be canonically expressed between two persons who are capable of giving it. The parties themselves must give their consent; no human power can replace or supply it. Matrimonial consent is defined as the act of the will by which a man and a woman, in an irrevocable covenant, give and receive each other in order to make a marriage (c. 1057). The couple, by their free, mutual consent, make a marriage covenant, and on that covenant they build a life partnership (*consortium totius vitae*).

The basic human right to enter into marriage is acknowledged in the canons: all persons not prohibited by law can contract marriage (c. 1058). The marriages of Catholics (even when only one partner is Catholic) are ruled by canon law as well as by God's law. Civil authority has competence over the civil effects of marriage, e.g., registration, change of names, inheritance, etc. (c. 1059). Marriages are presumed valid until the contrary is proven (c. 1060). Valid marriages are called "ratified only" until the partners have had sexual intercourse, thereafter they are called "ratified and consummated," and cannot be dissolved by any human power or for any reason, save death (cc. 1061, 1141).

Pastoral Care and Marriage Preparations. Pastors are to see that their church communities support and assist married couples: with instruction about the meaning of marriage and parenthood, with personal preparation for entering into marriage, with a fruitful liturgical celebration of their weddings, and with ongoing help as they live their married lives (c. 1063). Bishops are to organize this support and assistance in the diocese (c. 1064).

In preparation for their marriage, couples are urged to be confirmed, if they have not been, and to receive the sacraments of penance and holy eucharist (c. 1065).

Before a marriage is celebrated, it must be established that nothing stands in the way of its valid and licit celebration (c. 1066, 1113–1114).

This is the pastor's responsibility, but the faithful are obliged to reveal to him or the bishop any impediments to the marriage of which they are aware (cc. 1066, 1069–1070). Pastors are to try to prevent those who are too young from marrying, and they must refer certain problematic marriages to the bishop (cc. 1072, 1071).

Diriment Impediments. A diriment impediment renders a person incapable of contracting marriage validly (c. 1073). Impediments are canonical obstacles to marriage. They are circumstances or conditions of a person or of the relationship between persons which prevent them from validly marrying. (The adjective diriment, from the Latin *dirimere*, to interrupt, hinder, break up, means nullifying.)

The Code lists twelve diriment impediments to marriage:

1. **Age.** A man under sixteen or a woman under fourteen years of age (c. 1083).
2. **Impotence.** The inability to have sexual intercourse, on the part of the man or the woman; a permanent condition, existing before the marriage, either absolute or relative, i.e., impotent with anyone, or only with this partner (c. 1084).
3. **Prior Bond.** One who is still bound by an existing valid marriage. If the prior marriage was null or was dissolved, this must be canonically established before another marriage can be entered (c. 1085).
4. **Disparity of Cult.** One partner is a baptized Catholic, or has been received into the church, and not formally left it, and the other person is not baptized (c. 1086).
5. **Orders.** Those who have been ordained deacons, presbyters or bishops (c. 1087).
6. **Vow of Chastity.** Those who are bound by the permanent vow of chastity taken in a religious community (c. 1088).
7. **Abduction.** A man who abducts or detains a woman for the purpose of marriage cannot validly marry her, at least not until she has been freed and willingly agrees to marry him (c. 1089).
8. **Coniugicide.** One who causes the death of one's own spouse or the spouse of an intended marriage partner, or conspires with that person to kill the spouse of one of them (c. 1090).
9. **Consanguinity.** Blood relatives. In the line of direct descendants (i.e., grandmother, father, daughter, grandson, etc.) marriage is invalid, and it is also invalid in the collateral line (i.e., brother, sister, cousins, aunts, uncles, etc.) up to and including the fourth degree (i.e., first cousins). (cc. 1091, 108)

10. **Affinity.** Relatives by marriage. All degrees of the direct line, ancestors or descendants (cc. 1092, 109). For example, a man cannot marry his former wife's mother or daughter, nor a woman her former husband's father or son.
11. **Public Propriety.** Those who have lived together in an invalid marriage or in public concubinage may not in the future marry one another's blood relatives in the first degree of the direct line (c. 1093). (Same example as for affinity.)
12. **Adoption.** Legal relationship resulting from adoption; all degrees of the direct line, and the second degree of the collateral line, e.g., an adopting parent cannot marry the adopted child, nor may the adopted child marry a brother or sister in the family (c. 1094).

Some of the marriage impediments can be dispensed. That is, church authority can relax the law or set the impediment aside in a particular case for a good reason (cf. cc. 85–93). For example, disparity of cult is frequently dispensed. The impediments which can be dispensed are purely ecclesiastical rules, i.e., of human origin and changeable, for example, holy orders, age, or public propriety. But some impediments are considered to be of divine law, that is, either from God's revelation or in the very nature of things, for example, impotence, the bond of a prior marriage, and the closest degrees of consanguinity. These cannot be dispensed.

The diocesan bishop (or other local ordinary) is the authority who usually grants dispensations from matrimonial impediments (c. 1078), and his authority to do so is expanded in danger of death or when a marriage is imminent (cc. 1079–1080). In those special circumstances, pastors, confessors, and the minister delegated to assist at the wedding can also dispense from most impediments. Dispensations from holy orders, the public vow of chastity, and coniugicide are normally reserved to the Holy See (cc. 1078).

The bishop can also delay the marriage of those who are under his jurisdiction, but he must have a serious reason for doing so (c. 1077).

Consent. Consent makes marriage. Matrimonial consent is the act of the will by which a man and a woman mutually give and accept each other in order to establish marriage (c. 1057). The couple must be present together (in person or by proxy) for this exchange of consent (c. 1104), and the internal consent of their minds is presumed to accord with the words they speak (c. 1101.1). Even if they think that their marriage is null, they are still able to give consent (c. 1100), and their matrimonial consent is presumed to continue, even if the marriage is actually null for some reason (c. 1107).

Ordinary people are quite capable of giving consent to marriage. However, over the years the church has declared many marriages invalid because of inadequate consent. The canons enumerate eight possible defects of matrimonial consent:

1. **Incapacity.** Those who lack sufficient use of reason, who lack due discretion of judgment about the rights and duties of marriage, or who are unable to assume the obligations of marriage for psychological reasons, are incapable of contracting marriage (c. 1095).
2. **Ignorance.** Those who do not understand that marriage is a permanent partnership between a man and a woman which is ordered toward the procreation of offspring by means of sexual cooperation are unable to give valid consent (c. 1196).
3. **Error about Person.** Mistaken identity about one's partner renders marriage invalid, but a mistake about some quality of the partner does not, unless that quality was directly and principally intended by the other partner (c. 1097).
4. **Fraud.** One who is deliberately and fraudulently deceived about an important marital quality of the partner enters marriage invalidly (c. 1098).
5. **Error about Marriage.** One who is mistaken about the unity, indissolubility, or sacramental dignity of marriage contracts invalidly, if that person's will was determined by the error (c. 1099).
6. **Simulation.** If, contrary to their spoken words, one or both partners positively exclude marriage itself or some essential element or property of marriage, they contract invalidly (c. 1101.2).
7. **Condition.** Marriage based on a condition concerning the past or present is valid or invalid depending on the actual fulfillment of the condition; marriage based on a future condition is invalid (c. 1102).
8. **Force or Fear.** If someone is compelled to marry by force or grave fear, which is inflicted from without, the marriage is invalid, if marrying is the only way to be free from the fear (c. 1103).

Form. Catholics are required to be married within the church, rather than in a civil ceremony or in some other religious setting. This means that the members of the church must observe a certain canonical form when they celebrate their marriage, or else the church does not recognize the marriage, it considers the marriage to be invalid.

Canonical form must be observed whenever at least one of the marriage partners is a baptized Catholic, or was received into the church, and has not formally left it (c. 1117). The form consists in the marriage taking place with the assistance of an authorized minister of the church and in the presence of two witnesses. The minister assists by asking the couple for the expression of their consent and receiving it in the name of the church. The minister is either the bishop (local ordinary) or the pastor, or a priest or deacon delegated by either of them (c. 1108).

The bishop and pastor, in virtue of their office, validly assist at marriages within their territory, whether those marrying are their subjects or not, as long as at least one of those marrying is a Catholic of the Latin rite (c. 1109). The bishop and pastor can delegate to priests or deacons the faculty to assist at marriages within their territory, either for a specific marriage or for all marriages (c. 1111). Where priests and deacons are lacking, the bishop can delegate suitable laypersons to assist at marriages (c. 1112).

There is also an extraordinary canonical form for marriage. If it is not possible, without grave inconvenience, to have access to a person who is competent to assist at a marriage, then the partners may marry before the witnesses alone. However, this is permitted only when the lack of access is foreseen to continue for a month or when one of the partners is in danger of death (c. 1116).

In a mixed marriage, i.e., between a Catholic and another baptized Christian who is not Catholic, the bishop of the Catholic partner can dispense from the canonical form, if there are serious difficulties with its observance (c. 1127.2). This provision affords the possibility for the marriage to take place in a non-Catholic church.

Celebration. Marriages are to be celebrated in the parish of either of the partners; they may be celebrated elsewhere with the permission of the pastor or bishop (c. 1115). As a rule, marriages are celebrated in the parish church (c. 1118). The pastor assists at marriages, or he permits a delegate to do so (cc. 530, 1114). In the celebration of marriages, the approved liturgical rites and legitimate customs are to be observed (c. 1119). The celebration should show that the spouses share in the mystery of Christ's unifying and fruitful love for his people (c. 1063.3).

For a serious and urgent reason the bishop (local ordinary) can permit a marriage to be celebrated secretly (c. 1130). This means that canonical form is observed, but the marriage takes place in private, and those who witness it are held to secrecy. This procedure is rare, and is only justified by the serious harm which might befall the parties, e.g., political persecution, deportation, continued concubinage, etc.

Records. The pastor of the parish in which the marriage was celebrated makes a record of it in the marriage register, noting the names of the spouses, the person who assisted, and the witnesses, along with the place and date. Records are also to be made when the extraordinary form is used, or when the bishop dispensed from the observance of form (c. 1121). The pastor sends notice of the marriage to the parishes where the partners were baptized, so that it can be entered on their baptismal record (cc. 1122, 535.2).

Mixed Marriages. Marriages between Catholics and baptized non-Catholics are forbidden unless the bishop gives permission for them. Mixed marriages are those between two baptized persons, one of whom was baptized in the Catholic Church or received into it after baptism and has not formally left it, and the other is a member of a church not in full communion with the Catholic Church (c. 1124).

The bishop (local ordinary) can give permission for a mixed marriage only if he has a just and reasonable cause to do so, and if three conditions are fulfilled. He must have the same reasons and assurances in order to grant a dispensation from the impediment of disparity of cult, that is, to permit a marriage between a Catholic and a non-baptized person (cc. 1086, 1129). The three conditions are:

1. the Catholic party declares that he or she is prepared to remove the dangers of falling away from the faith, and makes a sincere promise to do all in his or her power to have all the children baptized and brought up in the Catholic Church;
2. the other party is to be informed early on of the promises which the Catholic has to make, so he or she is aware of the obligations of the Catholic party;
3. both parties are to be instructed about the essential purposes and properties of marriage, so that neither party excludes them (c. 1125).

The requirements of canonical form are to be observed in mixed marriages (as well as those involving a dispensation from the impediment of disparity of cult), unless the bishop dispenses from them in view of serious difficulties which might stand in the way of their observance. There is to be one celebration of the marriage, one exchange of consent, not two (c. 1127). Ecumenical celebrations are possible, but they are not to involve duplicate rituals.

Pastors are to see that Catholics in mixed marriages are given the spiritual support they need to live up to their responsibilities, and that the couples and their families are strengthened in unity (c. 1128).

Effects. The canons mention several effects of marriage. From every valid marriage there arises a permanent and exclusive bond between the spouses. When Christians marry, the sacrament they confer on one another consecrates and strengthens them for the dignity and duties of married life (c. 1134). Each of the spouses has equal rights and obligations regarding those things which pertain to the partnership of conjugal life (c. 1135). Parents have the primary right and serious duty to do all in their power to see to the physical, social, cultural, moral and religious upbringing of their children (c. 1136).

Children conceived or born of a valid marriage, or one which at least one partner thought to be valid, are legitimate (c. 1139). Illegitimate children are legitimated by the subsequent marriage of their parents (c. 1139). Illegitimacy has no canonical effects.

Convalidation. Convalidation means to make a marriage canonically valid which was actually invalid from the outset, although it may have had the appearance of validity. The process may seem to be pure legalism, but it can be pastorally helpful in reconciling persons to the church.

Marriages can be invalid for three reasons: 1) the presence of a diriment impediment, 2) a defect of consent, or 3) lack of canonical form.

1. To convalidate a marriage which is invalid due to a diriment impediment, the impediment must cease or be dispensed, and at least the party who is aware of the impediment must renew consent (c. 1156). The renewal of consent must be a new act of the will concerning a marriage which the person who is renewing consent knows or thinks was null from the beginning (c. 1157).
2. A marriage which is invalid due to a defect of consent is convalidated when the party who had not consented now gives consent, provided the consent given by the other party still exists (c. 1159).
3. A marriage which is invalid due to a defect of form must be contracted anew according to canonical form in order to become valid (c. 1160).

There is still another, more rare, kind of convalidation. It is called a radical sanation (*sanatio in radice*, a healing at the root) and, by a legal fiction, it has retroactive consequences. It is accomplished by church authority, and does not require the renewal of consent.

The radical sanation of a marriage is its convalidation without the renewal of consent, granted by a bishop or the pope, and including a dispensation from an impediment, if one existed, and from the canonical form, if it was not observed, and the retroactivity into the past of canonical effects. The convalidation of the marriage occurs at the moment it is granted, but it is retroactive to the time the marriage was celebrated (cc. 1161, 1165). The spouses' consent to the marriage must continue; it must appear that they are going to persevere in conjugal life (cc. 1162, 1161). However, the sanation can be granted without one or both of the partners knowing about it, if there are serious reasons to do so (c. 1164).

Separation. Spouses have both the right and duty to maintain conjugal cohabitation (c. 1151). However, there are certain serious causes which can justify separation. Chief among them is adultery (c. 1152). Physical, psychological or spiritual endangerment to the other spouse or to their children is another, and rendering common life excessively harsh is a third (c. 1153). In the event of a separation, suitable provision is to be made for the support and education of the children (c. 1154). In all cases, when the reason for the separation ceases to exist, conjugal living should be restored (c. 1153.2).

In the foregoing instances of the separation of married spouses, the matrimonial bond endures. However, there are three special circumstances in which the bond may be dissolved, thus enabling the parties to remarry:

1. A marriage which was never consummated by sexual intercourse. A non-consummated marriage between baptized persons or between a baptized party and a non-baptized party can be dissolved by the pope, for a just cause and at the request of one or both of the parties (c. 1142, 1697–1706).

2. The Pauline Privilege: a marriage between two non-baptized persons. A marriage entered by two non-baptized persons is dissolved by means of the pauline privilege in favor of the faith of a party who received baptism. The marriage is dissolved by the very fact that a new marriage is contracted by the party who has been baptized, provided the non-baptized party departs (cc. 1143–1147). The procedure is supervised by the bishop (local ordinary), and is based on the words of Paul in 1 Corinthians 7, 12–15.

3. The Privilege of the Faith: a marriage between a baptized person and a non-baptized person. The pope can dissolve such marriages in favor of the faith when one of the parties to the original marriage either becomes a Catholic or wishes to marry a Catholic.

Annulment. Some marriages fail. Separations often harden into divorces. The differences between the spouses become irreconcilable, and there is no hope of a return to conjugal living. Then, either one of the parties to the marriage may seek from the church a clarification of their marital status. Even a non-Catholic party might make this request, if he or she is thinking about remarriage to a Catholic. They ask whether their failed marriage was canonically valid at its outset. They do so by petitioning, in the church's court, for an annulment of the marriage. They ask the judges to declare their marriage invalid according to canon law. They request a declaration of nullity, usually in order for them to remarry.

The process normally begins at the parish, with an interview with the pastor or a member of the pastoral team. The petitioner tells the story of the marriage and its failure. Either the petitioner or the pastoral person puts the story in writing, and forwards it to the diocesan marriage tribunal. (Tribunal comes from Latin; it was the raised platform for magistrates, and came to mean a court or forum of justice.) The judges and other tribunal personnel follow the careful procedures of the Code (cf. cc. 1400–1650, 1671–1691), depending on the basis or "grounds" alleged for the nullity, in discerning whether the marriage was canonically valid or not.

The judges examine the petitioner's story for evidence of the general categories mentioned above, namely, the three possible causes of the invalidity of a marriage: 1) the presence of a diriment impediment, 2) a defect of consent, or 3) lack of canonical form. If they detect a basis for a formal petition, they seek further evidence in the form of documents and personal testimony, and try to reach a decision based on moral certitude. If they discover sufficient proof that the marriage was invalid from the beginning, they declare its nullity. (Some decisions are subject to a confirmatory review by the next level of tribunal.) The canonical annulment usually means that both parties are then free to remarry.

(See the *Rite of Marriage* (1969) from the Congregation for Divine Worship; the 1981 apostolic exhortation *On The Family* of Pope John Paul II; and L. Wrenn, *Annulments*, 4th ed. rev., Washington: Canon Law Society of America, 1983.)

Other Acts of Divine Worship

Sacramentals. Sacramentals are sacred signs, something like the sacraments, which signify spiritual effects obtained through the prayer of the church (c. 1166). Examples of sacramentals are: holy oils, altars, holy water, stations of the cross, blessed rosaries, etc. Ordained clerics are the ministers of sacramentals, but laypersons may administer some of them (c. 1168). Consecrations, dedications, e.g., of churches, and some blessings are reserved to the bishop or a specially deputed presbyter (c. 1169).

(Consult the *Blessings* section of the *Roman Ritual* (1984) from the Congregation of Divine Worship.)

Liturgy of the Hours. In carrying out the priestly function of Christ, the church celebrates the liturgy of the hours. In it God's people hear his words to them, and recall the mystery of His salvation. The church praises God in song and prayer, and importunes him for the salvation of the entire world (c. 1173).

Since the liturgy of the hours is the action of the whole church, laypersons are earnestly invited to share in it, while clerics and religious are obliged to pray it (c. 1174, 276, 663). (The liturgy of the hours was formerly called the divine office or the breviary. Consult the *Liturgy of the Hours* (1971) from the Congregation for Divine Worship.)

Funerals. In its funeral rites the church asks spiritual aid for the departed, honors their bodies, and brings the solace of hope to the living. The Christian faithful are entitled to funeral rites (c. 1176). No Catholic is to be deprived of the church's funeral rites except the following, if they died unrepentant: 1) notorious apostates, heretics and schismatics (c. 751); 2) those who chose cremation for reasons opposed to the faith; 3) manifest public sinners whose funerals would give public scandal to the faithful (c. 1184). The church recommends the practice of burying the bodies of the dead, but does not prohibit cremation (c. 1176).

The usual place for funeral rites is in the deceased's own parish church, but that person or those entrusted to arrange for the person's funeral may choose another church (c.1177). If the parish has a cemetery, the person is to be interred there, but everyone is free to choose the cemetery of burial (c. 1180).

The bishops of the province are to set limits on funeral offerings; the poor must not be deprived of the funeral rites which are due them on account of the offering (c. 1181). After the burial or cremation, it is recorded in the parish death register (c. 1182).

(Cf. the *Rite of Funerals* (1989) from the Congregation of Divine Worship, and *Christian Burial Guidelines* (1975) *Canon Law Digest* 9:688–702.)

Veneration of the Saints. The church recommends the veneration of the Blessed Mother and the cult of other saints. (c. 1186). Their images may be displayed in churches, but in moderation and good taste (c. 1188).

Vows. A vow is a promise made to God. It is an act of worship, and it obliges by reason of the virtue of religion. A vow must be deliberate and free, and it must be about something which is possible and good for the person making the vow (c. 1191). Examples: to make a pilgrimage, to remain a virgin, to abstain from alcohol or drugs, to devote oneself to the poor, etc. A private vow ceases when the time for its fulfillment has passed, or when there is a major change in the matter, or condition, or purpose of the vow; and the vow can be dispensed or commuted (i.e., changed to something else) by church authorities, namely, the pope, bishops, pastors, clerical religious superiors (cc. 1194–1197). (For the public vows taken in religious communities, see cc. 607, 654ff.)

Oaths. An oath is the invocation of God's name in witness to the truth of what is asserted or promised (c. 1199). It also obliges by reason of the virtue of religion (c. 1200). Examples: to give true evidence, to faithfully fulfill an office, to complete a task, etc. The obligation of a promissory oath (i.e., an oath to do something in the future) ceases if the beneficiary remits it, and it can cease in the same ways and by action of the same authorities as vows (see above; cc. 1202–1203).

Sacred Places and Times

Places. Sacred places are those which have been designated for divine worship or burial by a liturgical dedication or blessing (c. 1205). Hence, they include churches, oratories and cemeteries. The diocesan bishop dedicates sacred places and blesses churches, but he can depute a presbyter to do these things in his stead (c. 1206–1207).

Only those activities or events which serve the exercise or promotion of worship and religion are permitted in sacred places; anything not in keeping with the holiness of the place is forbidden. However, the bishop (ordinary) can permit them to be used for other purposes on occasion, as long as the uses do not conflict with the sanctity of the place (c. 1210).

Sacred places are violated by the occurrence of seriously harmful actions, e.g., murder, rape, assault, etc., which scandalize the faithful. When the bishop (local ordinary) judges them to be serious and contrary to the holiness of the place, then a liturgical penitential rite is to be held in the place to repair the harm, before services are resumed (c. 1211).

Churches. Churches are sacred buildings, intended for divine worship, to which the faithful have right of access for purposes of public worship (c. 1214). The permission of the diocesan bishop is required in order to build a church, and he is not to grant that permission unless he judges that it would genuinely serve the needs of the people, and that there will be adequate means to build and maintain it. He must consult the presbyteral council and the pastors of the nearby parishes before making that judgment (c. 1215).

The principles of both liturgy and sacred art are to govern the design and building of churches (c. 1216). They are to be dedicated or blessed as soon as they are completed (c. 1217). Churches are to be maintained with the cleanliness and beauty which befits the house of God; their sacred and valuable furnishings are to be safeguarded (c. 1220).

The faithful are to have free access to churches at the time of sacred celebrations; no entrance fee may be charged (c. 1221).

Churches may be relegated to other, non-sacral uses, as long as the pastoral welfare of the people is not jeopardized, but only after the presbyteral council has been consulted and those with legitimate claim to the church have agreed (c. 1222).

(Cf. the *Dedication of a Church and an Altar* in the *Roman Pontifical* (1977) from the Congregation for Divine Worship.)

Oratories. Oratories are places set aside for the divine worship of a particular community or group of the faithful, like a religious community or those who are connected to a school or hospital. Other members of the faithful may have access to an oratory if the competent superior agrees (c. 1223). The permission of the ordinary (diocesan or religious) is required in order to establish an oratory (cc. 1224, 608).

Shrines. Shrines are churches or other sacred places to which the faithful make pilgrimages (c. 1230). They can be diocesan, national or international, but must receive permission to use those titles (cc. 1231–1232). The faithful are to be provided with especially good preaching, liturgical celebrations and forms of popular piety at shrines (c. 1234).

Altars. Altars are the tables on which the eucharistic sacrifice is celebrated. Every church should have a fixed altar, i.e., one attached to the floor (c. 1235). Customarily, the top part of a fixed altar is made of stone, but other worthy and solid materials may also be used (c. 1236). Altars are to used exclusively for divine worship; fixed altars are to be dedicated, and should contain a relic of a martyr or other saint (cc. 1237, 1239). (See the *Dedication of a Church and an Altar* in the *Roman Pontifical.*)

Cemeteries. The church is to have its own cemeteries for the burial of the faithful departed, or space reserved for that purpose in civil cemeteries; both are to be blessed. But if neither is available, then individual graves are to be blessed as they are used (c. 1240). Parishes and religious communities can have their own cemeteries (c. 1241). (See the *Rite for Blessing Cemeteries* in the *Roman Ritual.*)

Sacred Times. Sacred times are those holy days or days of penance determined by the church. Only the pope can establish or change these days for the universal church (c. 1244). On the other hand, a diocesan bishop, a pastor or a clerical religious superior can dispense, in individual cases, from the obligation to observe holy days or days of penance (c. 1245).

Sunday, the Day of the Lord, is the primary holy day of obligation in the universal church. The other holy days are Christmas, Epiphany, Ascension, Corpus Christi, the Motherhood, Immaculate Conception, and Assumption of Mary, St. Joseph, Saints Peter and Paul, and All Saints. Of these ten, the bishops of the United States removed the obligation from St. Joseph's Day and the feast of Saints Peter and Paul, and transferred the obligation of Corpus Christi and the Epiphany to the nearest Sunday (c. 1246).

On Sundays and holy days the faithful are obliged to participate in mass, and to refrain from that work or business which stands in the way of the worship of God, the joy of the Lord's Day, and the relaxation of mind and body (c. 1247). The obligation of participating in mass may be satisfied by assisting at mass celebrated anywhere, in any Catholic rite, on the holy day or the preceding evening. If participation in the celebration of the eucharist is impossible, the faithful should share in a liturgy of the word, or devote some time to prayer personally, in their family, or in groups of families (c. 1248). (See the *Directory for Sunday Celebrations in the Absence of a Priest*, Congregation for Divine Worship, *Origins* 18:19 (Oct. 20, 1988) 301–307.)

Repentance and conversion are part of every Christian's life. All members of the faithful are bound to do penance. Days of penance have been established so that all may join in common observances of penance, namely, prayer, works of piety and charity, and that self-denial which comes from performing one's duties more faithfully, and from fasting and abstinence (c. 1249). The penitential days are all the Fridays of the year, and the season of Lent (c. 1250).

Abstinence from meat or some other food is to be observed on all Fridays. (The bishops of the United States recommend that Catholics abstain voluntarily from flesh meat on all Fridays, and that they maintain the traditional obligation of abstinence on the Fridays of Lent.) Ash Wednesday and Good Friday are days of fast and abstinence (c. 1251). Everyone over fourteen years of age is obliged to abstain from meat on those days. Only those over eighteen and under fifty-nine are obliged to fast (c. 1252).

Fasting is understood to mean taking just one meal in a day; however, some other nourishment may be taken at other times during the day, if necessary to maintain strength.

(Consult the apostolic constitution on fast and abstinence, *Poenitemini*, *AAS* 58(1966)177ff, English translation published by NCWC, and *Penitential Discipline in the United States* (1966), *Canon Law Digest* 6:679–685.)

THE GOVERNING FUNCTION

Book One of the Code

The first book of the Code, entitled "General Norms," defines the persons, offices, powers, legal instruments and acts which make up the church's canonical system. It is like the list of definitions which precedes a statute in modern civil law: "here is the official meaning of the terms used in the following piece of legislation." These general norms are the building blocks used in the rest of the canonical structure. They are basic elements of the church's ruling or governing function.

Persons

Personhood is a fundamental concept in any juridic system. It begins to define those whom the law recognizes, who are subject to the law and can act under it. It is analogous to citizenship in a state or nation. Citizens are fully subjects of civil laws, but aliens and the unborn are partially recognized as well. Children, the insane and convicts suffer some impairments of rights; they have an attenuated status.

Who are subject to the church's governance? Who have rights and duties in the canonical system? Canon law recognizes two kinds of persons: physical persons, i.e., individual human beings, and juridic persons, i.e., legally established aggregates of persons or things.

Physical Persons. Canonically, persons are those who have been baptized and are in full communion with the church. By baptism one is incorporated into the church of Christ and is constituted a person in it, with the rights and duties proper to Christians, provided that he or she is in ecclesiastical communion (c. 96). (A more complete description of the Christian faithful and what is meant by full communion is given in canons 204–205.) Those who were baptized or received into the Catholic Church are subject to its ecclesiastical laws, unless they are under seven years of age or lack the use of reason (cc. 11, 99). Divine laws and the natural law oblige everyone, those in the church and those outside it.

The canons describe physical persons in relation to their age, geographic location, relationships, and rite. A summary of each follows.

Age. Adults, who have full exercise of their rights, are those over eighteen. Those under eighteen are called minors, and they remain subject to their parents or guardians in the exercise of their canonical rights. Minors under seven are called infants, and cannot act for themselves canonically. Minors over seven are presumed to have the use of reason (cc. 97–98).

Residence. Canonical residence, called domicile, is acquired by actually residing within a parish or diocese for a period of five years or residing there with the intention of remaining permanently. One can also have a quasi-domicile by residing someplace, e.g., at college, for three months or going there with the intention of staying at least three months (c. 102). Members of religious communities acquire domicile in the place of the religious house to which they are attached (c. 103). Domicile is lost by leaving a place with the intention of not returning (c. 106). It is by domicile that one's proper pastor and bishop (ordinary) are determined (c. 107), because both parishes and dioceses are usually territorial.

Relationships. Relationships are by blood, i.e., consanguinity, or by marriage, i.e., affinity, the relationship between one spouse and the blood relatives of the other. They are calculated in lines and degrees: 1) in the direct line, there are as many degrees as there are generations or persons, not counting the common ancestors, e.g., mother and son are first degree, grandmother and grandson are second, etc.; 2) in the collateral line, there are as many degrees as there are persons in both lines together, not counting the common ancestors, e.g., brother and sister are second degree, aunt and nephew are third, first cousins are fourth, etc. (cc. 108–109). Children who are legally adopted are considered to be the children of their adopting parents (c. 110).

Rite. There are several different ritual churches within the Roman Catholic communion, distinguished chiefly by their diverse liturgical traditions. The Latin rite is one. Others include the Byzantine, Maronite, Melkite, Armenian and Chaldean. Persons normally belong to the rite in which they were baptized. A child of parents who are both Latin rite Catholics is ascribed to the Latin rite by baptism. If one parent is not of the Latin rite, but they both agree that the child should be baptized in the Latin rite, then the child is a member of that rite. But if the parents do not agree, then the child is ascribed to the rite of the father. One who is baptized after the age of fourteen, may choose his or her rite. Transfers from one ritual church to another are possible under certain conditions, e.g., on the occasion of marriage (cc. 111–112).

Juridic Persons. Juridic persons are also subjects of obligations and rights in canon law. Juridic persons are aggregates of persons or things which are ordered toward a purpose in keeping with the church's mission, and which transcend the purpose of the individuals who belong to them. They are established by law or by the action of church authority (cc. 113–114). Some examples of juridic persons: the church itself, the Holy See, dioceses, religious communities, parishes, associations, foundations. Juridic persons are sometimes called moral persons, and they are analogous to corporations in civil law.

Some juridic persons are designated as public; they have a more official status than private juridic persons. A public juridic person is one established by church authority to carry out in the name of the church a function for the public good of the church (c. 116). It must have its statutes approved in advance (c. 117).

Juridic persons are represented by physical persons, i.e., someone who is authorized to act in its name, e.g., the bishop for a diocese, the pastor for a parish (cc. 118, 393, 532).

Collegial juridic persons are those in which the members determine its actions by their votes, e.g., the college of bishops, a monastic community (c. 115). Collegial actions, i.e., elections or other decisions, are accomplished by majority vote (c. 119).

An ancient canonical protection for the rights of individuals lies imbedded in this provision, namely, the rule that "what touches all, as individuals, should be approved by all" (*quod omnes uti singulos tangit, ab omnibus approbari debet,* c. 119.3).

Juridic Acts. Juridic acts are those human actions which the law recognizes as having juridic effects, i.e., effects related to rights and obligations. They can be the actions of individual human persons or of juridic persons represented by agents or groups, but in either case, they must be persons whom the law recognizes. Some examples of canonical juridic acts: marriage, ordination, conferral of office, sale of church property, establishment of a parish, judgment of a church court, admission to a religious community.

The Code states some general principles about juridic acts. In order that a juridic act be valid:

1. the person must be capable of placing it;
2. it must include all of its essential elements;
3. the formalities and requirements imposed by law for validity must be observed.

In the example of marriage, validity requires: 1) a person who is free to marry, 2) freely consenting to marriage, 3) according to the canonical form. A juridic act correctly placed with regard to its external elements is presumed to be valid (c. 124).

The canons recognize four factors which can radically affect a person's juridic act: 1) force, 2) fear or fraud, 3) ignorance or error, 4) the counsel or consent of others:

1. An act placed under irresistible extrinsic force or physical coercion is considered not to have been placed (c. 125.1).

2. An act placed because of unjustly inflicted grave fear or because of fraud is valid but rescindable (c. 125.2).

3. An act placed because of ignorance or error may be invalid or rescindable depending on the matter involved, but if the ignorance or error concerned a substantial element or a *sine qua non* condition, then the act is null (c. 126).

4. When the law requires that in order to place certain acts a superior must obtain the consent of or consult a group of persons, e.g., the finance council or the provincial council, the act is invalid if the consent of a majority of those present is not obtained, or if all present are not consulted. When the law requires the consent or consultation of certain individuals, e.g., the diocesan bishop for the establishment of a religious house, interested parties in the alienation of property (cc. 609, 1292), the act is invalid if the superior does not obtain the consent or seek the counsel (c. 127).

[A **Note on Canonical Consultation:** The canons often require some form of consultation before a person in authority, e.g., a bishop or religious superior, acts. Consultation is a safeguard against capricious or ill-considered actions, but in the ecclesial setting it is much more than that. Consultation is a way of acknowledging the presence of God's Spirit in the members of the community. Understanding, insight and wisdom are gifts which are not limited to appointed or elected office-holders; the faithful have them too, sometimes in abundance. All of the members of the church share, sacramentally and canonically, in the mission and ministry of Christ's church. Those who serve on councils, boards and advisory groups have a right to be heard.

For these reasons, canonical consultation is anything but perfunctory or *pro forma*. It is an authentic and serious process, rooted in the very nature of the church.

Consultation implies:

1. bringing together the members of the group to be consulted, not merely contacting them by mail or telephone;
2. fully informing them of the facts of the situation and its background;
3. encouraging a full and free discussion, an honest exchange of views about the decision to be taken;
4. each member expressing his or her own judgment sincerely and candidly;
5. the superior usually and normally following the consensus expressed by the group;
6. in the rare instance when the superior feels compelled to act otherwise, giving the group his or her reasons;
7. observing the confidentiality of the process, when this is called for (cc. 127, 166).

Canonical consultation should not be limited to the occasions demanded by the canons, e.g., the bishop must consult the presbyteral council before starting or suppressing a parish (c. 515.2). Leaders should consult the appropriate group in all important matters. Consultation should be the prevailing pattern for responsible action in the church, the course normally followed in taking decisions or forming policies.]

Offices

Governance in the church is exercised, in large part, by officeholders, i.e., by those in official positions. Ecclesiastical office is broadly defined as any function (*munus*) established in a stable manner by divine or church law which is to be exercised for a spiritual purpose. The obligations and rights attached to individual offices are determined by the canons or the authority which established them (c. 145). Examples of ecclesiastical offices: diocesan bishop, vicar general, religious superior, pastor, administrator, chaplain.

Qualifications. Formerly, ecclesiastical offices required a participation in the powers of orders or jurisdiction, and could only be held by clerics. That is no longer the case, and laypersons are now eligible for many offices (c. 228).

In order to hold office a person must be in ecclesial communion and endowed with the qualities canonically required for the position (c. 149). An office which carries with it the full care of souls, e.g., the office of pastor, requires the order of priesthood; it cannot be validly conferred on one who is not ordained to that order (c. 150).

Provision. The process of conferring and acquiring an ecclesiastical office is called the canonical provision of office. It takes place in one of four ways:

1. Free conferral. A diocesan bishop, for example, provides for offices in the diocese, e.g., appoints priests as pastors of parishes, by freely conferring them on the persons he judges best suited to exercise them (cc. 147, 157). Most offices in the church are filled by free conferral.

2. Presentation followed by installation. If someone has the right to present a candidate, a church authority must still confirm or install the candidate. For example, when a bishop has entrusted a parish to a religious community, the superior of the community might have the right to present a candidate for pastor, and then the bishop names him pastor (cc. 147, 158–163, 682).

3. Election or postulation followed by confirmation or admission. In religious communities the major superiors are usually elected, and their election sometimes requires the confirmation of their highest authority or of the Holy See. Postulation means that the electors request a higher authority to dispense from an impediment which stands in the way of their electing the person they feel is best suited, e.g., the person is too young, or has already served the maximum number of terms. At least two-thirds of the group must vote to postulate. The favorable response of the authority is called the admission of the postulation (cc. 147, 180–183).

4. Election and acceptance. The election of the pope is the clearest example. His election by the college of cardinals requires no confirmation, only his acceptance (cc. 147, 176–178).

Loss of Office. Ecclesiastical offices may be lost in seven ways:

1. Expiration of the stated term of office. Pastors are often appointed for six-year terms; religious provincials for three or four years (c. 184).

2. Arrival at the canonical age limit. Bishops and pastors are requested to submit their resignations at age seventy-five; cardinals over eighty cannot serve as papal electors (cc. 184, 401, 538).

3. A vicarious episcopal office when the see becomes vacant. Vicars general and episcopal lose their authority when the diocesan bishop dies or departs, i.e., resigns or is transferred or removed (cc. 481, 416). (But judicial vicars do not lose office when the see is vacant, and parochial vicars assume added responsibilities when their parishes become vacant. Cc. 1420, 541.)

4. Resignation. Any person of sound mind can resign an ecclesiastical office for a just cause. With the notable exception of the papal office, most resignations require acceptance before they are effective (cc. 184, 187–189, 332).

5. Transfer. A person can move from one office to another, willingly or unwillingly, e.g., when a pastor is transferred to another parish in the diocese (cc. 184, 190–191, 1748–1752).

6. Removal. Persons can be removed from office for cause by higher church authority, e.g., a pastor whose ministry has become a detriment, or by law, when one loses the clerical state, leaves the Catholic faith or communion, or when a cleric attempts marriage (cc. 184, 192–195, 292, 1740–1747).

7. Privation. One can be deprived of office as a penalty for a canonical offense, but only after the penal procedures are observed (cc. 184, 196, 1336, 1341–1353, 1717–1731).

Power of Governance

Governance in the church is an exercise of ruling power, *potestas regiminis*, better translated as the power of governance, also called jurisdiction. *Regimen* comes from the Latin verb *regere*, which does not mean to rule over or dominate, but to guide or direct, as a rider does a horse or a helmsman does a ship. The power of governance is the name given to the authority of leadership in the church. Such authority must always be seen as service, as ministry, in imitation of the Lord's own servant leadership (Mt 20,25–28, Mk 10,42–45, Lk 22,26–27).

Those who have received sacred orders are eligible to receive the power of governance, and lay members of the Christian faithful can cooperate in its exercise (c. 129). There is a deliberate ambiguity in the Code's basic statement about those who can exercise the power of governance. Formerly, it was reserved exclusively to the ordained, but now the canons clearly recognize the reality of lay participation in leadership roles (c. 228).

The power of governance is intended for and normally exercised in the external forum, that is, in the arena of the church's public life, not in the internal forum, the forum of conscience (c. 130).

The power of governance is distinguished into ordinary and delegated. Ordinary power is that attached to an office by the law itself, i.e., a person possesses it in virtue of office; it ceases with the loss of office (c. 143). Delegated power is granted to a person, but not by means of office (c. 131).

The ordinary power of governance is further distinguished into proper, i.e., that exercised in one's own name, like a bishop, or vicarious, i.e., that exercised in the name of another, like an episcopal vicar; the authority of an episcopal vicar comes with his office, but that office is vicarious, that is, a "stand-in" or substitute for the bishop (cc. 131.2, 475–481).

Ordinaries. Some of those who possess the ordinary power of governance are called "ordinaries." Canonically, the title ordinary is quite important. It designates the highest levels of office-holders in the church. (Clearly "ordinary" in this usage does not mean common and undistinguished!) The following have the title of ordinary:

———the pope;
———diocesan bishops, and those equivalent to them, i.e., those entrusted with a particular church like a diocese (c. 368);
———vicars general and episcopal vicars (cc. 475–481);
———major superiors of clerical religious communities of pontifical right (c. 620).

These ordinaries, except the pope and the religious superiors, are also called "local ordinaries," meaning that their authority is related to a diocese or other particular church. The canons often explicitly reserve certain acts of authority to diocesan bishops; but sometimes the canons say simply "the ordinary" or "the local ordinary," meaning that vicars general or episcopal are also included. It is an important distinction to note in each case (c. 134).

The power of governance is distinguished into legislative, executive and judicial (c. 135). This threefold description of governmental authority is familiar because it is commonplace in civil government. However, in the church it means a distinction among three kinds of authority, not a division into three branches of government. At the papal and episcopal levels of church authority, these three kinds of power are joined in one office; the three are united—there is no real separation of powers, except when it comes to those who assist the pope or diocesan bishops, e.g., the vicar general in executive matters, the judicial vicar in judicial matters.

Legislative Power. Legislative power is exercised in keeping with the canons, especially canons 7 through 22, and, below the level of the pope and the college of bishops, it cannot be delegated. A bishop or a general chapter of a religious community, for example, cannot delegate their law-making prerogatives to anyone else. Laws cannot be enacted at lower levels which are contrary to those from higher levels (c. 135).

Judicial Power. The judicial power possessed by judges also cannot be delegated, and is to be exercised in accord with the canons, especially canons 1400–1731 (c. 135). Note that in canon law the decisions of judges do not create precedents, as they do in the common law tradition. Interpretations of the canons contained in judicial decisions do not have the force of law; they oblige only those for whom the decision was given (c. 16.3).

Executive Power. A person, e.g., a bishop, can exercise executive authority over his own people even when he or they are outside his territory, and he can also exercise it over those passing through his territory, i.e., those not residing there (c. 136). Ordinary executive power can be delegated, either for a single act or for all similar cases and, most often, it can be subdelegated (c. 137). Delegated power ceases:
——when the mandate has been fulfilled;
——when the period of time for which it was given has elapsed;
——when the number of cases for which it was given is completed;
——when the purpose for the delegation has ceased;
——by the revocation of the one who granted it, or;
——by the resignation of the delegate, accepted by the one delegating (c. 142).

The church supplies (*ecclesia supplet*) executive power to one who lacks it in two special situations:

1) common error, that is, when the community mistakenly assumes that the person has the authority, e.g., the priest appears on the altar to witness the marriage or sits in the confessional to hear confessions;

2) positive and probable doubt, that is, when the person is not sure whether or not he has the authority to perform the act in question, but has positive and likely reasons to think that he has.

The church, through this canon, also provides the needed authorization for the sacraments of confirmation, penance, and marriage in the two situations above (c. 144). *Ecclesia supplet* (the church supplies) is a clever canonical contrivance to avoid the nullity of administrative or ministerial actions caused by the negligence or mistake of those who act without proper authorization.

Instruments and Acts of Governance

Governance is exercised in the church in many ways. The canons touch on only a few. Some church leaders govern by their example, by encouragement and exhortation, by planning and assessment, by personnel and resource management, or by all of these. The canons present some of the juridical instruments and actions which are available to those with the power of governance.

A. Laws and Their Equivalents

Laws. The Code gives the following general principles about all canonical "laws":

——a law comes into existence when it is promulgated, i.e., published, but it goes into effect only after the church has had time to learn of it (cc. 7–8);

——laws look to the future, not to the past (c. 9);

——laws which invalidate actions or incapacitate persons must expressly say so (c. 10);

——when there is a doubt of law, the law does not bind (c. 14);

——when there is a doubt of fact, the law obliges, but ordinaries can dispense from it (c, 14);

——ignorance or error about a law or penalty or fact can excuse one from observing a law (except one which is incapacitating or invalidating), but it is not presumed, i.e., it must be proven if challenged (c. 15);

——laws enacted later usually supplant earlier ones (c. 20);

——the church "canonizes" some civil laws, e.g., on contracts, on wills (cc. 1290, 1299), and they should be observed as though they were canonical (c. 22).

Universal laws, that is, those enacted for the entire Latin or Western church by the highest authority (pope or ecumenical council), are promulgated by their publication in the *Acta Apostolicae Sedis* (*Acts of the Apostolic See*), a monthly official register published by the Vatican Press, and they normally become effective three months after the date of their publication (c. 8). Universal laws bind those for whom they were enacted everywhere they are (c. 12). Universal laws do not suppress particular laws unless they expressly say so (c. 20).

Particular laws, that is, those enacted for a particular church (e.g., diocese), province or nation, by the legislative authority proper to each, are promulgated in the way the legislator determines, and they normally become effective a month later (c. 8). Particular laws are presumed to be territorial rather than personal, that is, they bind those who have residence in the territory or are actually present in it, but usually do not oblige non-residents passing through the territory or residents while they are absent from the territory (cc. 12–13). Laws enacted by the chapters of religious communities are presumed to be personal rather than territorial, and oblige the members of the community for whom they were given.

[*A Note on Particular Laws and Subsidiarity:* The principles which guided the revision of the Code urged the application of the principle of subsidiarity and a healthy decentralization in the church. Particular legislation was suggested as one way to achieve those goals. No one desires to proliferate rules unnecessarily but, in the interests of pastoral adaptation to local needs, perhaps too little use is made of legislative initiatives. Both bishops and the chapters of clerical religious communities have ample legislative power (cc. 391, 631). A prudent use of this rule-making ability might contribute to a fuller realization of subsidiary function and the healthy autonomy of particular churches.]

Customs. Customs are the practices within the Christian community which eventually obtain obligatory force. They commanded high respect and exercised great influence in the formation of canonical discipline. Now, however, custom is so circumscribed in canon law that it is of negligible rule-making effect. For a custom to become a rule, i.e., have the force of law, it must:
——be approved by the legislator, at least by tacit toleration,
——be reasonable, which means never expressly disapproved by law,
——be observed by a community capable of receiving a law, i.e, one that is stable, definable, and not too small,
——be observed with the intention of introducing a law,
——be observed for thirty continuous years.

If, however, the legislator gives specific approval to such a custom, even though it was outside of or contrary to canon law, then it obtains the force of law (cc. 23–26).

General Decrees. General decrees are like laws, that is they are common prescriptions, obligatory norms of action, given by one having legislative authority, for a community capable of receiving laws, e.g., a diocesan bishop for the diocese (c. 29). (The term decree comes from the Latin verb *decernere*, to decide.) Those with executive authority, e.g., congregations of the Roman curia, cannot issue general decrees unless the legislator (the pope or ecumenical council) expressly gives them that authority in a particular case (c. 30).

B. Subordinate and Subsidiary Norms

General Executory Decrees. General executory decrees determine how laws are to be applied or simply urge their observance. They can be issued by those with executive authority, e.g., Roman congregations, but they stand under the laws and cannot change them. They are sometimes called directories, norms for implementation, or ordinances (*ordinationes*) (Cc. 31–33).

Instructions. Instructions reiterate or clarify laws and specify ways to implement them. They oblige those charged with carrying out the laws. Instructions also are issued by those with executive authority, and cannot alter the laws which they explain (c. 34).

C. Individual Administrative Acts

The Code here describes a series of administrative actions which emanate from those with executive authority and are directed to individuals or particular groups, rather than the community at large. Some may be obligatory, but they are not to be extended to other persons or other cases than those expressed in the acts. They are to be given in writing (cc. 35–37).

Individual Decrees and Precepts. An individual decree is an administrative act issued by an executive authority giving a decision or making a provision, e.g., a letter of appointment, in a particular case, not necessarily in response to a request. An individual precept is a decree which orders a person or persons to do or refrain from doing something, especially in relation to the observance of the law, e.g., a letter of reprimand. (Precept comes from the Latin *praecipere*, to tell beforehand, advise, warn, admonish.) The authority is to investigate the matter and hear the interested parties before issuing such decrees and, if it is a decision, the reasons for it should be included. Such decrees have force only with regard to the matters decided and only for the specific persons involved (cc. 48–52). These individual decrees are normal administrative communications. They can be disciplinary in nature, but they are not penal sanctions.

Rescripts. A rescript is an administrative act granting a privilege, dispensation or another favor, in response to a request (c. 59). An example: the bishop's letter granting a requested dispensation. (Rescript comes from *rescribere*, to write back, to answer.)

Privileges. A privilege is a favor granted to certain persons, either individuals or juridic persons, by special action of a legislator or someone with executive authority deputed by a legislator (c. 76). The reason why privileges are tied to legislative authority is found in the etymology of *privilegium*; it comes from *privi legis*, a private law, an ordinance in favor of an individual. Privileges are permanent (c. 78). An example: the privilege of celebrating the liturgy in a rite other than one's own, i.e., the biritual privilege.

Dispensations. A dispensation is the relaxation of an ecclesiastical law in a particular case. It is granted by those with executive authority or those who have been given the power of dispensing (c. 85). Dispensation is one of the principal ways by which canon law allows pastoral adaptation to the needs of the people. The word comes from *dispendere*, to weigh out, divide, arrange, dispense. A common example: the bishop's dispensation from the matrimonial impediment of disparity of cult.

No one can dispense from divine or natural law, and not even all church laws can be dispensed. Those which define the essential constituents of a juridical institute or act, e.g., the essential properties of marriage or religious life, cannot be dispensed (c. 86). A diocesan bishop can dispense his people from both universal and particular laws, except for procedural and penal laws and those matters especially reserved to the Holy See, e.g., from the obligation of celibacy (cc. 87–88). A pastor, other presbyters and deacons can dispense from certain laws, e.g., marriage impediments, private vows, observance of holy days or penitential days, in special circumstances (cc. 89, 1079–80, 1196, 1245). The person who dispenses from a law must have a just and reasonable cause for doing so, in view of the circumstances of the case and the seriousness of the law (c. 90).

D. Statutes and Rules of Order

Statutes. Statutes are ordinances for juridic persons, i.e., aggregates of persons or things, like universities, associations, hospitals, etc. The statutes spell out the purposes, constitutions, governance and policies of such institutions. They resemble articles of incorporation and bylaws. They bind only the members or those who govern the juridic person (c. 94).

Rules of Order. Rules of order are the norms to be observed in assemblies or in celebrations, e.g., synods, chapters, conventions, etc. They set forth the organizational structure of the gathering, its leadership and procedures. They oblige those who participate (c. 95).

TEMPORAL GOODS OF THE CHURCH

OF THE CHURCH

Book Five of the Code

This part of the Code is all about stewardship and accountability. The temporal goods in question belong to portions of the People of God. The property is cared for by office-holders, e.g., bishops of dioceses, pastors of parishes, superiors of religious houses. They are the stewards of the goods; the properties are entrusted to them, and they are held responsible for their safekeeping, maintenance and disposition.

Temporal goods, in contrast to spiritual goods, are those which have economic value. They include real estate, personal property, money, securities, entitlements, etc. The Catholic Church has the right to acquire, retain, administer and alienate (i.e., transfer) temporal goods in pursuit of its own ends, namely, to conduct divine worship, to provide for the support of its ministers, and to perform works of the apostolate and of charity (c. 1254).

The universal church, the Apostolic See, particular churches (e.g., dioceses), and all the other juridic persons within the church, are capable of acquiring, retaining, administering and alienating temporal goods (c. 1255). Juridic persons in canon law are those aggregates of persons or things which are recognized as subjects of obligations and rights (cc. 113–123). Some examples: parishes, seminaries, religious communities, monasteries. The juridic person which acquired the goods, owns and controls them. This is of fundamental importance: the dominion over temporal goods belongs to the juridic person which acquired them (c. 1256).

Dominium means more than title and possession; it also implies use, benefit, income, management, and the right to convey the property to someone else, but subject to canonical regulation.

[Note: The reason for insisting on the canonical rule that the juridic person owns the property which it acquires, is that in the United States the rule is frequently obscured by the property-holding structures of dioceses. Dioceses in the U.S. hold property, under the laws of the several states, in four different ways: corporation sole, corporation aggregate, charitable trust or fee simple. Only the corporation aggregate (in which each parish is a distinct corporation) comes close to the canonical principle embodied in

165

canon 1256. The others, especially corporation sole, give the impression that the diocese owns and controls the property of all of the juridic persons within it.]

Only those temporal goods which belong to the universal church, the Apostolic See, or another public juridic person within the church are "ecclesiastical goods" and subject to the canons as well as to the statutes of the juridic person which owns them (c. 1257). Public juridic persons are those established by church authority to function in the name of the church; for example, dioceses and parishes (c. 116). Goods which belong to individuals, lay or clerical, or to private juridic persons, are not ecclesiastical goods and therefore not subject to these canons.

Acquisition. The church can acquire temporal goods by any just means (e.g., subsidies, bequests, endowments, purchases, etc.), but ultimately the principal source of its goods is the free-will offerings of its members. The church claims the right to require from the faithful the means to achieve its ends (cc. 1259–1260). The members of the church have the right and obligation to assist the church with its legitimate necessities, and the diocesan bishop must remind them of that duty and urge its fulfillment (cc. 1261, 222).

The customary offertory collection at Sunday mass, which includes parish envelopes, is the ordinary way the faithful support their local church (c. 1262). Collections for special needs (parochial, diocesan, national or universal) are an additional way the the faithful assist specific projects. The bishop can order such special collections to be taken up in all the churches and public oratories of the diocese (c. 1266).

The diocese and its various agencies are supported in large part by a system of parish assessments. The diocesan bishop can levy a moderate tax on all of the public juridic persons of the diocese. The tax is to be proportionate to the income of the juridic person. The bishop can impose the tax only after consulting the finance council and presbyteral council. In addition, the bishop has the authority to levy an extraordinary tax on individuals as well as all juridic persons, but only in the event of a grave necessity (c. 1263).

Private individuals and associations are forbidden to solicit funds without the written permission of their own bishop and the local bishop (ordinary) of the place where they are soliciting. This refers to personal appeals, not to advertising or direct mail requests, and mendicant religious are exempted from the prohibition (c. 1265). (Mendicants, from the Latin *mendicare*, to beg, are those who live from alms, e.g., Franciscans, Dominicans, Carmelites, Augustinians.)

Offerings which are given to the superiors or administrators of juridic persons, e.g., those in charge of parishes, shrines, monasteries, retreat houses, etc., are presumed to be given to the institution and not the individual. And offerings given for a specific purpose may be used only for that purpose (c. 1267).

The Holy See receives a major portion of its financial support from "Peter's Pence," the offerings which the bishops send each year to the pope from their dioceses. These funds, given in proportion to the resources of the diocesan church, enable the Holy See to serve the universal church. This support, which is based on the unity and charity which bond the churches together, is a powerful sign of the communion of the churches (c. 1271). (Another such sign is the reminder that wealthier dioceses are to aid poorer ones. C. 1274.3.) (Cf. *Principles and Guidelines for Fund Raising in the United States*, NCCB, 1977, *Canon Law Digest* 8:415–421.)

Administration. The pope is called the supreme administrator of all ecclesiastical goods, in virtue of his primacy in governance (c. 1273). This enables him to issue guidelines for other administrators of church property, and would justify his intervention in an administrative emergency. Next in the line of administrative supervision is the ordinary, e.g., diocesan bishop or major religious superior. The ordinary is to issue instructions about the administration of church property, e.g., spending limits, bookkeeping procedures, and watch over those juridic persons, e.g., parishes or religious houses, entrusted to him or her (c. 1276, 1279.2).

The one who governs the juridic person to whom the goods belong has the responsibility for their administration, e.g., the pastor of the parish or the superior of the religious house (c. 1279.1). That person is the administrator, but there is to be a finance council or at least two advisors to help him or her with the administration of property (c. 1280, 537).

The diocesan bishop, in administering the goods of the diocese, has a finance council and a financial officer to assist him (cc. 492–494). The bishop must consult the finance council on administrative matters of importance, and in some instances, he must obtain their consent along with that of the college of consultors (cc. 1277, 502).

All administrators of church property are to act as faithful stewards of what is entrusted to them. They are obligated to follow the canons, and they take an oath to be good and faithful administrators. They are to make inventories of the goods under their care, see that they are insured, comply with relevant civil laws, collect revenues, pay interests, invest funds, keep accounts, prepare budgets, make annual reports, safeguard records, and pay employees decent family wages (cc. 1282–1284, 1286–1287). To do something beyond these acts of "ordinary administration," e.g., to make major expenditures, construct a building, establish a school, etc., the administrator must have the written authorization of the bishop or major religious superior. If the authorization is not obtained, the action is invalid (c. 1281).

Contracts. The church accepts the local civil law on contracts and payments. Whatever the civil law of the terrritory determines about contracts is to be observed in canon law with the same effects (c. 1290). This is the most prominent example of the church's "canonization" of an area of civil law (c. 22).

Alienation. Alienation, from the Latin *alienare*, to make something another's, to transfer property, means the transfer or conveyance of temporal goods. The canons require authorization for the transfer of church property, over a certain value, which is part of the "stable patrimony" of a juridic person. Stable patrimony means the land, buildings, and stable or fixed capital, i.e., funds designated and invested for a specific purpose. The same permission is required for any transaction by which the patrimony of the juridic person is jeopardized, that is, might be diminished, e.g., mortgage, lien, pledge as security for a loan, etc. If the permission is not obtained, the transaction is canonically invalid (cc. 1291, 1295).

Each conference of bishops sets minimum and maximum value amounts, in reference to the alienation of property, for the territory. For transactions below the minimum, no higher authorization is needed. For transactions between the minimum and maximum, the bishop's permission is required. This applies to juridic persons subject to the bishop, e.g., parishes, or the diocese itself. Before a bishop can grant the permission, the finance council, the college of consultors, and the interested parties, e.g., donors, must consent. When the value of the transaction exceeds the maximum, or when the goods are of special artistic or historical value, the permission of the Holy See must be sought (c. 1292). (In the United States, in 1987, the maximum value amount was set at $1,000,000.)

In religious communities, authorizations for transactions below the maximum value amount are given by the competent superior with the consent of his or her council. Over the maximum amount, the permission of the Holy See must be sought (c. 638).

In all proposed transactions over the minimum value amount, a good reason for it must be given, and appraisals of the value of the objects must be obtained (c. 1293). The objects should not be sold for less than their estimated value, and the money realized is to be used for the stated purposes (c. 1294).

Wills and Foundations. Those who are able to dispose of their goods, may leave them to the church and its purposes, while such persons are still living or at their death. In regard to bequests to the church at death, the civil law formalities are to be observed, if possible, but the intentions of the deceased should be honored by the heirs, even if those formalities were neglected (c. 1299).

The wishes of donors to the church are to be fulfilled with the greatest care, whether the gifts were accepted during their lives or after their deaths (c. 1300). The ordinary, e.g., bishop or major religious superior, is the canonical executor of all such gifts to the church, and must oversee their fulfillment (c. 1301).

The ordinary is to be informed about the terms of all trusts and other fiduciary arrangements on behalf of the church (c. 1302), and is to give advance approval for all foundations, funds or endowments which involve long-term obligations (cc. 1304–1307).

SANCTIONS IN THE CHURCH

Book Six of the Code

Punishment may seem entirely out of place in a community of grace and charity. However, the church is a community in which every member is acknowledged to be a sinner as well as a saint. In spite of the Lord's leadership and the Spirit's guidance, some members, even ordained ministers, go astray on occasion. Sometimes, when their misdeeds are serious and public and clearly contrary to the faith or discipline of the church, the community must respond with a sanction. Such things happened in the time of Jesus (Mt 18,5–9,15–18), in first-century Corinth (1 Cor 5), and in every subsequent age of the church's history.

Punitive action is sometimes required for the good of the individual offender and for the integrity of the community. Those are the two purposes of penalties in the church: 1) the conversion, repentance and reconciliation of the offending person, and 2) the restoration of order and reparation of scandal, i.e., the repair of harm done to the community and the deterrence of abuse (see c. 1341).

Still, punishment is a last resort. Pastoral exhortation, kind admonition, familial correction, earnest entreaty and even firm rebuke should all precede penalties (c. 1341). And even in its application, leniency and mercy should temper the severity of a canonical penalty.

Offenses. The church claims the right to punish its offending members with penal sanctions (c. 1311). However, not every offense a member commits is punishable. Not every mistake, sinful action, or violation of a canon can be punished by church authority. Only canonical offenses can be punished. A canonical offense has three essential elements: 1) it is an external violation, 2) which is gravely imputable to the person by reason of deliberate intent or culpable negligence, 3) of a law or precept to which a penalty is attached (c. 1321). An external violation means that a canonical offense is an infraction committed in the realm of the church's public life, not something which is solely in the world of intentions or in the forum of conscience (cf. c. 1330). The next two sections treat the other two elements of a canonical offense.

173

Penal Laws and Precepts. Laws are general rules issued for the entire community by those with legislative authority. Precepts (from *praecipere*, to warn or command) are orders given to individuals or specific groups by those with executive authority (c.49). Here, the subject is penal laws or precepts, i.e., those with penalties attached.

The canons of the Code contain most of the church's penal laws: canons 1364–1399. The pope can add to or alter these rules for the universal church, and he can issue penal precepts as well. Penal regulations may be given for particular churches, e.g., dioceses, in keeping with the following guidelines.

Those who have legislative authority, e.g., bishops, can make penal laws, and they can also attach penalties to the laws of higher authorities (c. 1315). However, they should do so sparingly, i.e., only with great restraint and when truly necessary (cc. 1317–1318). Such laws are to be interpreted strictly, i.e., narrowly (c. 18). This reflects the church's longstanding attitude toward penalties: they must be interpreted benignly, in order to protect the rights of alleged offenders. (*Regula iuris* number 49 reads: *in poenis benignior est interpretatio facienda.*)

Those who have executive authority, e.g., bishops, major superiors of clerical religious communities, can issue precepts with penalties attached, but they should do so rarely and only after mature consideration (c. 1319).

Religious can be penalized by bishops (local ordinaries) in those areas in which they are subject to their authority, e.g., pastoral care, liturgy, apostolates (cc. 1320, 678).

Those Subject to Penalties: Imputability. When an external violation of the penal canons occurs, imputability is presumed, unless it is evident that the person was not imputable (c. 1321.3). However, if the person violated the penal law or precept simply because of a lack of due diligence, i.e., unintentionally, he or she is normally not punished (c. 1321.2; 1389.2 contains an exception).

The grave moral imputability required for a punishable offense implies a free and deliberate human act. Some persons are incapable of such acts, e.g., those who lack the use of reason, and therefore are incapable of an offense (c. 1322). Many others have their freedom or awareness diminished, and they are not subject to penalties: those under sixteen years of age, those unaware that the action was a violation, those who acted accidentally, while drunk or mentally disturbed, or under duress, grave fear, necessity, serious inconvenience, or in self-defense or the defense of another (and persons who only thought themselves to be in one these latter situations) (c. 1323).

Some persons may suffer a partial impairment of their freedom or awareness, and for them punishment should be reduced, e.g., those with imperfect use of reason, those under eighteen years of age, those unaware of a penalty, those who acted in the heat of passion, while voluntarily drunk, compelled by fear, under provocation, or otherwise without full imputability (even if the person erroneously thought him or herself to be in a situation of grave fear, necessity, serious inconvenience, or acting in self-defense). It is very important to note that none of these persons incur any automatic (*latae sententiae*; see explanation below) penalties, e.g., that for abortion (c. 1324).

Accomplices, i.e., those who cooperate or collaborate in the commission of an offense, may also be punished, depending on the circumstances (c. 1329).

Application of Penalties. The ordinary, e.g., bishop or major superior of a clerical religious community, is the one who initiates penal procedures, but he is only to do so as a last resort, when all other pastoral means have failed to repair scandal, restore justice, and reform the accused (c. 1341). He must observe canonical procedures; the faithful have that as a basic right (c. 221.3).

The ordinary makes a preliminary investigation into the alleged offense and its imputability (c. 1717). Then he makes a decision about taking punitive action, and chooses whether to proceed judicially or administratively. The canons clearly favor a judicial process, because of the greater safeguards for the rights of the accused (cc. 1342, 1718, 1721, 1723, 1481.2). In either process, the accused must be given the opportunity to be heard in his or her own defense and should be provided with canonical counsel (cc. 1720, 1725, 1723, 1481).

The judge or ordinary (depending on the kind of process chosen) is given considerable discretion in applying the penalties, if it is determined that the accused actually committed the offense (cc. 1343–1349).

Since medicinal penalties (see explanation below) are aimed at the reform of the offender, censures cannot be imposed validly until the accused has been warned to repent and given suitable time in which to do so. If the person is truly sorry for the offense and seriously promises to make amends, then he or she cannot be censured (c. 1347).

The foregoing paragraphs describe the usual and preferred procedures for applying or declaring penalties. They call for the intervention of a person in authority, an investigation, some due process, and a subsequent judgment. Penalties applied in this way are said to be inflicted by a sentence (*ferendae sententiae*). There are a few penalties which can take effect by the very commission of the offense, *ipso facto*. It is possible for offenders to "bring on themselves" these penalties "automatically" by the performance of the prohibited act. These penalties (all censures) are called *latae sententiae*, a sentence already given (c. 1314). Some examples: procuring an abortion, a cleric or religious in permanent vows attempting marriage, a bishop ordaining without proper dismissorial letters, violating the eucharistic species. Actually, *latae sententiae* penalties are very rarely incurred, because of the prevalence of mitigating circumstances (cc. 1323, 1324; see imputability, above).

Penalties bind guilty parties wherever they are, unless the penalty is explicitly limited (c. 1351). Penalized clerics are to be given decent support in order to live (c. 1350).

Penalties are suspended in five situations: 1) while they are under appeal, 2) while the guilty person is in danger of death, 3) when a censured person must care for someone in danger of death, 4) while an automatic (*latae sententiae*) penalty is not known to others and the offender cannot observe it without causing scandal or infamy, or 5) when someone requests a sacrament or other pastoral assistance from a censured person (cc. 1335, 1352–1353).

The statute of limitations, for most offenses, on taking penal action against an alleged offender is three years (c. 1362). The same statute of limitations applies to the enforcement of a penalty after judgment has been given (c. 1363).

Penalties. The church employs four forms of canonical punishment; the first two are less serious and more readily applied (c. 1342.1), the last two categories are penal sanctions, i.e., penalities strictly speaking:

1. *Penal Remedies.* In order to prevent offenses, an ordinary, e.g., bishop or major religious superior, may admonish or rebuke someone who is behaving in a disorderly or scandalous manner, is very close to committing an offense, or is suspected of having already committed one (cc. 1312, 1339).

2. *Penances.* As a substitute for a penal sanction, an ordinary can impose some work of religion or charity on an offender, e.g., a retreat, a fast, alms, abstinence, a specific task or service, etc. (c. 1312, 1340).

3. *Expiatory Penalties.* To expiate means to make satisfaction for or atone for. These penalties are intended to repair the harm done to the community and to deter others from similar offenses. They include such things as deprivation of offices, powers, faculties or rights, or a

prohibition from exercising them, a prohibition from living in a certain territory, or an order to live some specific place, a transfer to another office as a penalty, or dismissal from the clerical state. These penalties can be imposed for a time, for an indefinite period, or permanently (c. 1336).

4. *Medicinal Penalties or Censures.* As the name implies, these penalties are intended to heal or cure the offender. (The word censure means a reprimand.) There are three such penalties: excommunication, interdict, and suspension. Excommunication means partial exclusion from the communion of the faithful. It does not separate a person from the church, but it implies an impaired participation. The excommunicated person is forbidden to celebrate or receive the sacraments or to carry out any offices or ministries (c. 1331). Interdict has the same sacramental restriction, but not that on governing functions (c. 1332). Suspension forbids either some or all acts of the power of orders, of the power of governance, or the exercise of the rights or functions of office; suspension applies only to ordained ministers (cc. 1333–1334). Since the purpose of medicinal penalties is conversion, a censure must be lifted when the offender repents and is willing to repair the harm done or the scandal caused (c. 1358).

Cessation. Expiatory penalties, if imposed for a specified time, lapse upon the expiration of that time. All other penalties cease by remission, that is, the lifting or cancelling of the penalty by a church authority. Penalties and their remission are *per se* matters of the external forum of the church; that is why the remission of a penalty is normally given in writing (c. 1361). By exception, some penalties can be remitted in the internal sacramental forum, i.e., in confession (cc. 1355.2, 1357).

A censure, since it is a medicinal penalty aimed at healing the offender, cannot be remitted unless the person has repented for the offense and is willing to make reparation for the harm or scandal caused by it. If, however, the person has repented, the penalty must be remitted (cc. 1358).

External forum. Some few penalties are reserved to the Holy See for their remission, e.g., the unauthorized consecration of a bishop, the violation of the seal of confession. All other penalties can be remitted by the bishop or religious superior (ordinary) who imposed them, or the bishop (ordinary) of the place where the offender lives, or someone delegated by those ordinaries (cc. 1354–1356).

Internal Forum. Any bishop can remit *latae sententiae* penalties in sacramental confession (c. 1355.2). Any priest can remit any censure when the penitent is in danger of death (c. 976). Any confessor, in sacramental confession, can remit the *latae sententiae* censures of excommunication or interdict, if it would be burdensome for the penitent to remain in a state of serious sin until recourse could be had to the proper authority. (The confessor must have the penitent make such recourse within a month, however, or he can make it on the penitent's behalf.) (c. 1357) [Note: Canons 1355.2 and 1357 do not apply to penalties which have been declared, i.e., *latae sententiae* censures which are formally declared or announced by church authority after they were incurred.]

Penalties for Specific Offenses. The canons list specific offenses to which penalties are attached. Some of the penalties are explicit, e.g., excommunication, but others are generic and discretionary, e.g., a just penalty. These penal canons are divided into the following six categories (with some examples of each kind of offense):

1. Offenses against religion and the unity of the church. This category includes apostates, heretics, schismatics, perjurers, blasphemers, and parents who have their children baptized and educated in another faith (cc. 1365–1369).

2. Offenses against church authorities and the freedom of the church. Here are such offenses as using physical force against the pope, bishops, clerics or religious, teaching doctrines condemned by the church, and stirring up hostilities against church authorities (cc. 1370–1377).

3. Usurpation of ecclesiastical functions and offenses in their exercise. Here are found penalties against those who are not ordained priests but who attempt to say mass or give absolution, usurpers of ecclesiastical office, simoniacs (simony, named after Simon Magus of Acts 8, 9–24, is the exchange of something spiritual for temporal goods), and priests who in confession solicit penitents for sexual sins (cc. 1378–1389).

4. The crime of falsehood. One who falsely accuses a priest of solicitation, injures the good reputation of another, or falsifies a public church document is assigned suitable punishment (cc. 1390–1391).

5. Offenses against particular obligations. This includes clerics who attempt marriage or live in concubinage or practice pedophilia, as well as those who fail to observe their obligation of residence (cc. 1392–1396).

6. Offenses against human life and freedom. Murder, kidnap, mutilation, assault and abortion are assigned penalties here (cc. 1397–1398).

A final canon permits penalties for offenses not listed. Especially serious violations may be punished when there is an urgent need to prevent or repair scandal (c. 1399). This runs counter to the cherished principle that there should be no crime or punishment which is not stated in the law (*nullum crimen nullaque poena sine lege*). It opens up the possibility of arbitrary punitive action, and should be used only with the greatest caution.

PROCESSES

Book Seven of the Code

The last book of the Code contains 352 canons on judicial and administrative processes, i.e., the legal acts and procedures to be observed in solving disputes and questions. Most of them concern the church's judicial (court) system, but some are administrative, i.e., related to uses of executive rather than judicial authority.

These procedural regulations are quite important, e.g., a bishop cannot dispense from them (c. 87); they relate to matters of justice and the protection of rights. However, detailed knowledge of these procedural canons is generally regarded to be above and beyond an introductory knowledge of canon law. For that reason, only a brief summary of the procedural canons is offered here, enough to see the outline of the processes and to recognize the personnel involved in them.

The church's processes for doing justice are very ancient. For example, there were already sophisticated rules for judges in the third century. The church's system depended heavily on Roman law, but it has been modified many times through the centuries.

Avoiding Trials. All the Christian faithful, especially bishops, are to strive earnestly to avoid lawsuits among the People of God, and to settle disputes peacefully and as soon as possible. Equitable solutions, mediation, negotiated setttlements and even arbitration are warmly recommended as alternatives to contentious trials. Judges and administrators should encourage such alternative dispute resolution procedures at the outset of disputes or even during litigation. Dioceses do well to have such "due process" systems available (cc. 1446, 1713, 1733; cf. *On Due Process*, Washington: NCCB, 1970).

Judicial Trials. The general rules for trials (canons 1400 to 1655) apply even to the various special procedures, e.g., matrimonial and penal processes.

The purposes of judicial trials are to pursue or vindicate rights, to declare juridic facts or to impose penalties. But disputes which arise from administrative actions, e.g., the decision of a bishop, can only be taken to an administrative superior or to the Apostolic Signatura (cc. 1400, 1445.2).

The church claims jurisdiction over spiritual matters and violations of church laws (c. 1401). Anyone, whether baptized or not, can bring a case before a church court (c. 1476). The faithful have access to the courts to vindicate and defend their rights (c. 221), and there is a legal action available to defend every right (c. 1491).

The judge or court before whom cases can be brought, i.e., the tribunal which can hear a case, referred to as the competent forum, is carefully regulated. The pope, as supreme judge for the whole Catholic world, reserves certain cases to himself, and any one of the faithful can bring their case to the Holy See at any time (cc. 1442, 1405, 1417). Ordinarily, cases may be brought to the court of the diocese of residence of the parties to the dispute, of the place of contract, the place where the thing in dispute is located, or place where an offense was perpetrated (cc. 1407–1416).

Diocesan courts, in actual practice, are almost exclusively occupied with matrimonial cases, i.e., adjudicating the validity or nullity of marriages. The four competent tribunals for these cases are: that of the place where the marriage was celebrated, where the respondent lives, where the petitioner lives, or where most of the evidence is located (c. 1673; note that the latter two options are available only under certain conditions).

There are, in effect, three levels of church courts: the first is the diocesan tribunal, the second is metropolitan (archdiocese of the province) or regional, the third is the Holy See. At the Holy See, the Roman Rota is the appeal court and the Apostolic Signatura is the supervisory court (cc. 1419, 1438–1439, 1442–1445). Cases are usually reviewed or appealed in the order of the three levels.

The bishop is the judge in the diocese, but he normally exercises this function through a judicial vicar (also called an *officialis*). The vicar heads the diocesan court, and is assisted by diocesan judges. Every marriage case must be heard by a panel of three judges (cc. 1419–1426, 1447–1457). In clerical religious communities, the provincial is the judge (c. 1427).

Within the diocesan court there are:

——petitioners, those who bring cases, who petition the court;

——respondents, those cited or brought in, the other parties;

——a promoter of justice, who provides for the good of the church;

——a defender of the bond, who stands for the bond of marriage;

——procurators, who represent and act on behalf of the parties;

——advocates, who look out for the rights of the parties (cc. 1476–1477, 1430–1436, 1481–1490).

Cases are to be heard in the order they are received (c. 1458). Evidence is collected, arguments made and judgments are given in writing, rather than orally (cc. 1472, 1610). (The Code provides for an oral procedure, but not in marriage nullity cases, cc. 1656–1670, 1690). Cases are to be expedited, and concluded within a year (c. 1453). Parties are asked to contribute to court costs (c. 1649).

A trial has three stages:

1. A person initiates a case by bringing a petition. The judge decides the court's competence, the petitioner's standing, and whether the petition has a basis. The judge cites the respondent, and fixes the legal grounds on which the case is to go forward (cc. 1501–1525, 1677).
2. Evidence is collected, e.g., by interviewing the parties, gathering relevant documents, hearing witnesses, and calling in expert witnesses (cc. 1526–1600, 1678–1680).
3. The entire case, including arguments submitted by advocates and the defender of the bond, is discussed, orally or in writing, and decided by the judges; one of them writes the deciding opinion (cc. 1601–1618).

The judgment can be appealed to the next level, and all affirmative decisions (that is, judgments that the marriage was null) in matrimonial cases require a confirmatory review by the appeal court (cc. 1628–1640, 1681–1684).

[Note: Some marriage nullity cases may be decided through a simple documentary process. That is, marriages which were invalid because of some diriment impediment or due to a lack of canonical form, may be declared null after an examination of the relevant documents, e.g., baptismal certificate, marriage license, etc. (cc. 1686–1688).]

(Cf. L. Wrenn, *Procedures*, Washington: Canon Law Society of America, 1987.)

Administrative Recourse. This is a process of appealing to the one who has taken administrative action or to his or her hierarchical superior. Administrative acts cannot be challenged in church courts (c. 1400.2), so the alternative procedures are set forth here.

Administrative acts include a wide range of decisions, orders, policies and decrees which are issued by those with executive (rather than judicial or legislative) authority. For example, they would include the administrative actions of a bishop, vicar general, chancellor, superintendent of schools, diocesan director of an agency, clerical provincial superior, or pastor. But these procedures cannot be applied to the acts of the pope or an ecumenical council. They have no human superior to whom appeal can be made! (c. 1732)

Administrative recourse here takes three forms: 1) conciliation, 2) request for reconsideration, and 3) recourse to the hierarchical superior. They are not necessarily pursued in sequence.

1) The church tries to avoid contentious conflicts. When one feels aggrieved or harmed by an administrative action of another, some form of conciliation or mediation between the two parties is strongly recommended in order to find an equitable solution. This can be attempted either before or during the request for reconsideration and hierarchical recourse. Offices or agencies for such conciliatory and mediatory functions should be made available (c. 1733). (Cf. *On Due Process* (1970) Washington: NCCB.)

2) A reconsideration of the administrative action should be sought within ten days of notification. That is, the aggrieved person should petition the one who took the action for its revocation or modification within that time. The request includes a petition for suspension of the action. When the one who took the action is subject to the bishop, the request for reconsideration may be addressed directly to the bishop (c. 1734).

The one who took the action or the bishop has thirty days in which to respond to the request for reconsideration. If he or she denies the request or modifies the earlier action, time for recourse runs from that notification. If there is no response, the time for recourse runs from the thirtieth day (c. 1735). The effect of the original action is suspended during recourse, or its suspension can be sought from the hierarchical superior (c. 1736).

3) One who claims to have been injured by an administrative action can make recourse for any just reason to the hierarchical superior of the one who took the action. (He or she need not have followed the other two forms above.) This must be done within fifteen days of the notice of the original action or of the response or non-response to the request for reconsideration (c. 1737).

Recourse can be made directly to the superior. For example, if the recourse is against an action of a diocesan bishop, it may be sent to the appropriate congregation in Rome, e.g., the Congregation for the Clergy in case of a removal of a pastor. (The names and addresses of the congregations are listed in the front of *The Official Catholic Directory*.) Or the recourse may be sent to the one who took the original action, who is obliged to forward it immediately to the appropriate superior (c. 1737.1). The one taking recourse has a right to counsel (c. 1738).

The hierarchical superior has full authority to confirm, rescind or modify the orginal action (c. 1739).

Removal of Pastors. Pastors are to have stability in office. Hence, they are named for either an indefinite term or, more commonly, for a relatively long term, e.g., six years, renewable once (c. 522). Sometimes it becomes necessary to remove a pastor who is unwilling to leave his position. The Code provides a special administrative (not judicial) procedure for this purpose. It is not a penal proceeding; it does not presume or imply that a pastor has committed a canonical offense. It further specifies the general provisions for removing a person from any church office (cc. 192–193).

The reasons are given first. A pastor can be removed from a parish when his ministry has become detrimental or ineffective for any reason, even if it was through no grave fault of his own (c. 1740). Some salient examples are offered: disruption of ecclesiastical communion, incompetence or inability to perform his duties because of physical or mental infirmity, loss of good reputation or aversion on the part of the people, grave neglect of parish duties (e.g., cf. cc. 519, 521, 528–530), bad administration of temporal goods which caused grave harm to the church (c. 1741). There could be other reasons, especially in relationship to the needs of a particular parish.

The bishop is to conduct an inquiry to see if, indeed, cause for removal exists. Then he is to discuss the matter with two pastors, selected from among a group of pastors which has been agreed upon in advance by him and the presbyteral council of the diocese. If the bishop remains persuaded that the pastor should be removed, he tries to persuade him to resign within fifteen days. The bishop must give him the reasons for his request (c. 1742).

In the case of a pastor who is a member of a religious community, the bishop communicates with the pastor's religious superior; either can remove him after informing the other (c. 682.2).

The pastor may agree to resign, and he may attempt to attach conditions to his resignation (cc. 1743, 187–189).

If the pastor does not respond within the fifteen days, the bishop is to repeat the invitation to resign, giving him additional time. After the extension of time has expired, or if the pastor simply refuses to resign, the bishop may remove him (c. 1744).

If the pastor opposes the original attempt to remove him and the reasons behind it, the bishop is required to invite the pastor to submit a written refutation, after he has had a chance to see all the evidence which has been gathered. The bishop then must discuss the whole matter again with the two pastors, come to a decision about removal and, if his decision is still the same, issue the order removing the pastor (c. 1745).

The pastor who has been removed must stop exercising the office of pastor, and hand over control of the parish to the one assigned to replace him. He can appeal the decision to the Holy See and, if he does so, the bishop cannot name another pastor of the parish while the appeal is pending, but he can name a parish administrator (c. 1747).

The bishop is to provide for the removed pastor. He is either to give him some other assignment or support for his retirement (c. 1746).

Transfer of Pastors. The transfer of pastors from one parish to another, or from a parish to another form of ministry, is a routine matter. It does not imply any deficiency in the pastor's performance; it is not a punishment. However, sometimes a pastor is very reluctant or unwilling to accept a transfer. The final canons of the Code provide a procedure for such a situation. They further specify the norms of canons 190–191 on transfer of offices.

If a transfer seems to be necessary or useful for the church, the bishop is to propose it to the pastor in writing and try to persuade him to accept it (c. 1748). If the pastor is still unwilling, he is to explain his reasons to the bishop in writing (c. 1749). Then the bishop must consult with two pastors selected from the group of pastors named for this purpose (cf. c. 1742). If the bishop decides to go ahead with the transfer, he repeats his request to the pastor (c. 1750). If the pastor still refuses, the bishop can order the transfer, and the parish becomes vacant, i.e., can be given to another (c. 1751). The pastor must relinquish the office to his successor, but that does not preclude the possibility of his having recourse to the Holy See (c. 1752).

*   *   *

Like the prominent inscription of a noble ideal on the entablature of a building, the Code of Canon Law closes with the maxim, "The salvation of souls is the supreme law of the church" (*salus animarum suprema lex*, c. 1752). This ancient motto, which sounds old-fashioned and otherworldly to the modern ear, is cherished by canonists as a powerful reminder that the church's rules must serve the church's primary religious purposes. It puts canonical rules in proper perspective.

APPLYING THE RULES

"What are we to do?" is the question people bring to a book of rules. They come asking, "What are we supposed to do?" "What's the right thing to do in this situation?"

Understanding the canonical rules and applying them to specific situations is the critical piece. The carryover from theory to practice, the move from abstract rule to human action, is the crucial step. What follows are some things to recall when taking that step. They are aphorisms, from the Code, from the canonical tradition, and from common sense, which are good to bear in mind when applying the canons to real life. The aphorisms are reminders about rules and communities and people.

About the Rules

The salvation of souls is the supreme law. The old canonical maxim, enshrined in the last canon of the Code, is a way of saying what canon law is all about. It is to serve the church, the people on their pilgrimage to God. The canons must always be viewed in that context. They are rules for a *church*, not for any other kind of society. They must always serve the church's religious purposes. Pope Paul VI said:

> Canon Law has its foundations in Christ, the Word Incarnate, and hence, serves as a sign and instrument of salvation, but it does so only because of the works of the Holy Spirit, who imbues it with power and strength. Thus Canon Law must express the life of the Spirit, produce the fruits of the Spirit, and reveal the image of Christ. (*The Pope Speaks* 22(1977)169–170.)

Faith, hope and love come before law. It is not by law that we are saved, but by faith. Order and discipline are only facets of the church's life; they are always subordinate to its primary realities. Saving faith is the first bond which unites the church. Loving concern is our common striving. These supreme values must guide and limit the application of rules.

191

The canons must be viewed in the light of faith, understood in ways consonant with the expressions of faith, and applied so as to foster faith, hope and love.

The Council governs the Code. The Code of Canon Law of 1983 has been called the final document of the Second Vatican Council. Its express purpose was to bring the vision and teachings of the council into practical application. The ties between the council and the Code are many, and the canons must be viewed, understood and applied against the background of the council. It is in the documents of the council that the true and full meaning of the canons will be found.

Find the rule. Look up the canonical text itself. Do not be satisfied with a summary or paraphrase or news report. Whether it is a canon of the Code, a part of a sacramental ritual, a diocesan statute or guideline, a religious constitution or article of the community's rule, or a new instruction from a congregation of the Roman curia: get the text and examine it. Never apply a canonical rule unless you are quite sure of the official text and its meaning. It is a matter of justice, fairness and intelligent ministry.

Learn the meaning of the words. Ecclesiastical laws are to be understood according to the proper meaning of their words considered in their text and context (c. 17). Before applying a rule, one must be sure to understand it correctly. The first thing to do is to find the right meaning of the words which express the rule. What is their technical meaning in canon law? What do they mean here, in this section of the Code? What kind of writing is this canon, e.g., doctrine, exhortation, recommendation, command?

Purpose is the soul of the law. *Ratio legis est anima legis.* A rule is a means to an end. An understanding of the end or purpose for which the rule was made is essential to understanding the rule itself. What pastoral circumstances occasioned this rule? What was its historical and social setting? What abuse did it try to correct; what problem did it try to solve; what value does it inculcate? The legislative history should lead to the reason for the rule, the *finis legis*. The footnotes to the canons and the explanations of commentators are aids in this search.

Interpret strict laws strictly. Laws which establish penalties, restrict the free exercise of rights, or contain an exception to the law must be interpreted strictly (c. 18). It is long-standing canonical tradition that restrictive laws must be narrowly applied. Two of the ancient rules of law

(*Regulae Iuris*, compiled in the year 1298) state that: "adverse laws are to be restricted, favorable ones amplified," and "penalties are to be interpreted benignly." Strict interpretation means that the sense of the words of the canon and the scope of its application are limited as much as reasonably possible.

Rules tend to remain the same. Stability and continuity are highly valued in canon law. Later laws are to be related to earlier ones, and, insofar as possible, harmonized with them (c. 21). The canons of the Code, to the extent that they restate earlier law, are to be understood according to their meaning in the canonical tradition (c. 6.2). Often the best way to understand a canonical norm is to find the meaning of its predecessor, i.e., read the commentaries on the corresponding canon in the 1917 Code, and see what it meant and how it was applied.

Lawmakers also interpret the law. Laws are authoritatively interpreted by the legislator or someone deputed by the legislator. Such official interpretations become part of the law itself. Unlike many other systems of rules, the decisions of the church's courts and administrative agencies do not have the force of law, i.e., do not establish precedents (c. 16). The "Council on the Interpretation of Legal Texts," an agency within the Roman curia, occasionally issues official interpretations of canons. (They are published in *Communicationes*, and can be found in *Canon Law Digest*; those issued since the 1983 Code are gathered in the *Jurist*, vol. 50, 1990.)

About the Community

Communities apply rules differently. The existing conditions of the various communities within the church qualify their use of canon law. Communities range from new to well-established, from a handful of members to millions, from very rustic to very sophisticated people, from extremely poor to quite wealthy, from homogeneous to very diverse, from oppressed to free, from troubled to tranquil. The church's disciplinary rules are understood and applied quite differently in these widely diverse situations.

The community knows best. Custom is the best interpreter of the law (c. 27). This canonical rule means that the practice of the community clarifies and confirms the meaning of the law. The way that a law is actually regarded and followed by the people is the best measure of the law's intent. This rule is based on the conviction that the members of a community understand the real purpose of the law, and that they observe it so as to achieve that end. At a deeper level, the rule reflects the belief that the Holy Spirit dwells within and guides the community of the faithful; the Spirit's direction can be discerned in the actions of the people as well as in the enactments of the legislator.

The community's reception of a rule is decisive. The authority and force of a law depends in part on its reception by the community. By receiving, i.e., obeying, a rule the Christian community affirms its truth, its validity, and its suitability for them. When the community fails to observe a rule, it often means that the rule is impractical or unsuited to that community; the people perceive it as "not right" for them. The result of the non-reception is that the rule is ineffective. This doctrine of reception is a time-honored canonical tradition.

About the Person

Know yourself. Rules are not self-implementing. All rules are applied by persons. Persons differ one from another, and each one is affected by moods, attitudes, prejudices and passions. Personal disposition influences the way that individuals impose or obey rules. For example, most agree that it's not a good idea to make serious decisions hastily or to write letters in anger. Always take stock of your personal situation before applying the canons. Never discount the human factor.

Exercise discretion. Applying canonical rules always involves a certain measure of discretionary judgment. (Discretion comes from the Latin *discernere*, to distinguish or discern; it means the power of choice.) Pope Paul VI said that the purpose of the entire array of laws is to help the faithful in their spiritual lives, which must be inspired by personal conscience and a sense of responsibility rather than by precepts. A suitable discretionary authority (*congrua potestas discretionis*) belongs to both pastors and faithful. [*The Pope Speaks* 22(1977)178.]

Practice prudence. Being prudent, at least in St. Thomas Aquinas' thinking, does not mean acting hesitantly or warily. Prudence is the virtue which helps persons to rule themselves and others rightly and reasonably. It is the habit of practical reason which directs persons and communities to do what they ought in each particular situation. Prudence is the virtue which enables us to select and put into operation the most suitable means to an end.

Every prudent act involves taking counsel about available options, making a choice among them, and putting the decision into action. Prudence is a good guide when applying canonical rules.

Observe economy. The principle of economy (from the Greek *oikonomia*, management, stewardship) means administration of the church in imitation of God's stewardship of human salvation. It is based on St. Paul's use of economy when referring to God's plan of salvation (Eph 1,9), the divine management of history (Eph 3,9), the stewardship of God's mysteries (1 Cor 4,1), and the direction of the church (1 Tim 1,4). In the canonical tradition of the Eastern churches economy means both the prudent management of the church and accommodation, adaptation or compromise in certain matters. It flows from the contemplation of God's powerful purpose in the church, and it can lead beyond the limits of the church's law. Economy is not so much an exception to the law as an obligation to decide individual issues in the general context of God's plan for the salvation of the world.

Remember epiky. Epiky (or *epikeia*) is a virtue, a part of justice, which enables one to correct the deficiencies of general rules when they are applied to particular situations. It takes account of the inherent inadequacy of all human laws by applying them sensibly and wisely to individual cases. For example, there is a general rule against Catholics marrying non-Christians (c. 1086), but pastoral judgment sometimes counsels a dispensation from the general prohibition. Epiky is morally superior to a merely verbal or rigid application of rules, and therefore a better form of justice.

Do equity. Pope Paul VI said that in canon law equity is to govern the applications of norms to concrete cases. Equity takes the form of mercy and pastoral charity, and seeks, not a rigid application of the law, but the true welfare of the faithful. Canonical equity is the fruit of kindness and charity. It combines two notions: 1) seeing that the ideal of justice is actually realized in a fair result, and 2) justice tempered with mercy, the softening of the rigor of justice under the influence of charity. Canonical equity is mentioned in one of the early canons of the Code, and recalled in its final canon (cc. 19, 1752), as though the lawmaker would keep it always before our eyes.

APPENDIX I:
DOING RESEARCH
IN CANON LAW

Find the Rule

In order to answer a canonical question, the first task is to locate the official text of the authoritative rule:

1. For canons in the *Code of Canon Law* of 1983: Canons are always cited by number; if one has the number, finding the canon is simple. If not, the Code's table of contents is a good outline in which to find the proper section, or there are very good subject matter indexes:
    (a) In the official Latin text (*Codex Iuris Canonici, Fontium Annotatione et Indice Analytico-Alphabetico Auctus*; Libreria Editrice Vaticana, 1989) there is a 122 page index;
    (b) Xaverius Ochoa, *Index Verborum ac Locutionum Codicis Iuris Canonici* (2nd ed.; Libreria Editrice Lateranese, 1984) is an exhaustive 600 page book of indices;
    (c) *The Code of Canon Law: A Text and Commentary*, eds. Coriden, Green, Heintschel (New York: Paulist Press, 1985) contains a 55 page, three-column index;
    (d) The Canon Law Society of Great Britain and Ireland published an index in a separate volume: *Index to the Code of Canon Law* 1984, 98 pages;
    (e) the French, German, Italian and Spanish translations of the Code include indexes as well;
    (f) Luigi Chiappetta, *Dizionario del Nuovo Codice di Diritto Canonico* (Naples: Dehoniane, 1986) is an alphabetical listing of canons by topic.
2. For sacramental or liturgical rules, consult the appropriate ritual or *ordo*, and look for the introduction (*praenotanda*) and the instructions for people and ministers within the text of the rite. *Documents on the Liturgy, 1963–1979*, International Commission for English in the Liturgy (Collegeville: Liturgical Press, 1982), and *The Rites of the Catholic Church* (two vols., New York: Pueblo, 1976 & 1980) are convenient collections.

3. For universal rules outside the Code: consult the official register, *Acta Apostolicae Sedis,* published monthly by the Vatican Press, with a thorough index at the end of each calendar year, or the periodical *Communicationes,* formerly the journal of the Commission for the Revision of the Code, now published by the Council on the Interpretation of Legal Texts; or go to the *Canon Law Digest,* a multi-volume publication of documents which affect the *Codes of Canon Law,* i.e., both the 1917 and 1983 *Codes.* It is now published by the Canon Law Society of America. The *CLD* is organized according to the numbers of the canons; each volume contains a subject-matter index, and a chronological index based on the date of issuance of the documents.

4. For particular regulations, i.e., those given by the bishops' conference for the nation, those issued by the bishop for a diocese, those enacted by the chapter of a religious community, consult the official publication of each source.

Check for Changes

One must be certain that the rule is current (*ius vigens*), i.e., that it is the one presently in effect, or that it has been modified or superseded by subsequent legislation. Changes, additions and interpretations of canonical norms occur with some frequency and, since they are not inserted into the Code, it is not always easy to discover them.

After locating the appropriate canon or other rule, then one must check the *Canon Law Digest* or other publication to see if some change has been made which affects the rule. From time to time someone will compile, on private authority, a volume of post-Code regulations. (None have appeared since the 1983 Code.) Canon law commentaries which are up-to-date include such alterations. The standard canonical journals (see below) usually carry important modifications. *Origins* and *La Documentation Catholique* are also good sources for official documents. The newsletters of the Canon Law Societies of America, Canada, Great Britain and Ireland keep their members informed of such changes. The Canon Law Society of America also distributes annually a booklet of *Roman Replies and Advisory Opinions,* which can assist with this updating task.

Consult a Commentary

The purpose of canonical commentaries is to explain the rules, give the reasons for them, and suggest how they should be applied. They are very helpful when one is trying to understand the norms. It is highly recommended that one consult at least one commentary to gain perspective on a canon, even if one is fairly sure of its basic meaning. Referring to several commentaries often gives insight and reveals additional information.

Presently the major commentary on the 1983 Code in English is *The Code of Canon Law: A Text and Commentary*, eds. Coriden, Green, Heintschel (New York: Paulist Press, 1985). The French, Italian and Spanish translations of the Code also contain valuable commentaries. There is a German commentary in a looseleaf format: *Munsterischer Kommentar zum Codex Iuris Canonici*, ed. K. Ludicke (Munster: Ludgerus, 1986ff).

Since many of the canons of the 1983 Code remain substantially the same as those in the 1917 Code, the commentaries on the earlier Code are still quite useful for understanding the meaning of the canons. Some of the above-mentioned commentaries contain tables which give the corresponding canon numbers in the two Codes. The comments on individual canons will usually mention the number of the corresponding canon in the earlier Code. Once the number of the 1917 canon is in hand, then it is a simple matter to find the commentary which explains it. (Of course, one must be very attentive to any changes made in the 1983 version of the canon.)

Some of the standard English language commentaries on the 1917 Code include: Bouscaren, Ellis, O'Connor, *Canon Law: A Text and Commentary* (Milwaukee: Bruce, 1946, and later editions); Abbo, Hannan, *The Sacred Canons* (St. Louis: Herder, 1952); Woywod, Smith, *A Practical Commentary on the Code of Canon Law* (New York: Wagner, 1925 and subsequent editions); Ramstein, *A Manual of Canon Law* (Hoboken: Terminal, 1947); Augustine, *A Commentary on the New Code of Canon Law* (St. Louis: Herder, 1918 and following, 8 vols).

Some of the standard Latin commentaries on the 1917 Code are: Vermeersch, Creusen, *Epitome Iuris Canonici* (Malines: Dessain, 1931ff); Beste, *Introductio in Codicem* (Naples: D'Auria, 1956); Regatillo, *Institutiones Iuris Canonici* (Santander: Sal Terrae, 1956); Sipos, *Enchiridion Iuris Canonici* (Rome: Herder, 1954); Wernz, Vidal, *Ius Canonicum* (Rome: Gregorian, 1952); Coronata, *Institutiones Iuris Canonici* (Rome: Marietti, 1949); Cappello, *Summa Iuris Canonici* (Rome: Gregorian, 1951).

Go to the Sources

There is no better way to find the original purpose for a canonical regulation than to study its authentic source, i.e., the document which actually gave rise to the rule.

The footnote references to each of the canons of the 1983 Code are the keys to tracing the source documents of those canons. These footnotes, found in the 1989 annotated and indexed volume of the *Codex Iuris Canonici*, reveal three categories of sources:

1. the corresponding canons of the 1917 Code (for the sources of those canons, see below);

2. the documents of the Second Vatican Council, 1962–1965: to find those documents, consult the collections of the constitutions, decrees and declarations of the council, e.g., *The Documents of Vatican II*, ed. W. Abbott (New York: Guild, 1966);

3. other specific, official documents issued after the 1917 Code and before the 1983 Code: The original Latin versions can be found in the *Acta Apostolicae Sedis*, and the translations can usually be found in the *Canon Law Digest* or such documentary services as *Origins* and *La Documentation Catholique*, the publications of the National Conference of Catholic Bishops, or the canonical journals.

The sources for the canons of the 1917 Code are to be found in three distinct collections:

1. The *Corpus Iuris Canonici*, the monumental set of canonical collections which was finally compiled about the year 1500. It is most readily available in the two-volume edition of Richter and Friedberg (Graz: Verlagsanstalt, 1959). The *CIC*, which was the classic canonical source before 1917, consists of six collections of canons. The first two (Gratian's Decree and the Decretals of Gregory IX) are very large, and the last four rather small. Each collection has its own peculiar reference symbols:
   (a) *Concordantia Discordantium Canonum*, or *Decretum Gratiani* (1140) is divided into three parts:
   Part I is signified by the letter "D" for distinction (e.g., the reference "c. 7, D.I" stands for Gratian's Decree, Part I, Distinction I, canon 7);
   Part II is signified by the letter "C" for causes (e.g., the reference "c. 116, C. I, q. 1" stands for Gratian's Decree, Part II, Cause I, question 1, canon 116; but note that question III of Cause XXXIII has the special abbreviation *de poenit.* for its subject, *de poenitentia*);

Part III is signified by the abbreviation *de cons.* which stands for *de consecratione* (e.g., "c. 18, D. I, *de cons.*" stands for Gratian's Decree, Part III, Distinction I, canon 18).

(b) *Decretales Gregorii IX* (1234), is signified by the letter "X" (when it was compiled it was referred to as the *Liber Extra*, the book outside of Gratian's Decree, and was assigned the letter X; e.g., the reference "c. 13, X, I, 2" stands for the Decretals of Gregory IX, Book I, title 2, canon 13).

(c) *Decretales Bonifatii VIII*, the so-called *Liber Sextus* (1298; it was referred to as the sixth book because it came after the five books of the Decretals of Gregory IX), is signified by the symbol "in VI°," (e.g., the reference "c. 5, I, 3, in VI " stands for the Decretals of Boniface VIII, Book I, title 3, chapter 5).

(d) *Constitutiones Clementi V*, or *Clementinae* (1317), is signified by the words "in Clem" (e.g., the reference "c. 2, III, 7, in Clem" stands for the Constitutions of Clement V, Book III, title 7, chapter 2).

(e) *Extravagantes Ioanni XXII* (John XXII was pope from 1316 to 1334, but the collection was compiled about 1500) is signified by its own name (which meant twenty constitutions from John XXII in effect outside the already recognized collections). E.g., the reference "c. un., VII, in Extravag. Ioan. XXII" stands for the Extravagantes of John XXII, title 7, the only chapter.

(f) *Extravagantes Communes* (the commonly occurring decretals issued by popes who ruled from 1261 to 1484 which were outside the foregoing collections; it was also compiled about 1500) is signified by its own abbreviation, e.g. the reference "c. 3, V, 7, in Extravag. com." stands for the Extravagantes Communes, Book V, title 7, chapter 3.

2. The *Codicis Iuris Canonici Fontes*, a nine-volume collection of the sources for the canons of the 1917 Code, compiled after the Code was issued, by those who took part in that codification, Cardinals Gasparri and Seredi. They assembled almost 6500 documents which were cited in the footnotes to the canons of the Code, documents other than the canonical collections which made up the *Corpus Iuris Canonici*. These volumes of the *Fontes*, published during the 1930s, were reprinted by the Vatican Press in 1948. The documents are organized into categories, e.g., from councils, popes, congregations, and are in chronological order within them. The ninth volume is an index to the *Fontes*.

3. The declarations and decrees of the Council of Trent (1545–1563). These are published in various collections. Among the most modern is

Conciliorum Oecumenicorum Decreta, eds. Alberigo, Joannou, Leonardi, Prodi, Centro de Documentazione, Istituto per le Scienze Religiose, Bologna (Freiburg: Herder, 1962). The documents from the Council of Trent are on pages 633 to 775. An English source is *Canons and Decrees of the Council of Trent*, trans. Schroeder (St. Louis: Herder, 1941).

Review the Literature

Authors have commented, theorized and speculated on the canons for centuries. There is a large body of canonical literature, both medieval and modern. To gain perspective on the state of a canon law question, it helps to survey the literature.

Monographs and commentaries by major scholars are at the heart of this canonical literature. However, doctoral dissertations by younger scholars offer valuable background on special topics; some universities publish canon law dissertations in series, like the Canon Law Studies at The Catholic University of America.

Much contemporary research and writing appears in canonical and theological journals. A very helpful English language key to the journals of the last thirty years is *Canon Law Abstracts*, a biannual publication of the Canon Law Society of Great Britain and Ireland, which gives brief abstracts of the canonical articles published in nearly ninety periodicals worldwide.

The leading canonical journals in English are:
The Jurist, Washington
Studia Canonica (English and French), Ottawa
Canon Law Society of America Proceedings, Washington.

Other canonical journals include:
L'Année Canonique, Paris
Apollinaris, Rome
Archiv fur Katholisches Kirchenrecht, Mainz
Ephemerides Iuris Canonici, Rome
Il Diritto Ecclesiastico, Rome
Ius Canonicum, Pamplona
Ius Ecclesiae, Rome
Monitor Ecclesiasticus, Rome
Oesterreichisches Archiv fur Kirchenrecht, Vienna
Periodica, Rome
Revista Española de Derecho Canonico, Salamanca
Revue de Droit Canonique, Strasbourg
Universitas Canonica, Bogota.

APPENDIX II:
CASES AND QUESTIONS

The "case study method" can assist the learning process very effectively in the study of canon law. The following ten cases are provided for that purpose.

The class should be assigned a case in advance of its discussion. The students should be asked to answer the questions at the end of the case by locating the applicable canons, and giving their reasons for their responses. They should search the Code and its commentaries for the relevant canons; they should not be satisfied with the summaries and restatements of the canons found in this book. More important than correct answers to the questions is the exposure to the canons, and the quest for good canonical and pastoral reasoning. The class discussions of the cases can be lively learning experiences.

The cases do not follow the order of the Code or of this book. The questions will lead students to various parts of the Code.

AUGUSTUS HAWKINS AND THE ELIJAH TEMPLE

Father Hawkins, 40 years old, 15 years ordained and a nationally known charismatic preacher, told Archbishop Haney in February that he had decided to leave the priesthood and "found my own church." He said that he wanted to create a faith expression for African American people which would integrate their own history, spirituality and culture with Roman Catholicism.

Hawkins had been the pastor of St. Agnes' Parish on the south side for twelve years. In that time he built the parish from 200 members to 2000 families; the Sunday collection increased from $400 to $8,000.

At the Archbishop's request, Hawkins consulted with Archbishop Jackson, a prominent black bishop, and Father Daniels, a priest-counsellor. Sometime later, Hawkins confided to Jackson that he had decided not to leave the priesthood, that he was going to stay in the church. He said, however, "There needs to be a split in the Catholic Church. I don't want to call it a schism, but there needs to be a movement in the Catholic Church where blacks finally say, 'We've had enough. We've come to the point where we realize that we are a token expression in your church, a token presence.' "

207

In late June Hawkins announced that he was going ahead with the establishment of his own congregation, "Elijah Temple African-American Catholic Congregation," a non-territorial faith community which happens to be in Gotham. He said that he hoped that it was the first step toward the establishment of an African-American rite within the Roman Catholic Church. He insisted that he was not schismatic, and still a Roman Catholic priest. Archbishop Haney warned that the new congregation cannot be considered a Roman Catholic parish of the Archdiocese of Gotham, and he forbade Hawkins to celebrate Mass in any parish of the archdiocese.

On Sunday, July 2, Hawkins celebrated mass at the chapel of City University Law School, and about 3,000 people participated. He announced a collection of $16,000. One thousand persons joined the Elijah Temple. The next day the Archbishop, calling his liturgy a destructive act of disobedience, suspended Hawkins from his priestly duties. On subsequent Sundays Hawkins led the celebrations, which he says are modelled on an approved experimental ritual from Zaire, at Lane High School. Attendance has been about 2,000, and several hundred more persons have joined the Temple.

(1) Is Augustus Hawkins a schismatic? (2) Are his followers excommunicated? (3) Did the Archbishop act properly in suspending him? (4) Do those who attend his liturgies satisfy their Sunday obligation? Are the eucharistic celebrations valid?

SARAH FORTHRIGHT AND PLANNED PARENTHOOD

Sarah Forthright has been the state director of Planned Parenthood for years. She is also a lifelong, staunch Roman Catholic, married in the church to a Catholic man. They send their children to Catholic schools. Sarah is an outspoken champion of women's rights, and is "pro-choice" on abortion.

When Sarah's oldest daughter, Jane, was thirteen she joined Sarah at a pro-choice march at the state capitol in late August. Jane was pictured in the local newspaper carrying a pro-choice banner. Father Murphy, the pastor of the Forthrights' parish who had very strong feelings on the abortion issue, immediately told the Forthrights that Jane was no longer welcome in the parish school. He cancelled her registration for the Fall semester. The Forthrights appealed to the Diocesan Superintendent of Schools, and then to the bishop, but no one wanted to overrule the pastor's decision, even though they disagreed with his action, because they didn't want to "send the wrong message on the abortion issue."

Jane enrolled in the local public school. Two years later she joined the parish course of preparation for confirmation. She attended faithfully and completed the course successfully. Two days before confirmation was to be administered, Father Murphy sent word to Jane that he wanted to talk to her about her views on abortion before he could recommend her for confirmation. The Forthrights were upset by this, and Jane's parents accompanied her to Father's office. They challenged him for singling out their daughter for this last-minute, extraordinary interrogation. The pastor replied that he had been asked by the diocesan chancellor to question Jane because of her mother's prominent role in the pro-choice cause. Jane responded to Father Murphy's question that she didn't like the idea of abortion, and earnestly hoped that she would never have to have one. She was confirmed the next day.

The Forthrights remained incensed about the way their daughter had been treated, and they asked the chancellor for an explanation. The chancellor responded with a letter which declared that Sarah had incurred the automatic excommunication for abortion (canon 1398) because of her public statements in defense of abortion and her position with Planned Parenthood, which sponsors a clinic where abortions are performed. The letter became public knowledge, and the bishop forbade any priest to give Sarah holy communion until she had been reconciled with the church.

(1) Were Jane's rights in the church infringed by Father Murphy's earlier action? (2) by his subsequent questioning of her? (3) Did Sarah incur the excommunication of canon 1398? (4) If she was excommunicated, how can she be reconciled to the church?

JOHN ORLICH AND THE DIOCESE OF OSTRAGOTH

John Orlich entered the affiliate program for the Diocese of Ostragoth after two years of college. When he graduated from college he entered the diocesan theological seminary. He accommodated well to the life of the seminary and did reasonably well in his studies. He moved easily through the theology program, and was ordained a deacon after his third year. John was assigned to a parish for that summer. He loved the ministry, and he was very positively evaluated by four different members of the parish ministry team, women and men. They found him to be outgoing, generous, sensitive and open.

A few weeks after classes began in the fall, the rector of the seminary called John into his office and informed him that he would not be ordained to the priesthood in the spring with his classmates and, as far as the diocese was concerned, never. The rector said that John was reported to have had homosexual relationships in the parish during the summer. The rector had investigated the matter, and became convinced that there was enough truth to the allegations that John should not be ordained. John denied that he was a homosexual, and declared that his associations with young men in the parish were honest and innocent. Those with whom he had ministered believed him, but the rector would not budge from the decision he had made. John was dismayed and at a loss.

The two priests in the parish where he had served were religious, members of the Order of Christ Jesus (OCJ). They suggested to John that he might apply for admission to their community, and they offered to vouch for him. John applied, was accepted, did a year's novitiate, completed his fourth year of theology, ministered in a parish for a year, was perpetually professed in the order, and was ordained a priest. He served, happily and successfully, in OCJ parishes in the Diocese of Ostragoth for eight years after ordination.

Then the OCJs' provincial council selected John to serve on the team at their house of formation in Thuringia. John declined, first tentatively, then adamantly. Ostragoth was his home, he loved the people, and wanted to stay in parish ministry. The provincial decided that John had an authority problem, and he put him under obedience. John refused the assignment, and petitioned for an indult to leave the community. The former rector of the diocesan seminary was now the bishop of Ostragoth, and despite John's negative feelings about him, he asked the bishop to incardinate him into the diocese. With great reluctance the bishop agreed to take John into the diocesan presbyterate on a probationary basis. Six years later the bishop wrote John a letter refusing him incardination because of some liturgical irregularities John was reported to have engaged in.

(1) Were John's rights violated by his seminary rector? (2) Did he have a right to ordination to the priesthood? (3) Was John's profession in the OCJs valid? (4) What is John's status in the diocese?

THE SISTERS OF JUSTICE AND
ARCHBISHOP O'DONNELL

The Sisters of Justice (SJs) is an institute of consecrated life of diocesan right. It is dedicated to serving the poor by working for the change of the unjust structures of society. It is a small group of strong, well-educated and progressive women. Most of the sisters live and work in the archdiocese headed by the vigorous and astute Archbishop O'Donnell, and many of them work for church-sponsored agencies.

The sisters held a renewal chapter on the twenty-fifth anniversary of Vatican II's Decree on the Appropriate Renewal of Religious Life. After long and prayerful deliberations the sisters agreed that they would no longer submit their governing documents to church authorities for approval, that they would admit married persons, including couples, as members, and that they would not have any formally established religious houses. They took these steps, and several others, not out of any spirit of defiance, but as expressions of the legitimate autonomy of mature Christian women who desired to relate to contemporary culture in meaningful ways. They felt that such measures were in keeping with their charism, would assist them in fulfilling their purpose as a community, and were in accord with the gospel. They professed full communion with the Roman Catholic Church and respect for its authority.

The sisters promptly informed the archbishop of their actions. He asked to speak to the council, and then to the full chapter. He spoke as a loving father. With understanding, empathy and sensitivity, he entreated them to reconsider some of their policies, not because he disapproved of them or because they were unreasonable, but because they were contrary to canon law. The sisters reconvened their chapter, reconsidered the issues seriously, and decided to maintain the policies they had adopted.

When the sisters communicated their decision to Archbishop O'Donnell, he responded with a letter in which he begged them to reconsider, but warned that if they did not, he would terminate the employment of those members who worked for church agencies, dismiss each member from the community, suppress the community, and distribute the community's assets to the poor. A month later he sent another letter threatening the same actions, but offering to dialogue on the issues. The sisters replied that their minds were made up, and that they stood in sisterly solidarity on the entire matter. They declared that they would remain true to their calling and their convictions even if they were no longer recognized as religious by the church.

(1) Are the SJs' new policies against canon law? (2) Can the Archbishop do the things he threatens? (3) If they wished to take the initiative, what could the sisters do canonically?

BISHOP NOVAK AND THE DIOCESAN SYNOD

Bishop Novak announced a synod for the Diocese of Hippo. Bishop Novak is a liberal, and a consensus-type leader. He wanted the synod to help renew the Christian life of the diocese. He appointed preparatory commissions, and they consulted the people, the priests, religious and lay ministers. They used theological and pastoral consultants, worked out drafts of policies, and circulated them for reactions.

The Liturgical Commission formulated a series of guidelines for worship in the diocese. For the most part they reflected practices already common within the diocese; they were intended to affirm those practices and make clear what was permissible. Among the guidelines were: 1) permission for pastors to give general absolution to the people who attend penance services during Lent and Advent; 2) permission for children to receive their first holy communion before first penance, if their parents preferred; 3) permission for Catholics to receive communion as often as they participate in the eucharist, even if this was more often than once a day; 4) authorization for non-Catholic Christians to be invited to share the eucharist when they attend weddings or funerals or ecumenical celebrations in Catholic churches.

When the Vicar General of the diocese, who is also a canonist, received the draft of these liturgical guidelines, he protested to the Bishop that all of them are contrary to the Code of Canon Law, and that the bishop could not allow them to be promulgated. Bishop Novak responded that he wanted unity of practice within the diocese, and if these policies commanded a consensus among the presbyterate and laity, he would agree to their enactment by the synod. The bishop went on to say that the Code gave him all the power he needed to exercise his pastoral office (canon 381), that he was the sole legislative authority at the synod (canon 466), and that he had the power to dispense from the universal law of the church (canon 87). So, even if these guidelines are contrary to the canons, he said that he would not hesitate to endorse them, if the synod accepted them.

(1) What is a diocesan synod, and what authority does it possess? (2) Are the proposed liturgical guidelines contrary to the canons of the Code? (3) Is Bishop Novak's response to the Vicar General correct?

BIRTH CONTROL AND TEACHING AUTHORITY

Pope John Paul III reexamined the issue of artificial contraception in response to many expressions of pastoral concern from bishops in various parts of the world. The pope appointed a commission of experts—theologians, demographers, doctors and married couples—to study the matter. After two years of work, the commission reported to him, and he issued an encyclical letter reaffirming the church's previous position, namely, that artificial birth control is always morally wrong under all circumstances.

Bishop Walters of the Diocese of Nirvana sent copies of the encyclical to all of the priests in the diocese along with a cover letter in which he said that he expected them to conform their teaching, preaching and counselling to the papal message. Twenty-five pastors (about one-fourth of the total number of pastors) of the diocese met and agreed to disagree with the encyclical to this extent: they respected the pope and his teaching authority, but in the application of the teaching on birth control to individual situations, they held out for the possibility of some pastoral accommodation. They said that they would be guided in their pastoral activities by both the papal teaching and the principle of accommodation. The pastors communicated this view to Bishop Walters.

The bishop called in each one of the pastors individually, listened to them, tried to convince them to conform to the papal teaching and, finally, threatened to suspend them if they refused. Nearly all of them, for what they said was the pastoral good of their people, refused to change their views. After two weeks and another warning by mail, the bishop suspended them from preaching, counselling or hearing confessions.

Bishop Walters also ordered the religious sisters and priests (all of whom happened to belong to institutes of pontifical right) who owned and operated four Catholic high schools in the diocese to stop using the religion texts which presented the accommodation theory on birth control, and to adopt the new textbooks which conformed to the papal encyclical.

The religious principals respectfully declined to make the change in texts, saying that their religion faculties considered the new texts to be inferior, and that the position on birth control set forth in the present texts was held by the majority of the papal commission, most moral theologians, and many local pastors.

(1) Did the bishop act within his authority in his initial demands upon his priests and the religious? (2) Was his suspension of the pastors lawful? (3) Could he require the high schools to change textbooks? (4) Could he have the religion teachers dismissed?

ST. MARK'S PARISH AND FATHER STURDY

Father Gentle had been the pastor of St. Mark's for ten years when Bishop Murphy asked him move to another parish. He hadn't been an ideal pastor: the parish income didn't keep pace with inflation, the buildings weren't very well-maintained, and the school closed during those years. But Gentle was a "people person"; he related well, trusted the laity, supported many of their initiatives, and promoted good liturgical celebrations. He worked closely with the elected parish council, and that group became the effective leadership organ of the parish.

Bishop Murphy assigned Father Sturdy as pastor at St. Mark's, even though people had complained about him at his last two assignments. The bishop didn't have many choices, and thought that the finances and physical plant needed attention at St. Mark's. He urged Sturdy to work collaboratively with the people, as Gentle had.

Sturdy was young and vigorous, a runner, who also worked out with weights every day. He regarded himself as a leader of men. He played by the rules. He said his prayers, and he preached pretty well. As soon as he arrived, Sturdy fired the janitor and the housekeeper and hired new ones, and he had all the locks changed on all the buildings. He made an assessment of needed repairs, and began to talk to the people about the money to pay for them. He met with the parish council, and laid out his agenda. They responded unenthusiastically, and suggested a plan of their own. Sturdy gradually stopped calling regular council meetings. He consulted them less and less, and postponed the elections of new members. The council appealed to the bishop about the pastor's disregard for them, but the chancellor wrote back that in canon law the pastor is responsible for the parish, and the parish council has only an advisory function.

Father Sturdy sought to economize by not replacing the liturgical coordinator when she resigned, and by cutting the music budget in half. As the eucharistic celebrations became more perfunctory and less participative, parishioners began to look around for better liturgy. Sunday and weekday mass attendance began to decline, although the collections actually increased due to the new program of tithing which Sturdy had introduced.

Father Sturdy went to the deanery meetings and insisted that his neighboring pastors not enroll St. Mark's parishioners, and that any St. Mark's envelopes which showed up in their collections must be returned to him. Their parishes were territorial, and he said the priests and people must observe the boundaries in order for pastoral care to be provided in an orderly manner. Sturdy complained to the bishop when one nearby pastor accepted three people who lived in St. Mark's parish into his RCIA program.

(1) What are the relative responsibilities of pastors and parish councils?
(2) What is the significance of parish boundaries for: a) mass attendance, b) baptisms, c) confession, d) marriages, e) anointing of the sick, f) funerals, and g) contributions.

SISTER JANET AND ST. JOSEPH'S PARISH

The availability of priests in the Diocese of Ruralia steadily declined, and Bishop Nolan was compelled to seek out someone else to run St. Joseph's Parish in Tinyville, after old Father Gilhooly died. Sister Janet Rice, OSB, who had several years of pastoral experience in other parishes, applied for the position, was interviewed by the Diocesan Personnel Committee and the bishop, and was given a five-year contract to lead the parish. She was the first non-priest to be appointed to head a parish in the Diocese, so everyone was a little uncertain about procedures and powers.

Janet was given the title of parish administrator, and she was told to report to her moderator, Father Smith over in Centerville, the county seat.

The first couple of years were very difficult for Janet and for the parish. Father Smith could come over for mass only twice a month, and the people were uneasy with the Word and Communion Service which Janet led on the alternate Sundays.

Janet was a strong person and a good minister, however, and gradually the people got used to her and appreciated her talents and her dedication to them. A few families avoided St. Joseph's and drove fifty miles to Centerville for mass, but the majority of the parishioners accepted Janet as the real leader of the parish community, and became devoted to her as their pastor.

Janet preached at the liturgy of the word, even on the Sundays when Father Smith celebrated the eucharist. She usually baptized the babies of the parish as well as the adult converts. Sometimes, when the couple asked, she would witness the marriages of the young people whom she helped to prepare for marriage. She routinely blessed the sick persons whom she visited in the hospital. Once, when she was unable to locate any priest in the county, Janet anointed an elderly lady who was dying. She carefully explained to the woman that she was not a priest, but the woman was greatly consoled by her ministry, and died peacefully a few hours afterwards. Janet preached at the funeral service, and the woman's family was reconciled to the church as a result. On a couple of occasions, when Father Smith failed to arrive for Sunday mass (he had a drinking problem), Janet mixed some unconsecrated hosts with those in the tabernacle so that there would be enough for everyone at the communion service. Father Smith had told her that was the thing to do.

The above activities were reported to Bishop Nolan by one of the alienated parishioners, and he reacted by terminating Janet on three weeks notice.

(1) Were Janet and Father Smith given canonically appropriate titles? (2) Was Janet able to do each of the things she did? (3) Did Bishop Nolan act responsibly in dismissing her?

JOE O'NEILL AND THE ORDER OF CHRIST JESUS

Joe O'Neill was one of the bright lights of the Order of Christ Jesus (a large and ancient religious institute of pontifical right) for thirty years. He was a Stanford-trained nuclear physicist when he entered the community, and he taught in a university run by the OCJs for nearly all of his religious life. He was an outstanding teacher and scholar, and a dynamic presence in the life of the school. Joe had keen pastoral interests, and engaged himself very effectively in campus ministry.

Joe was a social activist, and through the years he was outspoken in support of controversial causes. He denounced American involvement in Vietnam when John Kennedy sent in the first advisors. He solicited funds to send to the peasants who were fighting the rightist regime in El Salvador. He spoke out for the economic and social equality of women. Joe was moderately pro-choice on the abortion issue. He was a champion of gay rights on campus and in society.

Because of his effective support of such causes, Joe's superiors frequently received complaints about him. During one heated national election campaign, when the church mobilized its forces on the abortion and homosexual marriage issues, and Joe was loud in opposition, the OCJ provincial and council finally had enough. The heat from the hierarchy and the public was more than they could stand. They took action to dismiss Joe from the community. They warned Joe and threatened him with dismissal. He chose not to respond, figuring that they were just trying to shut him up. After Joe spoke at another rally, the provincial sent the request for dismissal to the general in Rome. The general and his four councilors, after long deliberation, voted three to two for Joe's dismissal. They issued a one-sentence decree of dismissal and sent it to Joe's provincial. By the time the provincial received the decree, the election was over, tempers had cooled, and the provincial council regretted its action. They wrote to the general and asked him to reconsider.

Meanwhile, the usually buoyant Joe became morose. All of his issues and candidates were defeated in the election, and all he could see around him on campus and in the country was growing materialism, selfishness, and callous lack of concern about the poor and oppressed. On top of it all, he simply could not believe that his community was trying to expel him after more than thirty years of faithful service. He was in his late sixties and very depressed. He began to doubt everything; in his homilies he spoke about his doubts of faith. Finally, Joe solemnly declared at Sunday mass that he no longer believed in God. He had his declaration published in the campus paper.

(1) Did the OCJ provincial council have cause to dismiss Joe? Did they follow canonical procedures? (2) Did the general council act properly? Was Joe actually dismissed? (3) Did Joe's loss of faith affect his status?

FATHER MUELLER AND THE NEW PARISH CHURCH

Father Mueller, a pastor in the Diocese of Smokey Mount, was an independent, tough, and enterprising priest of the old school. He was a man of action. When it became obvious to him that his parish, Holy Cross, in a remote resort community, needed a better and larger church, he went ahead and had one built.

Bishop Angelo of Smokey Mount was startled and angry when Father Mueller called him to come and bless the new church. It was the first the bishop had heard of the church. When the bishop came out for the blessing, he asked Father Mueller how he had financed the construction. Father Mueller proudly related how he had raised $75,000 from the parish over two years, and borrowed $425,000 from a local bank. When the bishop reminded him that the diocesan spending limit (the amount anyone could spend without the bishop's permission) was $10,000, Father Mueller assured him that he had never spent more than $10,000 at any one time; all the payments to the contractor were in amounts of $10,000 or less.

Bishop Angelo was forced to admire the fine, multi-purpose building which Holy Cross parish now owned, in spite of his exasperation at Father

Mueller's lack of notice to him and the financial arrangements. He asked the pastor how he got so much building for the money. Father Mueller was pleased to confide that he worked out a deal with the contractor which excluded union labor, avoided a performance bond, accident and workman's compensation insurance, environmental impact studies, and circumvented the state requirement for minority subcontractors. These special arrangements meant real savings in construction costs.

When the bishop asked how the small congregation was going to pay off the debt, Father Mueller was again happy to explain his plans. He was renting the church building to the local Methodist congregation for a service on Sunday mornings, to the Jewish community on Friday evenings, and to jazz and rock groups on two other weekday evenings. He explained that this was quite easy to do, because the Holy Cross parishioners had no need of the building at those times, and because he reserved the Blessed Sacrament at the rectory rather than in the church.

(1) Was there anything canonically wrong with Father Mueller's procedures in building and financing the new church? (2) Were his special arrangements with the contractor within canon law? (3) What about the leasing agreements for the use of the church? (4) Can Father Mueller reserve the eucharist apart from the church?

Index

219

error about, 136
form of, 136–137
mixed, 137, 138
in New Testament, 8
and persons in governing function, 150
preparations for, 133–134
records of, 138
and religious, 134, 178
and Roman Catholic Church, 132–133
and separation, 140
validity of, 152
Martin V (Pope), 21
Mass offerings, 124
Mass stipends, 15, 16, 124
Mediation, 186
Medicinal penalties or censures, 177
Melkite rite, 150
Metropolitans, 81, 184
Ministry of the divine word, 105
Missionary activity, 22–23, 48, 107–108
Mixed marriages, 137, 138
Moderator of the curia, 87
Modern Period, 24–25
Mueller (Father), 217–218
Murder, 98, 179
Mutilation, 179

Napoleon, 26, 27
National Conference of Catholic Bishops, 62
Natural law, 30, 33
Neller, Christoph, 24
New parish church, 217–218
New Testament, 7–8, 30
Nicea, Council of (325), 11
Nicene Creed, 11
Nomocanon, 16
Non-canonical associations, 59

Normalcy canons, 33
Norms of action, 32
Novak (Bishop), 211–212
Novella Commentaria, 18
Novitiate, 97

Oaths, 15, 16, 143
OCJ (Order of Christ Jesus), 210, 216–217
Observance canons, 33
Offenses, 173, 178–179
Offices, 153–155. See also specific titles of
O'Neill, Joe, 216–217
Old Testament, 30
O'Donnell (Archbishop), 210–211
Oratories, 144
Ordained ministers, 56
Order of Christ Jesus (OCJ), 210, 216–217
Orders, 129–132
Ordinaries, 156–157
Ordination, 61, 129, 132. See also Orders
Oriental churches, 47
Orlich, John, 209–210
Ostragoth diocese, 209–210

Panormia, 16
Papal decrees, 18
Papal legates, 72–73
Parents, 108–109, 118
Parishes, 88–89, 91, 144–145
Parochial vicars, 91
Particular norms, 32–33
Pastoral council, 85
Pastoring, 90
Pastors
and anointing of the sick, 128–129
authority of, 89–90
and baptism, 118

About the Author

James A. Coriden was born in Indiana in 1932. He was ordained a presbyter of the Diocese of Gary in 1957. He earned a bachelor's degree from St. Meinrad Seminary, a Licentiate in Sacred Theology and a doctorate in canon law from the Gregorian University in Rome, and a *Juris Doctor* from the Columbus School of Law at The Catholic University of America.

Dr. Coriden served in the tribunal and chancery of the Diocese of Gary from 1961 to 1968, on the faculty of theology at Catholic University from 1968 to 1975, and since that time at the Washington Theological Union, where he is Professor of Canon Law and Academic Dean. He has taught introductory courses in canon law for over twenty years.

The author has been an active member of the Canon Law Society of America since 1961. He organized and published several interdisciplinary symposia for the society, served on its board of governors, and was one of the general editors of *The Code of Canon Law: A Text and Commentary*, commissioned by the society after the promulgation of the 1983 Code. The society presented him its "Role of Law Award" in 1987.

Dr. Coriden has published many articles on canonical topics, especially in the areas of ministry, the rights of church members, teaching authority, church governance, and the interpretation of canons.